EASTON AREA PUBLIC LIB.

1901 9100 023 660 6

W9-CLB-820

NO LONGER PROPERTY
OF EASTON AREA
PUBLIC LIBRARY

HOUDINI

The Man Who Walked Through Walls

By the same author:

NIGHTMARE ALLEY

LIMBO TOWER

MONSTER MIDWAY

HOUDINI

The Man Who Walked Through Walls

BY

WILLIAM LINDSAY GRESHAM

HENRY HOLT AND CO.   NEW YORK

EASTON PUBLIC LIBRARY
EASTON PA

B H836G
cop 2

Copyright © 1959 by William L. Gresham

All rights reserved, including the right to reproduce this book or portions thereof in any form.

In Canada, George J. McLeod, Ltd.

FIRST EDITION

Library of Congress Catalog Card Number: 59-10470

JUN 1 3 1972

83280-1119

Printed in the United States of America

EASTON PUBLIC LIBRARY
EASTON PA.

To the greatest living escape artist
"The Amazing Randi"
(Mr. James Randall Zwinge)
this book is dedicated with the
sincere admiration of the author

Author's Acknowledgments

Above all, the author wishes to thank Clayton Rawson for his constant help and for making available his library of rare works on magic. While differing from the author in his opinions on "exposing" the tricks of the escape artist, he nevertheless assisted the research in too many ways to enumerate.

The author wishes to thank, in alphabetical order, the following:

Roy Benson, who grew up in vaudeville and magic;

Allan Bernard, old friend of Greenwich Village days, for his recollections of the late *Evening Graphic;*

Milbourne Christopher, past president of the Society of American Magicians, for permission to check through his collection of five hundred Houdini letters;

Mrs. Laura Abbott Dale, research officer of the American Society for Psychical Research, for her help in recommending sources;

Joseph Dunninger for personal recollections of Houdini, as well as for his contribution of photographs from his collection and permission to go through his amazing scrapbooks;

Bruce Elliott, my long-time mentor in things magical;

Al Flosso, magician and magic dealer, old friend of Houdini's;

Martin Gardner, who contributed his entire collection of Houdini clippings;

Walter B. Gibson, authority on Houdini and escape magic from whom, years ago, I got most of the carnival material for a novel, *Nightmare Alley,* for memoirs of the Great Escapist;

Lewis Goldstein, last surviving member of the original Houdini company, for his many anecdotes of the Prison Defier;

Renée Gresham for moral support and secretarial help;

Dr. John Henry Grossman, physician and chemist, for his researches into fire-resisting formulas; likewise his gift of two rare pamphlets;

Marcus Henvit for his long and informative letters;

Jean Hugard, dean of magicians, for special data;

Burling Hull for information on his Escape from Flames;

Dr. Stanley Jaks for Hungarian sources on Houdini's birth;

Fred Keating for his many helpful suggestions and his charity toward an "exposer" of secrets;

Robert Lund for his energetic leg work on the Belle Isle Bridge mystery;

Sam Margolies for his kindly contribution of sources;

Jay Marshall for his steady friendship through troubled years and his contribution of essential rare books and pamphlets from his collection;

Michael Miller, authority on the Houdini house;

David Moffett for research on underwater burial data;

John Mulholland, one of the best-loved figures in magic, for his help over the years;

New Rochelle Public Library staff for their patience and cooperation;

George Pfisterer for his many acts of kindness and his help with disputed points in Houdini letters;

Sidney Hollis Radner for the time given me in showing his Houdini collection as well as many hours spent in fascinating experiments with handcuffs;

Robert Towner for many odd bits of information;

The late Audley Walsh for Houdini anecdotes;

Dr. Martin Young for his ready cooperation in providing leads to source material;

To all these and many others who have been of assistance, I wish to extend my thanks.

Inaccuracies and defects in the book are to be laid at the door of the author and not of his sources.

—W. L. G.

Contents

HOUDINI

The Man Who Walked Through Walls

Prologue—The Shaking Tent

IF MAN has an instinct stronger than self-preservation it is the instinct to escape from bondage—"liberty or death!"

Cherished among folk heroes are the liberators: Moses and the Maccabees, Garibaldi and Bolivar. And down the years the adventures of great prison-breakers have made pulses race: Baron Friedrich von der Trenck, indefatigable digger of tunnels from the dungeons of Frederick the Great; Henri de Latude, who dangled his way precariously out of the Bastille down a rope ladder several hundred feet long, woven from linen threads. Such tales stir the soul as with the voice of a trumpet. But they are tales, at best, conveyed by the printed word.

Then at the turn of the twentieth century there arose from the ranks of obscure music-hall magicians a man who captured the imagination of two continents and held the limelight firmly focused on himself for twenty years. He did it by hammering out a brand-new form of entertainment in which he acted out the dream of every man—escape from bonds by magic.

Great as he was, his new art did not burst full-formed from his own genius. It had a long and fascinating history of gradual growth. . . .

The art has always engaged us; perhaps it touches us more deeply than we know. Glance first at these scenes. They are a part of our fabulous history of magic—and of the man who made its practice his life.

In the days before the white men came with their iron skins and fire sticks, the nation of the Anishinabeg lived in the lands

Longfellow described as being "by the shining big sea water." The Anishinabeg (other tribes called them Ojibwa) were great hunters, great fishermen in their big sea water—Lake Superior —and great warriors. But when decisions affecting the nation, a matter like war with the Fox tribes to the south, came before their councils, the elders sought advice from another world.

A circle drawn on the ground in the place-of-talking symbolized, for the council, the horizon on which rests the sky. Five stout saplings, trimmed of branches, were sunk three feet into the ground; earth was then packed hard around the saplings' base. A covering of moose hide draped the place of invocation so that no profane gaze could spy on sacred mystery.

Then the magician came forward to stand in the firelight, naked save for the pelt of a beaver worn like an apron and, on his head, a medicine bonnet bearing the stuffed heads of an eagle, owl, crane, and loon. He saluted the four winds with proper ceremony. At last he began to call down the spirits of the ancient great from their ghost dance in the northern heavens.

One of the tribe's bravest young warriors, known to be an expert at confining prisoners with strips of hide, then came forward. The magician held out his left wrist so that hide might be knotted firmly about it; he crossed his hands behind his back and the right wrist was tightly tied to the left. Other strips fastened his ankles. Though he was helpless now, his feet were drawn up and lashed to his wrists. Solemn braves lifted the trussed man and carried him into the tent, left open at the top to admit the spirits of the air.

Hoot of the owl, gabble of the loon. From the hide-walled enclosure, only wide enough to allow the jackknifed magician to lie across it, rose a chorus of unearthly sounds. The watching crowd moaned as ghostly fingers twitched the moose-hide walls. The medicine lodge shook, the poles bent from side to side. Obviously, spirits had descended. For a tied, helpless man could not make strong walls tremble.

The council fire died. Embers glowed. But the cries of bird

and beast still sounded; the howling of great winds, the snapping of ghostly fingers, the steady rasp of the tortoise-shell rattle came from the tent, shaking now as in great winds. As the embers lost their light, tiny flecks of green fire appeared around the tent. All knew that the shades of dead warriors would give wisdom to their people.

Now they announced their presence; each spoke his name. A chief whose deeds were tribal legend counseled war in a full-throated voice. (Who could think this was the voice of the conjuror?) The ghost chief hinted of danger. The tent's shaking made more awesome his words.

Then the spirits were gone; the strong saplings no longer shook. The elders found the conjuror as firmly bound as ever.

In a lecture hall ladies settled the enormous skirts decreed by fashion in the 1860's. There would be a demonstration now at which they could only wonder.

An old gentleman walked to the center of the platform and paused for quiet. With the silvery voice of a popular preacher but with an underlying note of complete sincerity, he told the strange history of the two young men now to appear, of their seeming power to call spirits from the vasty deep, of the motion incredibly imparted to objects placed near them—even though the lads would be firmly tied by volunteers from the audience. To a round of applause, broken by a few boos and hisses from skeptics, he introduced the wondrous brothers, Ira Erastus and William Henry Davenport.

The dapper, handsome youths took their places. Their hair was fashionably long, their sweeping mustaches and "imperial" beards neatly trimmed. Behind them rose their famous cabinet. It was no deeper from front to back than a narrow chair, no taller than a standing man. There were three doors. The center door had a tiny, curtained window.

A committee from the audience filed hesitantly onstage, a bit dazzled by the footlights, lamps in front of bright tin reflectors. The lecturer produced two short pieces of rope and

a single long coil. Volunteers agreed to do the tying "so that
the young men cannot possibly be accused of producing the
phenomena themselves." Ira Davenport extended his left arm,
the rope was tied around the wrist with a good square knot
over the pulse. The dashing young man with the dark curls
and mysterious black, flashing eyes placed his left hand behind
his back, then his right. He turned and the audience could see
that he held his right wrist against his left. The committeeman
settled one wrist firmly against the other, brought the ends of
the rope around the right wrist and tied them fast, inspected
the knots and tugged at the arms. The youth could not possibly
use his hands. With brother William Henry similarly secured,
the boys took their places inside the cabinet, one at either end,
where they sat on shelves facing each other. The committee
knotted the long rope about the knees and ankles of one; then
stretched it to tie the other's legs in the same manner.

A guitar, a tambourine, a horn, and a bell were placed in
the center of the cabinet as the doors were closed. Hardly had
the catch of the door snapped when tambourine and bell flew
through the center window. At once the master of ceremonies
threw open the end doors. Both boys were firmly tied.

In 1914 a forty-year-old man—an athlete, a veteran of
vaudeville and before that of the circus, the carnival midway,
the dime museum, the medicine show, and the beer halls—
began the last mystery of his now famous act.

He was well under average height, powerful without being
bulky, bushy-haired, and a little bowlegged. His face was
sharp-featured yet handsome, with intense blue-gray eyes. His
strong, agile fingers had—in the first minutes of the show—
unfastened the buckles of a strait jacket through heavy canvas.
Then, in an exhibition of straight magic, he had cut into a
length of cloth and magically restored it. This had been followed by his famous needle trick. He apparently swallowed
three packs of darning needles and thirty feet of white cotton
thread, then produced the end of the thread from his lips—

with a needle dangling from it! After handing the tip of the thread to an assistant, he backed across the stage. Little glittering steel points, each threaded on the cotton, emerged from his mouth. The needles had been threaded!

Now he announced that the evening's last mystery would be his own invention, the exciting and celebrated Chinese Water Torture Cell. The curtains revealed, ominous beneath a single spotlight in the center of the stage, a mahogany cabinet. A glass panel glittered in its front.

An excited audience watched, entranced, as assistants filled the cabinet with water from a fire hose. The man of mystery, offstage for a moment, entered in a dressing gown. Removing the gown, wearing only the bathing suit it covered, he lay down while an assistant imprisoned his feet in a mahogany square with two openings, not unlike the stocks of the seventeenth century. The "stocks" were fastened to a rope descending from the flies. The man was raised, then lowered head down into the water. Liveried attendants locked the top of the tank in place. A cabinet with metal-pipe frame, curtained with dark blue velvet, was lifted forward to enclose torture cell and the occupant, until now plainly visible upside-down in the water.

When the curtains closed, an assistant with a fire ax stood by. For two and a half agonizing minutes the audience saw imminent tragedy in the ax poised to smash the water prison. The ax never fell. The curtains parted and the magician stepped out, streaming water. Behind him stood the grim cell, its cover still locked and clasped.

When the applause finally began to dwindle, the man who had escaped raised his hand:

"Ladies and gentlemen," he spoke, in a rather high-pitched voice that somehow (he did not shout) carried to the top row of the balcony, "allow me to thank you for your generous applause. And to make the first public announcement of my most recent development in the field of mystery. On Monday, the sixth of July, when I open at Mr. William Hammerstein's Victoria Theater in New York City, I shall present a feat which

has, since the dawn of history, been considered an absolute
impossibility. I shall endeavor to walk through a solid brick
wall."

Harry Houdini did just that. Or seemed to. The wall was of
solid brick, built on a foot-wide steel beam by a squad of bricklayers before the eyes of the audience. Over a large carpet in
the center of the stage was spread a seamless sheet of cloth.
Members of a committee from the audience stood on its edges.
Screens were placed on each side of the wall and the magician
stepped behind one. They heard his voice from the screen,
"I'm going . . . I'm going . . . I'm gone!" Then quietly—from
the other side—"Here I am!" He stepped out to greet an audience at first stunned into silence. There was, everyone could
see, no connection possible by a tunnel under the wall. The
carpet and canvas made that impossible. There was no way
around the wall. The committee could see both ends. Everyone could see that he did not go over the barrier. . . . Then
how? How did a man walk through a wall?

In previous appearances, he had released himself from ropes
and handcuffs, from sealed sacks and bound trunks, from
packing cases nailed fast, from stocks and pillories, from coffins, from iron boilers riveted shut, from a giant milk can filled
with water, its lid secured with padlocks. But, until now, the
Escape King had always left the wondering spectators at least
a loophole for speculation. "He opens the handcuffs with mag-
nets." "The box is made to fall apart when it gets in the water."
"People come up out of the stage by trap doors and let him
out of the torture cell." All wrong, but something at least for
the mind to envision. Now there was nothing. Speculation was
simply torment. Houdini had done the utterly impossible.
Where would he go from here? Where? The following year he
entered a box and was buried deep in the ground. In twenty
minutes he reappeared. He had escaped from the box; he had
dug his way back to the air and light, to freedom. All escapes
were possible for the man who walked through walls.

When he was dead, myth made even more elaborate the legend built during his lifetime: that he had a Secret and he had carried this Secret to the grave. This legend died in the public mind only when Houdini again held the headlines. He had come back from the grave; the voice of a spirit medium had given a ten-word code message to his wife. It did not matter that Bess Houdini denied that it was a spirit message known only to herself. The legend grew. It is still talked about, as Houdini is still remembered.

Time, Lord Dunsany tells us, eventually will conquer even the gods. This book is an effort by one who remembers Houdini in the days of his glory to preserve the fascination of the legend, and at the same time to show a little of the man himself: stormy, and devoted; cruel, and warmhearted; unselfish, and egocentric, he is no easy subject. He was ruled by emotions. His natural shrewdness often was lost in impulse. He was one of the most annoying, most likable, most unpredictable geniuses that ever lived.

Can what he was, what he did, have any meaning for us?

The author wrote with that conviction. Harry Houdini began with nothing—nothing, that is, but courage and a belief in his own genius which amounted to obsession. As the archetype of the hero who could not be fettered or confined, he became the idol of a million boys, a friend of presidents, and the entertainer of monarchs.

This was the Houdini who stepped out of the wings as a legend in his own lifetime. What of the man hidden by the legend?

For all his crotchets, Houdini had one great source of power. Courage was that power, and he knew that courage must be practiced as diligently as sleight-of-hand. He was no master-manipulator of cards and coins, in spite of his ambition to be remembered as a wizard of dexterity. But he did manipulate life and circumstance and the imaginations of men.

By reviewing his life, let us see how he went about it.

1. *Discovery by Gaslight*

THE EARLY DARK of an autumn evening had fallen over Manhattan and now at the street corners night was dispelled by the glow of gaslights on their posts—a soft radiance soon to give way to the electric glitter of progress. Under the corner lamp the boy paused and opened his book. It was a battered specimen rescued from the ten-cent stall of a bookshop. The lad had counted out his pennies and found he could spare ten. He had to keep a nickel for his fare on the Third Avenue Elevated.

In one hip pocket he carried a dog-eared deck of playing cards. Ordinarily, on his way home from his place of employment, the necktie factory of H. Richter's Sons at 502 Broadway, he would practice a sleight known as *sauter le coup,* or "jump the stroke." But now he had found something infinitely more fascinating; a world of marvels to which the mastery of magic might admit him. And he had found himself! All the restless yearnings of youth for fame and wealth, travel and the friendship of the great were in this book; its author had known them too.

The book was *The Memoirs of Robert-Houdin, Ambassador, Author and Conjuror, Written by Himself.* If a young notary's clerk, Jean Eugène Robert, could rise by patient efforts and stout heart to be the "father of modern magic," then he, Ehrich Weiss, necktie-lining cutter, could do the same.

From that moment, as the events of his life make clear, Ehrich Weiss never doubted his destiny. Crushing defeats, snubs, family pleading for other ambitions did not stop him. Although tireless practice never gave him the polished ease of the star sleight-of-hand performer, he hacked and carved his

8

place on the heights by inventing a whole new form of magic. He hurled at the universe a challenge to bind, fetter, or confine him so that he, in turn, could break free. He triumphed over manacles and prison cells, the wet-sheet packs of insane asylums, webs of fish net, iron boxes bolted shut—anything and everything human ingenuity could provide in an attempt to hold him prisoner. His skill and daring finally fused deeply with the unconscious wish of Everyman: to escape from chains and leg irons, gibbets and coffins . . . by magic.

The Weiss family had come to the new world from Budapest, Hungary. Ehrich, the son of a rabbi, was born in the ghetto section of Pest shortly before the family came to America. In the excitement of the trip, the exact date of his birth was apparently forgotten. The Weiss family settled first in Appleton, Wisconsin. Since his mother always wrote him on April 6, Ehrich claimed that date as his birthday and Appleton as the place.

Just before the invasion by the Nazis in the Second World War, a Hungarian magic enthusiast, Dr. Vilnos Lenard, found in some synagogue records an entry describing the birth of a son, Ehrich, to Mayer Samuel Weiss on March 24, 1874. The records survived pillage, and examination of Dr. Lenard's discovery may finally settle the matter. The actual date and place of Ehrich's birth are not truly important. It is important that he took great pride in being an American.

The Weiss family was numerous. Ehrich was a fifth son. The first-born boy died in Hungary, the second-born in New York shortly after the family came from Wisconsin to settle there in 1888. Two living brothers were older than Ehrich; two were younger, as was his only sister. In their home on East 69th Street, the six Weiss children came quickly to know their parents' pride in family. They lived in an atmosphere of dignity and respect for learning, an atmosphere that contrasted sharply with the world in which Ehrich's destiny lay. If the fact that he never ceased to return to it is evidence, Ehrich loved his home.

He knew the record of his early life was obscure. Later, when he had fallen out of love with his first hero, he wrote of Robert-Houdin: "Because of his supreme egotism, his obvious desire to make his autobiography picturesque and interesting rather than historically correct . . . it is extremely hard to present logical and consistent statements regarding his life." The statement is equally true of Ehrich Weiss.

There is a romantic legend, built up from publicity material and souvenir-program biographies, which tells us that the performer called Houdini was an amazing infant who never cried and needed little sleep, who as a very young child showed so impressive a mastery of locks that a professional locksmith employed him. The legend adds that at the age of nine Houdini was discovered by Jack Hoeffler's Five Cent Circus when it played Appleton and was engaged to do an act he had originated—picking up pins with his eyelids while hanging head down from a trapeze!

The stories are apocryphal. It is probable that Ehrich Weiss was introduced to magic at the age of sixteen. His first teacher was Jack Hayman, who worked next to him in the necktie factory. This was the job to which Ehrich had gone after his father gently remonstrated with him about his being a newsboy. A man of impressive dignity, Dr. Weiss explained that selling papers in the street was no occupation for the son of a rabbi and scholar.

In his spare hours, Ehrich was a loyal member of the Pastime Athletic Club. He trained for and won some track events. He also gained skill as a swimmer, doing most of his practice in the garbage-laden waters of the East River, where he joined the other neighborhood boys.

Ehrich's interest in spiritualism was aroused when, with Joe Rinn, a friend from the Pastime A. C., he visited the home of the notorious spirit medium, Minnie Williams. Mrs. Williams' house on 46th Street had been acquired from an ardent believer who was advised by the spirits to sell for one dollar and no other considerations. As Mr. Rinn tells the story, when the young Ehrich Weiss entered this plush palace of ghostly mystery he nudged Joe and whispered, "There must be plenty of money in this game."

No wonder he thought so. This was probably the most ornate house he had ever seen. Certainly it was different from the crowded flat of the scholar and gentleman, Rabbi Weiss.

Ehrich sat beside his friend Joe while hymns were sung. The room was lighted only by the dim greenish glow of a lamp in a box. In time, spirit forms came from the curtained corner of the room which was called the "cabinet." Among the shades resurrected that evening was Dr. Henry Ward Beecher. The boys noted that the floor creaked in very unghostly fashion when the spirits walked across it.

As he left, Ehrich accurately estimated that Mrs. Williams had taken in forty dollars: forty people at a dollar a head. Even after paying two thugs who were her bodyguards, she had, he reckoned, a good net profit. Ehrich knew his factory labor could never give him the money taken in here. But, although he already had a deep interest in illusion, he was not then tempted to become a medium. There were other reasons than conscience and lack of experience. For one thing, his father wouldn't have permitted it. If being a newsboy was no job for a rabbi's son, being a spirit medium would have been infinitely worse.

Soon, Ehrich's hours of dedicated practice began to reward him. Every now and then he was able to appear in public as a prestidigitator. On even rarer occasions he was paid a dollar or two. This was a time-honored and practical course. The amateur gained the experience before live audiences that made possible a chance for professional appearances. For Ehrich, as for all newcomers then, professional life began in beer halls and cheap vaudeville theaters. He worked hard as an amateur to gain such stages.

In these early shows young Weiss was grandiosely billed as "Eric the Great." Frequently his assistant was his pal from the factory, Jack Hayman, who had not only shown Ehrich his first simple tricks but had taken him down to the Bowery where professional apparatus was glitteringly displayed behind the glass counters of magic shops. Such equipment was far beyond their means. Cards, however, were cheap, as were silk remnants. So Ehrich's act at first consisted mainly of effects with cards and silk handkerchiefs, though he also used a few magic boxes and other props that he had built himself.

Jack Hayman had introduced Ehrich to magic. Now he indirectly helped him to choose the name he made immortal. Jack told him that adding an "i" to a word in French makes it mean "like." Ehrich never questioned this. An "i" added to the name of his hero, Houdin, produced Houdini. (It was many years before Ehrich realized that the hyphenated Robert-Houdin meant that Robert was not his idol's Christian name.) And since a performer customarily has a given name, and since Harry Kellar was then the biggest "name" in magic, Ehrich Weiss became Harry Houdini. Perhaps the choice had been inevitable since the moment he opened Robert-Houdin's memoirs.

2. *The Book of Revelations*

NOW THE BOY who was Ehrich Weiss by day and Harry Houdini by night found direction and challenge in another book.

The second half of the nineteenth century was the great age of applied occultism. For forty years a movement called spiritualism had been growing in the face of skeptical scorn. It had begun in a farmhouse near Hydesville, New York, where in 1848 two little girls, Katie and Margaret Fox, began to tease their superstitious mother by tying an apple on a string and bumping it over the floor at night. Later the sisters learned to make rappings by snapping the big toe against the second toe. Under the management of their older sister, Leah, a hard-driving and money-hungry termagant, the girls toured the country giving séances at which rappings answered questions. Soon a sickly Scotch-American lad in Connecticut, Daniel Dunglas Home, began to produce rappings himself. And even before Home achieved fame and diamond cuff links for his endeavors, the Brothers Davenport had hit the lecture circuit with their cabinet in which ghosts romped.

At last, in 1891, a bombshell was heaved into the world of luminous nightshirts and self-playing accordions. It came in the form of a paperbacked book entitled *Revelations of a Spirit Medium, or Spiritualistic Mysteries Exposed/ A Detailed Explanation of the Methods Used by Fraudulent Mediums/ by A. Medium*. The price was one dollar.

The book was copyrighted under the name of Charles F. Pidgeon. Serious students of psychic research and its literature have since ascribed authorship to one Mansfield, to one Donovan—the list of possible authors is long. Whoever the author

13

was, he probably had been a professional "physical phenomena" medium—a producer of voices, spectral forms, raps, etc. At very least he had closely consulted one.

Angered mediums, so the story goes, began buying up copies and shoveling them into convenient furnaces. Sadly, their patronage couldn't save the publishers. They went out of business and the book soon became a rare volume.

One copy somehow came to the hands of the newly named Harry Houdini. At that moment he was disinterested (he would not always be) either in spiritualism or in charges of fraud against some spiritualists. He was, however, interested in how the fraud was managed. This slur on spiritualism made a superb text for an escape artist. There were, as an example, explanations in minute detail of the way a medium—or Houdini—might get out of ropes with which he had been tied. (The medium called this trussing a "control.") More, the text set out *with illustrations* the secret of a spirit collar, an iron band to be secured about a medium's neck with a padlock. Of course the collar never accomplished the announced purpose of holding a medium to a wall, since it could easily be opened by means of a cleverly-devised hinge. There were also explicit directions, and more pictures, about making "spirit" bolts, devices used to fasten a medium to a solid support. Harry learned how this ring-and-bolt contrivance opened to free the wearer. He also found directions for two very mystifying ways to escape from a sack when its drawstrings had been pulled tight, knotted, and sealed.

His preoccupation with escape was instant and intense. Moreover, it endured. Harry became an ardent, tireless student. As often as he could persuade them, he got his Pastime Athletic Club friends, who were doubtlessly puzzled, to tie him up. It was with this concentration of effort that, eventually, he achieved a mastery of the art that has never been surpassed.

On one occasion he saw the great Harry Kellar, in his full-evening magic show, use the famous Davenport wrist-tie for comic effects, shooting out one free hand to tap the volunteer from the audience, after the volunteer was sure that he had tied the magician so securely that he was helpless.

The trick itself delighted the youthful Houdini. He was particularly excited though, by Kellar's challenge: "I challenge you to tie my wrists together with this rope so that I cannot release myself!"

He loved that, and it was always to be so. The whole pattern of his career indicates how profoundly he must have been moved by the gesture Kellar handled so commandingly. But years separated Harry Houdini from realization of the full dramatic power of the challenge and full understanding of its most effective presentation. The story will grow with Houdini's growth. For he made the challenge a device peculiarly his. Year after year he defied the world to confine him—and year after year, or so he boasted, he never failed to escape.

At seventeen Harry made the great decision. He entered show business as a full-time professional. In April, 1891, he quit his job at H. Richter's Sons, taking with him a good recommendation from the boss and the prospect of trouble at home. It must have been impossible for his parents to appreciate this exchange of a decent job with assured income for the dubious standing and chance employment of an apprentice wonder-worker. For Harry there could have been no other decision.

Somehow during that spring he talked his way into a tryout at Huber's Museum on 14th Street, next door to the present site of Luchow's Restaurant. Presiding over the establishment was George Dexter, a tall, suave gentleman from Australia. Dexter, an eloquent "inside talker," introduced the acts, most of which were at the circus side-show level. Dexter was a man of the world, experienced in all kinds of variety entertainment, and, most important for Houdini, a master of rope escapes.

The rope-tie effects have been a favorite of traveling mountebanks as long as there have been fairs and festivals, circuses and amusement-seeking crowds. In fact, this form of escape antedates organized entertainment. Ojibwa sorcerers seemingly accomplished mysteries of tribal ritual after being bound. The trick probably was old when it came to the Ojibwa and must have begun its evolution deep in man's prehistory.

It seems appropriate that the great escapist should have started to learn the art at, quite literally, its beginning. Dexter was delighted to find that the young card-manipulator was fascinated by "escapery." Immediately he coached him in the essentials of the rope-tie artistry. He taught him, also, handcuff manipulation.

Somewhere along the line some enterprising carnival performer had found that the sight of a man with handcuffs on his wrists has a strong fascination for a midway crowd. Again it is the element of challenge—can he get out? And if so, how?

As presented, even to this day, on the "bally" platform of a carnival ten-in-one show, the handcuff escape has the simplicity of all good magic and, like all good magic, depends for its effect on the acting ability of the performer. Here is a presentation typical of the ones Houdini must have watched:

The crowd, idly sauntering along the shavings-cushioned earth of the midway, confused by a plethora of attractions, suddenly has its attention called by noise from the bally platform of a side show. A girl, clad in a costume as brief as the law allows, is being handcuffed by a large, official-looking man. The scene is arresting in itself. Here is beauty in distress!

The outside talker brings the crowd close. There is business back and forth between the officer and the talker on the platform. More business, back and forth, while the girl stands between them, the gyves on her wrists.

There is something archetypal and deeply stirring in the male human at the sight of a pretty girl in manacles or chains. While the audience stares entranced, the talker throws a cloth over the girl's hands. The crowd, or "tip," begins to sense that it is all a part of the show, but stays nevertheless. The girl, writhing as if in pain, struggles for a moment and then the handcuffs fall to the floor of the bally platform with a clang. The cloth is waved above her head and she dashes inside the tent followed by a portion of the tip—for no good reason that they could explain except that they want to see where she goes and what she is going to do when she gets there.

The official-looking person is any beefy individual who happens to be connected with the show or the carnival or, on occasion, a real detective who is *persona grata* with the showman. What the girl has done is to find the keyhole in the cuffs with a key, under cover of the cloth, and release herself, writhing the while as if she is squeezing her hands smaller than her wrists to slip the cuffs off. That, in essence, is the "handcuff trick"—as old, probably, as the invention of handcuffs.

Houdini's genius did not lie in invention of new effects from scratch; rather he was a developer of unsuspected potentials of drama in old effects. The uninspired midway performer, getting out of the cuffs with a duplicate key, seldom really plays it for drama. And for a long time Houdini, after he had acquired a pair of cuffs from some pawnshop, fell into the trap of showing his cleverness by making it all look *easy*. The drama lay, and he did not learn this for a heartbreakingly long time, in making the feat seem hard.

He was similarly tardy in seeing how he might put to use a special bit of information, a "secret" about handcuffs that is known to few except peace officers: *Nearly all cuffs of the same make and model (before 1920) opened with the same key.*

Most people believe a key is unique. If they buy a half-dozen padlocks, they expect to have six different keys. But the locks of handcuffs are more simple, as simple as the locks of brief cases. Local police may place five pairs of "regulation" cuffs on the escapist's wrists. If all are of the same make and model, one key often frees him.

Houdini early learned this about manacles, but he was slow to exploit what he knew. When he finally did, he used it with great imagination. With his own keys for all the makes of cuffs in current use in any city, he could safely challenge police officers to manacle him. In every city he could then extend his reputation as a magician who could free himself "by magic."

After his spring engagement at Huber's Harry decided to try his luck at Coney Island. He worked briefly with Emil Jarrow, a strongman who could write his name on a wall with a pencil while holding in the same hand, straight out from the shoulder, a sixty-pound dumbbell.

Jarrow and Houdini worked for "throw money"—that is, they put on their show in a tent and then passed the hat. Jarrow, after getting a page write-up in the New York *Sun*, went on to other activities and, with the irony of fate, he became one of the most adroit sleight-of-hand performers in the business at his own specialty (the trick where a borrowed and marked dollar bill vanishes and appears in the center of a lemon which, up until the moment of slicing, has been in the hands of a spectator)—whereas Houdini, the sleightster, grew to be something of a strongman.

It would be impossible to follow Harry from obscure booking to obscure booking. He went everywhere. In December, 1891, he sent a letter to Joe Rinn from Columbus, Kansas, saying that he was with a show in the ten-, fifteen-, and twenty-five-cent bracket, and that he was doing his own bill-posting. It's more likely that he was passing out handbills telling of his prowess, an inexpensive form of advertising he used all his life.

After Dr. Weiss died in 1892, the support of their mother and sister was up to Houdini and his brothers. Harry thus had one more motive for playing as many weeks as possible. He assured his mother that one day he would pour a stream of gold pieces into her lap. Mother Weiss had her doubts.

When Harry came home, it was not to rest. Day after day he practiced rope-tie escapes on the roof of the East 69th Street house. His kid brother, Theodore, who earned the nick-name "Dash" for his love of bold haberdashery, would enthusiastically spend hours tying Harry. Harry would spend more strenuous hours wriggling out. What the boys did mystified their mother. Never in all the history of the Weiss family, which had produced a number of rabbis and Talmud scholars, nor in the annals of her own family, the Steiners, had anyone senselessly allowed himself to be tied up with clothesline.

"*Nu,* so from this you should make a living, my son?"

"Never mind, Ma, I got an idea."

Ehrich had a secret. For the first time in his life he had borrowed money—enough to purchase a box trick from a broken-down magician. This box, which was the size of a small trunk, had a secret panel that opened inward. With a man inside, the box could be locked, then roped from side to side and from front to back. With a curtain drawn to conceal the method of escape, the imprisoned man would be outside in a few seconds, the locks and ropes undisturbed. The trick was originally the invention of the English illusionist John Nevil Maskelyne. With many modern improvements it is still being performed wherever magicians can find a stage. Worked by two people who are exceedingly agile, it becomes a genuine miracle.

Houdini was agile, and his kid brother Dash was willing. With Harry's box the Houdini brothers had an act. Both believed in giving audiences plenty of show for their money. Many observers thought it was too much. But Houdini was on his way!

3. *The Brothers Houdini*

IN 1893 the Midwest erupted with a skyrocket burst of out-door show business. Nothing like the Chicago World's Columbian Exposition had been seen before in the Americas.

The fair had been planned to commemorate the four-hundredth anniversary of the discovery of America, and was scheduled for 1892. But nobody minded the year's delay; it gave an extra twelve months for buildup in the papers.

Of all its attractions, the *Midway Plaisance* (which gave the English language a new word: *midway*) was a street of wonders—it featured an Eskimo village, a South Seas village, and "The Streets of Cairo," where Little Egypt gave the West its first view of the belly dance. Every outdoor act in the country seems to have headed for Chicago during that memorable season, and so did Harry Houdini with his new partner, Dash.

The boys, billed as the Houdini Brothers, took their trick box with them. In later years they remembered working in one of the side shows or a ten-in-one on the giant midway. They may have done so. The Fair seemed big enough for everybody. Even Minnie Williams was there with her bodyguard-manager, Bug MacDonald.

In the nineteenth century's biggest of big shows, an apprentice magician and his novice partner did not set Lake Michigan on fire. Of their fortunes, misfortunes, successes, and failures at the fair there is no trace. But there is evidence that Harry—without Dash—was booked by Kohl & Middleton's Dime Museum to do a single for twelve dollars a week.

Here was the place to get intensive experience. He gave twenty shows a day! Between shows he spent the little time he had observing the other acts. And a fascinating crew they were.

Many had been engaged because of some deformity or natural
anomaly—the midgets, the alligator-skinned boy, the bird girl.
Others produced gasps with stunts that mystified or startled
crowds, and these captured Houdini's professional interest. The
sword swallowers, he discovered, actually let the solid steel
blades slide down their throats; they had conquered the gag
reflex. He learned that fire-eaters may put in their mouths awe-
somely blazing materials, so long as they never forget to
breathe out gently to keep the heat away from the soft tissues
of the roof of the mouth.

Houdini admired these acts. His bête noire of the Dime
Museum, however, was Horace Goldin, whose rapid-fire illusion show was already winning fame. Goldin appeared in the
annex of the museum. This, in itself, was a mark of achieve-
ment, since admission here was a dime extra.

When Houdini approached Goldin on a one-master-of-mys-
tery-to-another basis, Goldin told him loftily: "Look here, kid
—you're getting twelve a week. I'm getting seventy-five. That
makes me six times as important around here as you." Houdini
boiled. It was twenty-five years before he forgave Goldin. In
the end they did become good friends, as great figures of
vaudeville's golden age.

Once back in New York, Harry's spirits, crushed during the
day by constant grinding attempts to book his act, were re-
vived at night by the tender scolding and fussing of Mother
Weiss.

For the Brothers Houdini, reunited and playing around New
York, times were so difficult that to anybody but Harry they
would have been considered impossible. But Harry never suc-
cumbed to the lure of a prosaic job and regular folding money
every week. He always knew what he wanted, and his determination to get it was extreme.

Harry had started his career with a number of formidable
handicaps. Most people who paid for entertainment expected
a magician to be a tall and impressive man, either slender, dark
and Mephistophelean (Hermann was the model) or big and

stately (Kellar set the style). Houdini was neither. He was short
—only about five inches over five feet—and, like many other
men who lack height, he wore his hair long and bushy. His
clothes, in youth as in middle age, always looked as though
he had slept in them. His speech connected one grammatical
error with another so that even booking agents not celebrated
for sensitive ears immediately graded Harry as small time.

He had also to remedy shortcomings more immediately
harmful. Although he had done magic before demanding and
potentially abusive audiences, he was still young; he worked
too eagerly and too hard. He had no flashy apparatus. He did
not do sleight-of-hand magic well. He was too proud to haggle
over the price of his services, and this was only one of his
faults as a businessman.

He was healthy, intelligent, and determined. To the casual
observer these might have seemed his only assets. No, there
was one more. His face was handsome—in moments of concentration its burning intensity could grip the attention of the
audience. Then he would smile and the gray-blue eyes, smol-
dering a moment before, would dance. He could smile a winning, enchanting smile that could make any crowd forgive a
bungled trick. That wholehearted, boyish smile stayed with him
all his life. It served him well in innumerable tight spots. He
needed the defense of a smile in the beer halls he played.

There are rowdy night clubs today where the customers gab
during the efforts of entertainers, but the basic toughness of
these spots lies in the relationship of the patrons to one another, rather than any concerted attempt to heckle the talent.
The beer hall of the nineties has no real descendant. The
tables were small and the aisles between them were just barely
wide enough to let a waiter wedge his way through. Fights were
frequent. The show went grimly on while waiters moved the
combatants to the sidewalk.

The performers were weary at times, although there were
"regulars" among the talent who seemed never to tire and

gave out with such volume of song that they drowned out the gabble of drunken conversation. The stage was usually a narrow platform with draw curtains. Sometimes it was without even this refinement. The girls of the "line," when there was a chorus, tended toward beef, as the taste of the times required. A novelty act had to fight extra hard to get a hearing. In such a "palace of amusement"—decorated with artificial autumn leaves tacked to the ceiling beams, foggy with smoke and acrid with stale beer—young Harry Houdini would step out "to show youse a few experiments in de art of sleight o' hand."

There was never any lack of volunteers to tie him up. The beer halls were well patronized by sailors.

At the blaring playground by the sea, Coney Island, was a street of cabarets called The Bowery, famous now for the start it gave to ambitious youngsters. Down the years Eddie Cantor, Irving Berlin, Jimmy Durante and Vincent Lopez all played here.

The Houdini Brothers came now to Coney's Bowery cabarets and cheap "vaude" houses. Harry had taken a step up from his tent show here with Jarrow. With Dash, he was in a theater performing the box trick.

They played it well. One was tied with a strip of braid around his wrists and locked in the box. The curtains closed. The other partner, putting his head through the curtains, counted, "One, two . . ." His head ducked out of sight. "Three." This time the other boy's head appeared. The curtains parted. The box was unlocked and inside, tied with the braid, was the Houdini who originally had been outside!

These were the last days of the Houdini Brothers as an act. Soon the billing became simply *The Houdinis*. For a girl had entered the picture—a tiny girl who weighed less than a hundred pounds and was just breaking into show business herself. Her stage name was Bessie Raymond. In later years Dash always claimed that he saw her first. But it was Harry she fell in love with and married.

4. *Magic Island*

In THE BIOGRAPHY authorized by Beatrice Houdini, *Houdini, His Life-Story by Harold Kellock, from the Recollections and Documents of Beatrice Houdini* (New York, 1928), the story of the Houdini's meeting, whirlwind courtship, and marriage is given in detail. While Houdini was playing a date at a high school, he spilled acid from a "water to ink" trick on little Wilhelmina Rahner's frock. He got her address, called to make his apologies and arrange for restoration of the garment. Later he took the girl on her first visit to Coney Island, kept her out late and, when she became panicky lest her mother punish her, he proposed marriage at once. They were married hastily by the boss of Coney Island, John Y. McKane, on June 22, 1894. So the Kellock account runs.

Something is wrong with this story on the face of it. The notorious McKane was on that date serving a sentence in Sing Sing prison. A reform movement had finally breached his stronghold and responsible authorities had inquired too closely into the way things at Coney Island were run.

An amusing glimpse of Houdini's life at Coney raises other doubts. In his earliest scrapbook, now in the collection of Mr. Sidney Hollis Radner of Holyoke, Massachusetts, there is a curious and interesting newspaper story pasted among Houdini's earliest press clippings. It is dated June 22, 1894, the date Bess always celebrated as their wedding anniversary, and it is written in the heavy-footed style of humorous newspaper features of the day. The story reports that one Risey, otherwise unidentified but treated as if he were a well-known character, apparently got a classic answer to his heckling of Houdini. The headlines give the flavor of the incident.

RISEY IN THE BOX

Much Merriment Along Coney Island's Bowery

A Veteran Theatrical Man Tries to Expose
the Hunyadi Brothers' Box Trick and
Comes to Grief—a Woeful Figure
on the Concert Hall Stage

The story, with a spectacular misspelling of Houdini and
with much topical reference that is obscure today, tells how
Risey—who bragged that he was a veteran of the circus and
concert-hall world for "thirty year" and considered himself the
"High and Mighty Muck of Vacca's Theater"—scorned the
box trick of the "Hunyadi" Brothers, saying that he had seen
the Davenport Brothers do a box trick twenty "year" earlier
and that he had then showed them up as fakes. The story
continues:

> Risey ran afoul of one of the Hunyadi brothers who was
> taking one of the Floral Sisters, "neat song and dance artistes"
> for a stroll between turns. He had heard of Risey's boasts and
> he glared at him. Risey passed the word about "fakers and fake
> box tricks." The Hunyadi heard the stinging words and turning
> quickly he shouted: "In de presence o' me lady fren' I'll say
> notin' but I'll do youse dirt when I git back." Manager Vacca
> at this point patched up a truce and the Brothers Hunyadi
> offered Risey $100 if he could fathom the secret of their box.
> Risey's confidence was as inflated as his self-esteem. That
> evening a sign was put up on one side of the stage: "Next:
> Risey's going into the box."

According to the reporter, the theater was crowded with newspapermen and local politicians who knew a promise of amusement when they heard it. Risey was first put into a silken bag
and then into the box. In five minutes he was calling for help.
He was released—but there was no escape from the delighted

crowd's derision. The reporter's overblown prose declines to a final gnomic understatement: "Risey," he concluded, "is now in a hole."

It is not too difficult to reconstruct the scene: a braggart who was employed around the theater in some humble capacity, but who imagined himself a performer, was encouraged—perhaps by the Houdinis, more probably by the theater manager— to try to get out of their box. It is even more likely that Risey was a paid stooge in a carefully arranged stunt, an old timer who for fifty cents' worth of beer would agree to go along with any gag.

Just why Houdini clipped this journalistic curiosity about the "Floral Sisters" and the "Hunyardi Brothers" is a mystery unless it had some special significance for him. In later years Dash, then known as Hardeen, told Sid Radner that his brother kept this story of the joke at Vacca's Theater because it marked the start of his courtship of Bess, who was one of the Floral Sisters. Dash apparently called on both sisters and arranged to meet them on the beach. Harry went as extra man and Beatrice Raymond, born Wilhemina Rahner, met Harry Houdini, born Ehrich Weiss. This has the ring of truth.

Another bit of evidence to substantiate Dash's story is an item pasted on the following page of Houdini's scrapbook. Taken from the *Clipper,* a New York weekly that carried theatrical news, the story is dated July 28, 1894:

> The Brothers Houdini, who for years have mystified the world by their mysterious box mystery, known as Metamorphosis, are no more and the team will hereafter be known as The Houdinis. The new partner is Miss Bessie Raymond, the petite soubrette, who was married to Mr. Harry Houdini on July 22 by Rev. G. S. Louis of Brooklyn. Harry has bought his brother's interest in the act and he and Miss Bessie Raymond will hereafter perform it.

There is little doubt that the Houdinis were married at least twice, once by a civil ceremony and again by a priest, since

Bess was a Catholic. They may well have been married a third time by a rabbi to please Mother Weiss.

Whatever the correct account of its details, the marriage lasted until Houdini's death, thirty-two years later.

Jerry Anderson, an Illinois collector of Houdini anecdotes, reports to *The Linking Ring* (official organ of The International Brotherhood of Magicians) that, when asked why she joined the act, Bess told this story:

"Two weeks after we were married, Harry was playing in a *musée* which kept open until late at night. Some gossip came to me that Harry had been seen with a redhead who worked on the same bill with him in the *musée*. I waited outside that night and when it was 'all out and over,' sure enough, Harry came out with this red-haired girl. I was boiling mad and I sailed into her with both fists. Harry had to pull me off. Finally he made me listen and told me that since it was a tough neighborhood he simply had agreed to walk the girl home. I was pacified when I went with them and, sure enough, the girl did live a few blocks from the *musée* and, as Harry had said, it was a tough neighborhood. The girl asked us both in for a midnight snack and it all blew over happily. But from there on in I determined to work with him. I fitted into the box better than Dash, anyhow. I was about half his size."

The newly married Houdinis could have no settled home. Often they lived in rooms upstairs from the places they were playing. Quarters were then a part of their pay. At other times they moved in with Mother Weiss in the ground-floor apartment on East 69th Street.

Bess Houdini claimed that Mrs. Weiss was like a mother to her. Bess might well have been hungry for parental love. Her own mother had become estranged when she married the son of a rabbi; and her father, a German immigrant, was dead. There are accounts which tell a slightly different story of the feeling between Mrs. Weiss and Bess, and the truth is probably somewhere in between. In any case, Bess must have known how to adjust to a large family; she had nine sisters and a brother. That fact may have made easier the times of sharing an apartment with the Weiss clan.

Harry evidently saved some money or talked fast to a job printer. Soon his act with his new wife-partner had a supply of playbills with illustrations showing every step of their trunk trick:

The Houdinis

present their . . . . marvelous mystery

METAMORPHOSIS

Exchange Made in 3 Seconds

The Greatest Novelty Mystery Act in the World!

All the Apparatus used in this Act is inspected by a Committee selected from the Audience

Mons. Houdini's hands are fastened behind his back, [he] is securely tied in a bag and the knots are sealed, then placed in a massive Box which is locked and strapped, the box is then rolled into a small cabinet, and Mlle. Houdini draws the curtain and claps her hands three times, at the last clap of her hands the curtain is drawn open by Mons. Houdini and Mlle. Houdini has disappeared, and upon the box being opened She is found in his place in the bag, the seals unbroken and her hands tied in precisely the same manner as were Mons. Houdini's when first entering the bag.

Just think over this, the time consumed in making the change is THREE SECONDS!

We challenge the world to produce an act done with greater Mystery, Speed or Dexterity.
Respectfully yours,
THE HOUDINIS

For this miracle of mystery, speed and dexterity, done sometimes twenty shows a day in a *musée,* they got twenty dollars a week.

The act wasn't easy to sell. Bess blamed the difficulty on herself. Her figure was too slender to be considered attractive in an era of ample beauties. The artist who did the playbill showed her dressed daringly in tights. He added curves of hip and bosom that the young bride didn't have. But she still felt that she was responsible for the difficulty in selling the act. For all Bess' misgivings, her lack of amplitude was not the sole barrier to bookings. The addition of a "petite soubrette" actually gave the turn more appeal.

Few accounts of Houdini's life fail to mention the advice that influenced his career. The manager of a Coney Island show (the story says it was the fabulous Sam Gumpertz, who plays hero in two Houdini legends) called the young magician aside one day and said something like this: "Harry, why do you say, 'Ladies and Gents, as youse can see I ain't got nothing up my sleeve!'?"

"Because I ain't. What's the matter with what I say?"

"Nothing. Except that it's bad grammar to say 'ain't.' "

The story probably had a background of truth. According to reliable reports, Houdini never used the expression again. He never was a polished speaker; because his parents spoke no English at home, he had learned the speech of the pavements. But he never said "ain't." He was eager to possess any kind of key—to any kind of door.

It is easy to believe the story Bess told of her spare-time activity in the early days. She put together card tricks from decks Harry got cheap from gambling houses. The Houdinis would pitch these tricks at the end of their act when playing *musées.* When times were at their toughest, the proceeds of this pitch kept the newlyweds eating.

Houdini never slept more than five hours a night. The minute he woke up he leaped out of bed, ready to grapple with any

problems the new day might bring. Always the first of these
was to provide breakfast, sometimes only a "growler" of coffee
from a lunch wagon. While Bess slept a little longer, Harry
would plunge out to the nearest market, jog-trotting more often
than walking, to keep himself in top condition. What he bought
for the day depended on what cash he had.

It was stew meat when times were prosperous, bread and
cheese when they were lean. At the rooming house or in one
of the chill, drafty dressing rooms of a small-town theater, Bess
would make coffee and cook on a little alcohol stove whatever
there was to cook. Years later, when he could afford to eat at
Delmonico's or Jack's, Houdini still enjoyed snacks cooked by
Bess on their little dressing-room "field kitchen."

At some time in this period it occurred to Harry to use his
handcuffs as an addition to the trunk trick. By now an actual
trunk had replaced the old box; a real trunk could work
"double" and carry wardrobe, props, and handbills on trips.
Gradually, although he had to skimp on food and other necessities, Houdini saved enough to back up his "challenge."

He offered one hundred dollars to anyone who could handcuff him so that he could not escape. The money always was in
hazard. Only much later did he learn a practically foolproof
stratagem by which the challenge money could be protected.
If a challenger tried freak cuffs, Houdini would ask to see the
color of *his* money. The challenge became a wager. Nobody
ever wanted to *bet* a hundred that the little Escape King
couldn't get out of anything.

The concert halls in the sticks provided a living so bare that
it just covered room and board. Getting railroad fare to their
next engagement took luck, ingenuity, and faith. This is the
way it was when the big chance came.

The Houdinis were playing the Deep South in the smallest of
small-time "vaude" when the telegram came that made Houdini
jubilant, and Bess ecstatic for him. It was from a New York
agent. He had booked them into the opening spot at Tony
Pastor's 14th Street Theater!

They could not afford to celebrate by treating the other acts to champagne or even to beer. The theater manager had to lend them the money for their fare back to Manhattan. But they left in a glow of expectation. The new year, 1895, promised great things.

5. *A Crowded House*

TONY PASTOR'S was three-a-day vaudeville with the first morning show at ten-thirty. The opening act on any bill, and this was the Houdini's spot, was usually a "silent," tumblers or jugglers. Dyed-in-the-wool fans often missed it entirely or filtered in while it was on. But Houdini was on a Pastor bill— even if his name was in the smallest type on the board outside, even if he was the opener. This was New York, and he was on the first rung of the highest ladder.

Harry and Bess played as if the all-but-empty cavern beyond the footlights were packed with a cheering throng. In his mind's eye Houdini filled it; he saw the rear of the theater jammed with standees. He was Houdini, the greatest magician in the world. What did it matter if the world didn't know it yet? It soon would. When a handful of paying customers gave the trunk trick a good reception, Houdini's smile was that of a conquering hero.

Years later Bess recalled that the other acts on the bill didn't know who the Houdinis were or what they did until a kindly trouper happened to notice Bess. Maggie Cline, who headlined the bill, dragged the little wisp of a girl into her dressing room a few minutes before the Houdinis were set to go on and asked, "My God, kid, who made you up?"

Bess admitted that the make-up job was her own. Maggie clucked in dismay, assaulted Bess' face with cold cream, and then made her up properly. When Harry saw Bess, he almost forgot the act. Elated by his wife's new beauty, he projected to his audience a fresh glow of confidence.

True enough, his dress suit had seen better days—much, much better, probably on the back of a waiter. The cards he spread in ribbon fans along his forearms, then flipped into the air and caught (with only one or two falling to the floor) had long since lost their crisp brilliance. The silks he made vanish, then triumphantly displayed with a borrowed handkerchief knotted between them were in obvious need of a hot iron. But it didn't matter that night. The audience caught fire from him; they enjoyed the tricks because the bustling young man was obviously having such a wonderful time doing them.

Of course, what the audience felt flowed back to Harry. He heard the spontaneous applause. With the substitution trunk number he produced true mystery, fast and inexplicable. It was the one trick in which Houdini's pace perfectly fitted the routine. Perspiring and triumphant, he and Bess took their bows hand in hand. The last thing the crowd remembered was the magician's smile. . . .

Curious about her new-found protégé, Maggie Cline decided to watch the act from the wings. More, she buttonholed the great Tony Pastor himself to watch with her. When the Houdinis came off, Pastor spoke a few kindly words to them. The next day he shifted them to the number-four spot on the bill.

Harry had never doubted his high destiny. The rest of the week was a vindication and promise. When the booking was over he asked for and got a note from Pastor which forever after remained a proud page in his scrapbook. Pastor's note was dated February 4, 1895, and said: "The Houdinis' act as performed here I found satisfactory and interesting."

But booking agents were not impressed. The Houdinis went back to Huber's Museum. Harry assured Bess that it was just fill-in time. The big circuits would soon be clamoring for their services.

Back at the *musées*, Harry was undismayed. He added another accomplishment to his repertoire, mastery of the "Punch whistle"—a device that produces the shrill, cackling voice of Mr. Punch: *"That's the way to do it!"* as he belabors his wife, Judy, with a stick.

In the spring of 1895 the Houdinis embarked on a new adventure. They made their way to Lancaster, Pennsylvania, winter quarters of the Welsh Brothers' circus, where they "joined on" by signing an impressive contract. Houdini was to do his card tricks and handcuff escape, Bessie a song-and-dance routine. In the side show she would do the mind-reading turn while Harry worked Punch. They would combine, of course, on their trunk trick. Further duties consisted of anything the management required of them, all disputes to be referred to the manager as "arbitrator"—a labor policy which other circuses might well envy.

The Houdinis arrived in Lancaster on a night of inky dark with chill torrents of rain falling. Somehow they found the circus "living car" on its siding. One of the Welsh brothers showed them to their quarters, a bunk behind a curtain. Welsh performers lived on this old freight car in which traveling apartments were made by panels of building board.

The Houdinis got twenty-five dollars a week and "found."

The Welsh Brothers Mighty Cavalcade and Giant Attraction was not quite a "mud sill" (wagon-borne) outfit. It lacked a menagerie, but it could boast that it traveled by rail. Houdini used to tell a story that gives an amusing description of this circus and of his position in it.

The show had a banner advertising a Wild Man, a remnant from a previous season when its personnel contained some muscular, dark-skinned lad who could portray a savage. The absence of the attraction usually went unnoticed. But one night a crowd of local toughs began clamoring for the wild man and threatening to "tear down the hull blame show" unless he was produced. John Welsh had for years survived by thinking fast in emergencies. He yelled to Houdini: "Hey, kid—you with the mop of hair—throw some paint on your face and get in that crate. We gotta have a wild man."

Harry did as his boss, and contract, said. He improvised a costume from gunny sacks, painted black rings around his eyes, red stripes along both cheeks and, inspired, painted his chin a bright blue. His grunts and growls were so convincing that the business stayed in the show.

Carried away by success, the ringmaster conceived a master stroke. He described the native lair of the wild man—the steaming jungles of Borneo—and told how, when captured, the creature would eat nothing but raw meat, although he had since learned to eat cigars. Spectators at once tested this statement. Houdini, by sleight-of-hand, seemed to put the cigars in his mouth. He chewed and swallowed with fine effect. Since Harry never smoked, the circus personnel shared the cigars afterward.

Among the circus acts was a troupe of Japanese acrobats, one of whom, Sam Kitchi, Houdini endeavored to teach English. In return, Sam prevailed upon an old Japanese with the troupe to teach Harry some of his feats. One of these was regurgitation; the old man was what is known in the side shows as a "swallower." He could produce ivory balls from nowhere, juggle them, catch one in his mouth and apparently swallow it. Certainly, when he opened his mouth there was no trace of it. Then with suitable grimaces he would produce it from between his lips. It did not remain in his mouth, nor was it actually swallowed. It was half swallowed—that is, he had mastered the technique of letting an object pass down his esophagus but stop halfway. By a retroperistalsis he could fetch it up again, none the worse. Accomplished performers of the art can do it with frogs, goldfish, watches, coins, and even live mice.

Houdini never tried it with any frogs or mice, but the feat itself, like all such side-show wonders, fascinated him. The old man told him to practice with a small potato on a string—so that if it got away from him it would be digested without harmful results.

Houdini enjoyed, and learned from, these unconventional experiences. But in spite of his early vagabond life, he remained at heart a fiercely conventional man. Thus one incident of the Welsh Brothers' tour rankled to the end of his days. He spent a night in jail!

6. *A Brace of Turkeys*

For YEARS the fact that he had spent a night behind bars was Houdini's most closely guarded secret. Then, as in many other cases, his driving commands to himself in the service of his legend finally worked their alchemy. The truth so shameful to him was transmuted. In his mind the episode became a triumph!

The circus had worked its way north, playing mostly one-night stands. In a small Rhode Island town not far from Providence the Welsh Brothers boldly opened on Sunday. Sunday theatricals and amusements were still against the state law and the sheriff was adamant. He stuck the entire personnel of the circus behind bars for the night, and there they stayed until John Welsh returned from New York the following day to make arrangements for their release.

That he had done nothing reprehensible or dishonest did not matter to Houdini. A son of Rabbi Weiss had spent a night in jail! He was convinced that if his mother ever found out about it the shock would kill her. Like many passionate, overly senti-mental men, Houdini underrated the toughness of mothers.

What he finally did with the incident gives a true insight into the man. Houdini made it an exploit, one of the adventures of his youth. With the touch of his legend-building genius, he added a dramatic ending: after the jailer had shut them all in the bull pen, Houdini borrowed a hairpin from Bess, picked the lock in a few seconds, and let out the incarcerated performers.

The experience of the circus was good for him. He still had not learned to "sell" the handcuff trick, but he used it to spice up the trunk mystery. Instead of the strips of braid, cuffs now

36

secured his hands behind his back. He escaped, appearing suddenly outside the trunk. Then he unlocked, unstrapped, unclasped and opened the trunk itself. When he untied the bag within—Bess was inside with the cuffs on her tiny wrists.

Harry now began studying handcuffs with his own special intensity. In pawnshops cuffs were displayed in windows, surrounded by blackjacks, revolvers, and field glasses. There were, it seemed, several kinds. He acquired pairs of different makes. But even when three pairs were snapped on his wrists at once, his escape (with his hands hidden by a magic *foulard*) caused no sensation. Many spectators guessed that he was only using duplicate keys.

Of their twenty-five-dollar circus salary the Houdinis sent twelve dollars home to Mother Weiss. They ate in the cook tent of the circus, slept on the cot in the living car, which at least offered shelter from the rain. They saved their money.

With the coming of fall the circus went back to winter quarters, leaving the Houdinis at loose ends once more. This time, however, Harry made his own new opportunity. His cousin, Henry Newman, was advance man for a broken-down burlesque company that bore an insouciant name, The American Gaiety Girls. Harry took his circus savings and bolstered up the company's tottering financial structure.

With the Houdinis, the cast numbered eight women and six men. There also were two child performers, the small sons of a couple in the cast. While the attire of chorines in those days was fairly voluminous compared to their costumes today, the company still had only one wardrobe trunk. This was just as well: freight rates were high.

Harry's first action as part-owner of the company was to censor out the "blue" material. He had a sense of humor, but he was forever Rabbi Weiss' son. The man who was "shamed" by spending a night in jail refused to have any lines or business in the show that would have offended his mother.

The show that emerged under Harry's management was frequently praised by the editors of small-town papers as being "clean, wholesome entertainment, fit for the entire family." It's only honest to report, however, that cousin Henry was liberal with cigars and free passes when he visited editors.

In spite of his scruples, Harry left in the show one feature that was standard in burlesque shows of the nineties. Audiences demanded the wrestling match between a stout comedienne and one of the comics. But though he left it in, he managed to tone it down.

So the Gaiety Girls limped along from one-night stand to one-night stand. No miracle resulted from the addition of the Houdinis. No crowds came to hear Bess' comic songs. She sang in a little-girl voice (which was no affectation) and with a big bow in her hair. Nor were there stampedes to see Harry's card magic, handcuffs, and trunk trick.

The season of exile with the Welsh Brothers, however, had given Harry something more than the funds to buy into a burlesque "turkey." He had acquired experience that now helped him, for a while at least, to keep his own show alive. He watched the unloading of baggage, made sure the hall was swept and garnished, and took care that the two "bananas"—comedians—were not too drunk to stand up on the stage. He also kept an eye on Mr. Harvey, the manager, who ran the ticket box. (In those pre-Equity days, managers of road companies were notoriously weak-willed.) But most important of all, he started now to master a new skill—handling the press.

A story in a Holyoke (Massachusetts) paper on December 5, 1895, generally is regarded as Houdini's first publicity break. This is not quite correct. Houdini's scrapbook contains earlier examples of what became a favorite device. The Springfield *Republican* and the Holyoke *Daily Democrat* both carried stories, on November 29 and December 2, respectively, about a young man appearing with the Gaiety Company who had visited local police, invited them to handcuff him, and—in a few minutes—had walked triumphantly from an adjoining room with the handcuffs open.

Harry was learning basic approaches he would later perfect. He understood that newspaper reporters could seldom be persuaded to cover the stunt in person but that the theater manager, or whoever spent money on newspaper advertising, could plant in the paper a story of such an encounter with the police.

Some editors were unresponsive to anything like show publicity. Others loved anything new. The headlines show mild success: DEMONSTRATES AT POLICE HEADQUARTERS—Worcester *Daily Star;* SLIPPED THEM ALL—Fall River *Daily Globe;* HOUDINI SURPRISES POLICE—Patterson *Guardian.*

But the Gaiety Girls were beyond the hope of ingenuity. The show finally expired in Woonsocket on April 14, 1896, where the *Evening Call* reported the tragedy:

MANAGER ARRESTED

Gaiety Girls Company in Great Turmoil Today

Harvey, it seemed, was accused of holding back profits and concealing assets. It was turmoil all right. The Gaiety Girls were through.

Houdini certainly was not. With the unquenchable optimism of a man who had a Napoleon-like imperative to follow his star, the twenty-year-old magician refused to give up. Show people traditionally said, "Every bad break brings you just that much closer to the good one that's waiting for you." For Harry this was doctrine, a tenet of absolute faith.

And the Houdini luck did seem to take a turn for the better when he and Bess met James Dooley, a kindly church organist recently turned professional magician. For many years an amateur of legerdemain, Dooley had invested his savings in a full-evening magic show. He had the good judgment to hire

professional help, however, and he signed Harry and Bess for
the show's tour.

For his stage name Dooley had chosen "Marco," which had
a nice exotic flavor. It proved, however, to be an unfortunate
choice.

The company opened in Nova Scotia, and it played to incredibly bad business. The few people who did drift in seemed
to like Marco. And their interest rose when, with a flourish, he
presented his company: "Ladies and gentlemen," Marco would
say, "being on my farewell tour, I have retired from all hazard-
ous work and will now introduce my daughter [Bess, of course]
and her husband, Houdini, who as my successor will do my
famous handcuff act!"

It was pleasantly obvious that the show played well enough.
It was painfully obvious that business was getting even worse.
Finally, Harry and Bess solved the mystery. In the previous
season, another performer using the name "Marco" had
"burned up the territory." He had billed himself luridly but
had performed in pitiful style. Nova Scotia was having no more
of "Marco." Money spent in getting paper up—putting posters
and ads in towns ahead—was buying empty houses.

This was Harry's second turkey in one year and he knew
something had to be done. Adversity had forced the growth of
his talent for publicity. He contrived what was essentially a
perfectly good stunt. He would be tied on a horse like a Western badman being brought in by the sheriff. His hands would
be bound behind him, his feet trussed together under the
horse's belly. Helpless and potentially in great danger, he
would then free himself!

To insure enough local publicity, he got the owner of the
local paper to come out of his den and witness the great escape.

But in the hurly-burly of setting up the stunt and persuading
the editor and other town celebrities to attend, Harry neglected
a first principle of the escapist's art: *try out the stunt ahead of
time and in private.* True, he had specified at the livery stable
that he must have the mildest-mannered horse available, but

the proprietor had either a perverse sense of humor or a bad memory. Houdini got a frisky, half-broken animal that started to buck the minute it was turned loose.

Since Harry was firmly tied, the horse could not buck him off. There was, of course, the chilling possibility that the horse would get tired of pitching and would, instead, roll. Harry knew horses did that; certainly the crowd knew too.

Never before in its life had the animal had a man tied to its back. It tried by every contortion to throw him. Finally Harry "rode the critter down." And he knew enough to kick it in the slats when it showed signs of slowing up. But by the time the horse had all the fractiousness "rode" out of him and Houdini could concentrate on getting out of the ropes, he was miles away down the road with not a soul in sight, newspaperman or otherwise.

The scrapbooks record no mention of the humiliating, dangerous, and funny episode. Houdini was always much too vain to clip unfavorable notices. But the local paper must have kidded him. To Houdini this must have been worse than being beaten half to death with fists. Never in all his life could he stand ridicule, or even a joke at his own expense.

Mr. John "Marco" Dooley by this time had lost most of his lust for show business and was ready to call it quits. With a grand Hibernian flourish he bestowed the name of Marco and the show itself—drops, props, paper—on his stage "son-in-law" and took himself back to Hartford, Connecticut, and his organ.

Beginning in Halifax, Houdini and Bess plugged away, playing it "blue sky"—going into a town cold, putting up posters, making agreements with local organizations to sponsor ticket sales on percentage. Often the rent of the hall went on the cuff. Except for playing for throw money in a saloon, what Bess and Houdini did is about the most discouraging operation in show business.

In St. John, Houdini made the acquaintance of a Dr. Steeves, the director of a large asylum for treatment of the mentally ill. The doctor asked the young magician to visit the institution.

Houdini was always to be fascinated by prisons and other places of restraint, and he managed in this case to view a part of the institution that few "trippers" ever see—the "closed wards." There, in a padded cell, rolling impotently on the floor, was an inmate wearing a weird garment of canvas and leather, his arms crossed and held in place by a heavy strap which buckled in back.

Very few normal folk set eyes on a strait jacket, in hospitals a "camisole" (from *camisole de force* or strong shirt). He saw that the principle of the jacket was identical to one of his favorite rope ties, often used by spirit mediums to render them apparently helpless and incapable of producing any ghostly high jinks. In this tie the wrists are firmly knotted into separate cords, the arms are crossed over the chest, and the ends of the ropes are firmly tied in back. This would seem to immobilize the subject completely. Not so. By working the uppermost arm strenuously he can lift the rope over one shoulder and then over his head. His wrists are still joined, it is true, but by a long enough piece of rope for him to use his hands effectively. The tie can very quickly be restored to its former position for inspection by the medium's "sitters."

Houdini wondered whether if he were placed in a strait jacket it wouldn't be possible to work his arms over his head and then—if his fingers were strong enough—unfasten the jacket buckles just above the leather cuffs, even though he would have to grip them through canvas. With typical intensity he lost himself in devising a method of escape from the jacket. Probably Dr. Steeves, impressed by Harry's ingenuity and determination, gave him an old strait jacket.

The experiments continued. For a long period of the heartbreaking tour, Harry struggled each morning—usually beginning in the first light of dawn—with the straps and canvas of a restraint so efficiently contrived that its name had become a synonym for helplessness.

Harry's reasoning had been right; escape from a strait jacket was possible. Many dawn work periods proved this fact, and confirmed his earlier hunch. He learned that he must manage to steal a little slack when his arms were being fastened behind him. The arm strap could be worked up and over his head by strength and persistence alone, but that step could be more easily managed if he could, as might be possible in some instances, loop the strap around something—a hook would be ideal. (Harry tested the procedure by using the strongest vertical brace available when he practiced at dawn—the brass knob of a bedstead!) He had also been right about the finger strength required to open the buckles with canvas-covered hands. Success required the pressure and twisting power of steel pincers, and the heavier the canvas the greater the effort demanded.

From his experience with the strait jacket, Harry began to learn another of the principles basic to the practice of his art: be ever on guard against the volunteer from the audience, who, by enthusiastic strength, clever reasoning, or chance action, can ruin a routine. For instance, the volunteers who put him in the jacket could always make escape impossible, if by care, craft, or a random movement one of them slipped an arm strap under one of the straps that fasten the back of the jacket.

Beyond any doubt the strait-jacket experiments helped make life bearable in Nova Scotia and New Brunswick. Harry's concentration on a new interest, his enterprise and confidence, apparently helped Bess endure days that grew ever more grim.

It was in those last grim days of the Marco show that Harry first tried the strait-jacket escape in public. He failed to set the St. Lawrence on fire or even heat the audience to the point of applause. He did the escape behind curtains and the crowd evidently assumed that somebody had sneaked in and unbuckled him. For the moment, he put aside the jacket—only for the moment—and began to plan another escape that might overcome the massive indifference to the name of Marco.

Again Houdini used a device from the asylum—the "crazy crib." This was an iron cot with rings welded to its frame. On it, violent mental patients were sometimes held immobile by straps at the ankles, wrists, and waist. The escape had merit as a spectacle. But using it meant dragging a rigid steel cot around with your baggage. The only alternative was to use a folding cot of the type that hotels supply for children, and the escape then lost much of its effect. The "crazy crib" was put aside with the strait jacket. Neither escape was good for the rapid-fire type of act demanded in the beer halls, the Houdinis' last resort in times of disaster, to which it now appeared they were sure to return. Harry went back to his cards and handcuffs, closing with Bess and the substitution trunk. And the Marco show continued dying.

Soon they were forced to sell draperies and props for money enough to move what was left of the show. Only Harry and Bess remained in the cast. Jack Kearny, who had joined the company as stage manager, prop man, carpenter, assistant to Marco, and general utility man, also stuck until the last horn blew.

It blew the night that the gross totaled ten dollars. Eight dollars went for the rent of an old church. The two bucks went for baggage hauling. The three troupers had no reserve. They bedded down in a hallway where the men covered Bess with their coats.

It was "the dark night of the soul." Most settled citizens agree that the worst that can happen, short of illness or death, is to be far from home, friendless, broke, and hungry. All these afflictions the Houdinis knew. But now, in addition, it was cold. The next morning they would be on the boat leaving for Boston. How they would pay for their passage was, in their situation, a minor problem. Survival was the concern.

Luck rejoined the troupe. The captain was realistic and kind. He agreed to let Bess and Harry put on a show to entertain the paying passengers. But when show time—fare-paying time—came, Harry was paralyzed by seasickness. He could remember being in no craft larger than a rowboat, and the Bay of Fundy was doing its worst!

The show did not go on. Passengers passed the hat and Bess finally got something to eat. But Houdini was not interested in food. He lay on the deck, his face green, wishing he were dead. Between waves of nausea he was thinking of strait jackets and "crazy cribs." The trip had been doubly valuable. It had given him a few more angles about operating "blue sky." Then, too, he had managed to see a place where confinement was not the challenge to skill that enchanted him—but was, instead, a terrible commonplace of everyday life.

7. *How Broke Can an Act Get?*

THE CHASTENING EXPERIENCES of Nova Scotia sat heavy on Harry's soul while he and Bess worked their way south from Boston. It had been a long way home. In New York Mother Weiss fussed over her errant son, clucking at how thin he was, and how thin Bess was too. Like every good, old-fashioned Jewish mother, Mrs. Weiss considered "a nice plate chicken soup" the cure for all ills, physical, mental, spiritual, and eventually financial.

She made a few pointed hints about how nice and safe a trade locksmithing was. Her Ehrich had other ideas; if he was to be in business, he'd pick his own.

He secured the New York agency for a line of magical apparatus put out by August Roterberg, a Chicago dealer. As a side line, Harry also announced—through his favorite advertising medium, handbills—that Professor Houdini would accept a few students in the art of magic. Nor did he stop there. In a catalogue of tricks and magical equipment which he issued, he also invited as students anyone who was planning to set up in business as a spirit medium: "I Teach and Instruct thoroughly by mail in all branches of Spiritualism, Slate Writing and Sleight of Hand," he proclaimed.

On another page he made another offer: "Spirit Mediums—lessons given in Rope Tying, Fantasmagoria, etc. Mediums instructed personally or by mail. . . . Terms on application." There were items to fit every purse: "How to read folded papers in dark rooms, 50 cents." "Spirit lock, complete, $2.00. Secret 50 cents." "How to cause a hand accordion to give music even though it is tied and sealed up. Secret, 50c." "How to materialize spirit forms; forms seemingly rise out of solid floor. Secret, $1.00."

For the chance reader of the catalogue who believed in clairvoyance, he added this interesting paragraph: "I give Scycrometric and Clairvoyantic Readings, telling you the Past, Present and Future. I will tell you your innermost secrets. Satisfaction guaranteed!! And I do not ask any questions! Can learn anyone. TERMS, Moderate."

These items were, in all fairness, incidental. The main part of the catalogue advertised straight magic. The Needle Trick which "was taught to me by Hindoos at the World's Fair of 1893" was priced at $5.00.

Professor Houdini would, another entry promised, teach anyone the "great Metamorphosis Substitution, my original act." This phrase can be taken two ways. It was, without a doubt, the act with which Houdini *originally* started. That he *originated* the act is something else, and no student of magic history would concede the point for a moment. The price was unspecified in the catalogue; however, the professor announced: "The price includes right of exhibiting same; drawings, complete instructions, explanations, introductory speech and all secrets of box, sack, coat, braid and quick method of working. There are several that try to imitate us, but unsuccessfully."

Offering the purchaser the "right of exhibiting" another's illusion is what Jewish people would call *hudspeh*—a quality for which the words "brass," "gall," or "nerve" give but a pale representation. An old Jewish joke best defines *hudspeh*: "A man that kills his parents and then throws himself on the mercy of the court on the grounds that he is an orphan—that is *hudspeh*."

Houdini seemed to have enough *hudspeh* for a half-dozen men. Without question, the tongue-in-cheek impishness of the pavement kid who grew up selling newspapers survived in the man who never doubted a high destiny—and could push toward it. But there was something else in his character. At first only a seed through the tough, beer-hall years, it grew, and grew until it seemed to distort his sense of reality and produce behavior which was, to put it as charitably as possible, eccentric.

Born with the pride of Lucifer, and a thirst for glory that amounted to an obsession, Houdini took the knocks of mischance with an optimism many could envy. He was simply convinced that he was great. Great at what, he had not yet decided.

In the magic catalogue, Harry listed his Punch-and-Judy show, complete with figures and personal instruction in mastery of the Punch whistle, for $10. And he had for sale ("If interested, write") his trick of getting out of regulation handcuffs and leg irons.

Orders did not come pouring in. Neither the secrets of handcuff escapery nor personal instructions in how to become a spirit medium seemed in demand. The finances of the Houdinis went from bad to worse than worse.

There is a saying in show business that you are never really broke until none of your friends can borrow any money to lend you. Houdini would seem to have gone beyond this point. He went to every newspaper in New York and promised secrets of the handcuff act for twenty dollars. He found indifference, amused tolerance, suspicion. But he found no money. At terrible cost to his pride he had bought only humiliation. He came back to the flat on 69th Street with his secrets intact.

Whenever the Houdinis were desperate they could often get a week or two at Kohl & Middleton's Museum in Chicago. The manager, Hedges, was a tough man, but he had a soft spot for performers down in their luck and had been known to wire railroad fare.

Harry and Bess started out again. After their stint at Kohl's they drifted south. In St. Louis they ran into one of the longest stretches of layoff time in the history of their act. To make things worse, winter was coming on and it was brutally cold. And their precious trick trunk, containing wardrobe and props, was being held by the freight office for an unpaid twenty-dollar charge.

Bess and Harry scraped up $1.50, for which they got a tiny hall bedroom for a week. The problem left was how to eat. The room was unheated, though it did contain a little cast-iron stove, and Harry was afraid that in the unheated room Bess— never a very robust girl—would catch pneumonia. He fell back on the "professional courtesy" then extended to performers by many vaudeville houses. He stuck Bess away safely in a warm balcony—to which she was, of course, admitted without charge —while he went out to search for work, groceries, and firewood for the stove.

Of work there was none—probably never in the history of St. Louis had its people so little need of a card manipulator and rope-tie artist. (Houdini had temporarily abdicated as the Handcuff King. The cuffs were in the impounded trunk.)

Then Harry, cold and savagely hungry on the strange streets of a strange town, surrendered to extremity. The young man who had been ashamed because he had been in jail overnight, who was the dutiful son of a scholar and teacher, stole a half-dozen potatoes. He used his magician's art of misdirection and snatched them from a grocer.

On the way back to his room—he had picked up Bess at the theater—he found a large packing case that had been set out for disposal. With six stolen potatoes for nourishment, and a supply of scrap wood for warmth, the youngsters returned to their rented room and closed their door against the darkness and the cold.

Minutes later, the ancient stove roared with a fire of packing-case wood. They roasted the potatoes, and waited excitedly as warmth spread throughout the room.

While knocking the packing case to pieces, Bess wrote later, Harry got the idea he later developed into his famous packing-case challenge escape. It had occurred when he struck the boards with his fists and said almost idly, "I wish they put these things together with shorter nails."

At the end of their week's rent Houdini refused to panic. He set out in the morning, as always filled to overflowing with confidence that *this* was his day. And this one was. He hurried back with the announcement that "The Houdinis" were temporarily no more. Now they were "The Rahners—Sparkling Comedy Team." Harry had talked his way into the Escher Music Hall by claiming to be a comedian!

Bess knew that life with Harry was a series of sudden shocks —she already had survived other bombshell announcements. But she did have reservations about her wardrobe. Harry stilled her doubts.

"You'll put a bow on your hair and come out wearing a nightgown pulled up like a kid's dress," he said. "I'll make up like a tramp."

He had no difficulty. His decent clothes were in the trunk with the handcuffs.

The big problem actually was material. Other variety performers faced with a sudden need for lines could invest a dollar in a copy of Madison's *Budget,* a yearly publication that contained jokes, skits, sketches, monologues, dramatic and comic recitations, minstrel gags, and odd bits. The Houdinis were too broke even to think of this bargain-basement rate. Harry sat in barber shops reading old humor magazines and evolved a routine of sorts.

Bess' chirping of the songs and Harry's frantic efforts as a tramp comic had an unexpected result. The audience liked them! Probably they found funny the youngsters' stern determination to *be* funny. In any event, Harry and Bess were held over—but at a salary cut. They got twenty-five dollars the second week instead of the original thirty. On closing night Harry proudly revealed himself to the manager not as a comedian but as Houdini, the King of Cards and Handcuffs! The manager bleakly said, "Never heard of you. What kind of act do you do?"

Harry described his routines in such hyperbole (but with such conviction) that he actually was told to get his magic props from the freight office and go on for a third week. That is, if he was half as good as he claimed. The audiences got plenty of magic that week. The Houdinis were held over again and the salary was raised to thirty dollars. Their fortunes were on the upswing once more.

But their fortunes declined. In Milwaukee a music-hall manager cheated the kids out of their pay. Another S.O.S. to Hedges brought them a week in Chicago. Feeling that his luck was due to turn again, Harry risked their all in a crap game—and lost. Now he had nothing—except the unshakable belief, serene and violent by turns, that he was great and that recognition was just around the corner.

What *was* just around the corner was The California Concert Company, a medicine show run by "Doctor" Hill. Hill was an impressively bearded man whose hair fell to his shoulders. His silver-tongued oratory about the virtues of his elixir was kept impassioned by whiskey. His partner, "Doctor" Pratt, played a small portable organ called a "melodian." He was an elderly gentleman who looked like a retired clergyman. The resemblance of the pair to Mark Twain's characters the King and the Duke suggested that nature had imitated art.

In the show Bess warbled a few sentimental numbers to entertain what street-corner crowds had gathered. Pratt was at the back-of-the-wagon console. Then Dr. Hill began a pitch that extolled the unique virtues of "the remedy." Houdini passed among the crowds distributing the bottles. The afternoon show also advertised the evening's "grand concert and dramatic entertainment," to be viewed at a local hall. Here Harry was something more than a passer-among-crowds. Still, it was a long way from Tony Pastor's.

Entertainers who signed with the company to keep eating, joyfully quit when anything better came along. The Houdinis' experience with the great pharmaceutical phantasmagoria was far from unique. The Keatons, Joe and Myra, also served time. They had a bouncy young son, still in the diaper stage, whom Houdini immediately called "Buster." Even with the California

EASTON PA

Concert Company he made a contribution to theatrical history.

For Harold Kellock's biography of Houdini, Bess provided anecdotes showing that the tour with the California Concert Company was not entirely dreary. Even for Houdini (when he could look back from success) their adventures made fine stories. But, at the time, little could amuse the proud young man whose afternoon job was carrying bottles into the crowd.

The Hill and Pratt business had ups and downs. After a week during which citizens of Galena, Kansas, showed a terrifying amount of sales resistance to Dr. Hill's elixir, the good doctor called his company together and announced a change of plans somewhat in this fashion:

"My dear friends—nay, closer than friends, for the bonds forged between us while experiencing the plaudits of the multitude as well as the slings and arrows of outrageous fortune have become stronger than ties of blood relation—as we all know, the proceeds of our attempts to bring culture and wholesome entertainment to the agricultural areas of our great nation have been fraught, during the past week, with singular lack of response on the part of the populace. In fact . . ."

Harry turned off the flow of eloquence: "Quit stallin', Doc, whatcha cookin' up?"

"Ah, yes, my dear boy, the fact is we're flat busted and we got to haul our rear ends out of this burg. Harry, you've got to help us. We're going to give a special performance on Sunday. Don't look alarmed." Pomposity returned. "It's going to be of an uplifting and semireligious nature. In fact, I have the handbills all printed up. Here, take a look."

EASTON PUBLIC LIBRARY
EASTON PA.

ANNOUNCEMENT EXTRAORDINARY

Opera House:

SUNDAY, JAN'Y 9

HOUDINI THE GREAT

Will give Sunday night A SPIRITUAL SEANCE in the open light. Only Time a Séance in Public Ever Given by HOUDINI except in large cities and then at advanced prices. HOUDINI'S work the past week in the Opera House releasing himself from handcuffs, leg fetters, chains and locks was seen and by that strange power, when the conditions are favorable, tables float through the air, musical instruments playing sweetest music, are seen flying through space all the spirit hands and faces are seen in full light. The representative businessmen of this city have kindly volunteered to act as an investigating committee which will insure honesty of purpose. The California Concert Company would not permit any imposition perpetrated on its patrons, at any rate. . . .

Admission 10, 20 and 30 c.
A NIGHT OF MYSTERY

The doctor, with his flowing beard, and his silky hair falling to his shoulders, looked more than ever like a picture of Jesus Christ on a lithographed Sunday School card. "You won't disappoint us, now, Harry."

Houdini's eyebrows drew down into his habitual frown of intense concentration. "Leave it to me," he said. "We'll slaughter 'em."

8. *The Beckoning Ghosts*

EVER SINCE the performance of Minnie Williams, whose heavy-footed specters had filled Houdini with a mixture of wonderment and disgust, Harry had carried a nagging suspicion that he could outghost any medium. He had been disgusted with the crudity of Minnie's show; its lack of "good theater." He had felt wonderment at the credulity of the suckers who patronized her. Well, here was a chance to give spiritualism expert production.

He saw the new enterprise as just another branch of his trade. Memories returned of the first professional big-time magician he had ever seen. Rabbi Weiss had taken little Ehrich with him on a trip to Milwaukee, where the boy got a view of Dr. H. S. Lynn and his magic show, complete with a section devoted to "mind reading" and "spirit phenomena."

As a professional himself, Harry knew that his colleagues had not been slow to hop on the band wagon set into such violent motion by the Fox sisters, the Davenport brothers, and Dan Home. In the furor of spiritism, many good magicians had presented mock séances in a half-serious manner, leaving it up to the audience to decide whether they'd seen the work of genuine telepathy and spirit return or simply clever trickery.

The borderline between honest magic and occult charlatanism is a tenuous one at times, and many a magician has crossed it when broke. Others have entered the twilight zone of occult claims out of pure cynicism, led to it by the refusal of seventy-five per cent of any audience to regard "mind reading" feats as anything other than genuine telepathy and clairvoyance—in spite of the magician's disclaimers at the beginning of the show:

"Everything I do is done by purely natural means. I make no claim to supernormal power whatsoever."

Hill's eloquent introduction gave Harry Houdini's first Sunday a proper setting. Galena had stayed away in droves from the straight variety show during the week, but the handbill's mention of spiritualistic wonders now sold out the house. Standees hemmed the rear of the hall.

Everyone with Hill doubled in brass; and it is likely that, before the curtain went up on Houdini's first performance as a spirit medium, Bess was on duty as the lobby hat-check girl. Letters left in coat pockets can be detected through the cloth. If the coat room has access to the auditorium, it would be possible for a keen-eyed girl to see in what part of the hall the customer took his seat. A quick look by her at the letter, bill, postcard, or receipt in the pocket of the coat—and the "medium" would get all he needed to give an impressive reading.

Houdini had all the equipment necessary for a raucous public séance. The trunk-trick cabinet and drapes served as a medium's cabinet; the sack in which he and Bess changed places in their metamorphosis illusion did double duty as a "control" measure for the "medium." Thoroughly bound, he could release himself fast, rattle and bang a tambourine and send it sailing above the cabinet. While it soared, the curtains would part to show Houdini still firmly encased in the sack.

But the "message" portion of the program was the clincher. The persuasive Dr. Hill had privately contacted two worthies of the town—one an old man who was sexton of the largest church, and another, popularly called Uncle Rufus, who was the town's encyclopedia of gossip. A five-dollar bill to each of these pipelines of information produced enough intimate knowledge of the skeletons in the town's closets to enable the young medium, Houdini, to "slaughter 'em!"

A few performances of this nature led the Houdinis to take stock of the situation. By this time they were the mainstay of the medicine show. It was logical that they break away and go in business for themselves, since the public was coming to see the spiritualistic phenomena, and receive the messages; the other acts were only being patiently endured.

So Harry became his own boss. He had slaved to perfect his act—and had wound up with a medicine show. But if the public wanted to believe in occult forces at work, even in his self-liberation from handcuffs, he would present the act that way.

The act was puzzling and mysterious. A bushy-haired young man, his brows drawn into an intense frown, intoned, "There is an old gentleman here; his name is Elias, or Elijah. Yes, it's Elijah. He has a message for his nephew, Oliver. He says 'Oliver, my dear boy, do not give up hope. Do not sell the farm to the first man who makes a bid for it. Better times are in store for you. And eventually the farm will be sold at a good profit. Be of good cheer.' "

How did the young man know enough to call the spectator by his first name of Oliver? And how did he know of Uncle Elijah and his legacy of the farm which was the pride of his life and might conceivably concern him even in death? Houdini had found out about Uncle Elijah from a visit to the graveyard and conversations with local gossips. For he and Bess kept their ears open. A small town discusses its intimate business. The talk in the general store, the barber shop, and the boarding house dining room were a gold mine of the little intimate details that make messages from the "happy summerland."

Houdini's manual of operations, *Revelations of a Spirit Medium,* pointed out that a glimpse into the family Bible of any household will give the reader a quick run-down on arrivals and departures, and the number of children who died at birth or early infancy (not an inconsiderable item in the nineteenth century). The Houdinis made contact with a firm which sold musical Bibles by door-to-door agents. (A tiny Swiss music box, mounted in the cover, played "Nearer, My God, to Thee.") Taking orders for the musical Bibles gave Bess and

Harry a good chance to see the family Bible and collect all its data.

To build their show and to give the public more for its money, they divided the performance into three parts. In the first, Houdini did handcuff and rope escapes but presented them in such a way that his audience believed he *hadn't* escaped. But things happened in the cabinet which could not have been performed by anyone tied hand and foot or fettered with handcuffs and leg irons!

Bess and Harry did their mind-reading routine in the second part. In principle, the trick goes back to the earliest printed history of stage magic. Early performers in England—Philip Breslaw in 1781 and the Chevalier Pinetti in 1784—had featured it, as had Houdini's early idol, Robert-Houdin, in France through the 1840's. Robert-Houdin was followed by Robert Heller, who based his entire act on mind reading and elaborated on the original simple methods by which an operator in the audience might code the names of coins and descriptions of jewelry for relay to the blindfolded "medium."

Possibilities grew. The magician could not only tell his assistant that he held a ring, but also transmit to her the initials engraved inside it.

Houdini had taught Bess his own version of the old Robert Heller verbal code and a variation, using silent signals of hands, feet, and positions of the head, signals Bess could spot from the stage through a trick blindfold.

It was the "spirit messages" which really "sold the medicine"—and in later years Bess told the story of a psychic feat that seemed almost miraculous.

The Houdinis had barnstormed their way north and over the Canadian border. As part of their act, they answered questions written by the audience. At one performance a woman who signed herself Mary Murphy asked, "Where is my brother John? I have not heard from him in nineteen years."

Questions about the whereabouts of missing persons require tactful handling. This time, however, Bess, who always had an impish sense of humor, felt an uncontrollable urge to "do a Brodie on it"—mind reader's slang for taking a long chance. She answered the question, not in the carefully worded ambiguity of the "reading medium" but with definite facts. "Your brother is in New York City," she told the woman. She gave an address on East 72nd Street, in Manhattan. Bess won applause but quailed inwardly; unlike her dynamic husband, she was not endowed with *hudspeh.*

The questioner, fortunately for Bess, did not take her life's savings and head for New York in quest of the missing brother. But she did send a wire. And she got back an answer. Bess had found John Murphy!

It was not reckless assurance on Bess' part, but one of those "flashes" that all people get who do a simulated clairvoyant act. Several blocks from the Weiss flat on East 69th Street was a soda and candy store. Its proprietress, Mrs. John Murphy, was well known in the neighborhood. Bess had conveniently recalled the name.

Harry also had a brush with the "miraculous." One evening he was sizing up the crowd as it filtered past his lobby post into the auditorium. His attention was diverted by a woman on her way to the show. She called a warning to her small son, who was riding his bicycle in daredevil "no hands" fashion, and went on into the theater. During the performance Houdini also decided to "take a Brodie." He got a spirit message for the woman. Her little boy had a broken arm—no, the accident had not yet occurred. It was coming closer, "down the pathway of time."

Sure enough, next day the boy fell off his bike and broke his arm! The tale spread through the town and the surrounding country and found its way into local papers. The Houdinis had a rush of business they had never known before. There was only one hitch: their audiences now expected them to perform miracles every night.

Perhaps Harry saw that demands must always grow. In any event, he was unhappy giving false consolation to the be' reaved—which his work as a medium forced him to do. That was not something the son of Rabbi Weiss would find easy to rationalize. He and Bess decided to "pack in the racket," to retire as psychics.

They had been eating regularly for some time. Bess was in good health, warmly clad. But customers—supplicants might be a better word—who had lost loved ones brought to the Houdinis their eagerness to reach the dead. Harry's conscience could not long let him exploit their grief, anxiety, and hope. When he found a touring stock company in need of a male lead and a soubrette, he was glad to fold up the psychic show permanently.

Bess and Harry had already signed up with the Welsh Brothers' Circus for the coming season but they did need a fill-in until the April opening. The stock company was the answer. The production was *Ten Nights in a Barroom,* and in "the great moral temperance play" Harry played Jim Morgan, the drunkard, while Bess (in her most pathetic little-girl voice) begged: "Father, dear Father, come home with me now, the clock in the steeple strikes one. You said you were coming straight home from the shop, as soon as your day's work was done."

The audience wept tears by the gallon, then brightened when Houdini—divested of mustache and the paper wads that had rounded out his cheeks and given him a proper bloated appearance—strode out and did his handcuff trick.

9. *Jail Break*

HOUDINI'S SECOND TOUR with the Welsh Brothers was fairly uneventful. He and Bess were doing a dozen different acts, always a tradition of small circuses, and this season Harry had worked into something new: acrobatics. When they played Harrisburg, Pennsylvania, in May of 1898, he tried his hand at the horizontal bar—one of the trickiest devices ever developed to tax human ingenuity and coordination.

Like any challenge, the horizontal bar brought forth an enthusiastic response from Houdini. It gave him an opportunity for dramatic display of his skill. But he was nonetheless dissatisfied: a "silent" act was frustrating for a natural-born talker who dearly loved to feel an audience hanging upon his every word. When the circus went back to winter quarters in September, Harry was about as close to discouragement as he ever got.

When they returned home, Bess' brother-in-law, William Bartholmes, offered to get Harry a job with the manufacturers of Yale locks. Locks were the only commercial product in which he had the slightest interest—and Houdini was tempted to leave show business. Other considerations increased the lure. It would be a great comfort to his mother to have him close at hand. Bess would be able to settle down as a housewife; no longer would she have to ignore illness, no longer push herself on stage.

Harry turned the idea over and over in his mind, walking the familiar streets of Manhattan for hours. He was always a great walker. He walked when he was depressed; he walked when he was elated. For days he walked and pondered. Then, after one long wandering, he made his decision: he would make one more stab at show business.

He knew that the eastern theaters were inhospitable to his magic act. But he could, he was sure, get a couple of weeks at Kohl & Middleton's. He never failed there; Chicago was always good territory for magicians.

Legend has it that, on this visit home, while talking to the soon-to-be-great Sam Gumpertz, Harry received a hint about publicity that helped carry him on to fortune. Legend or not, it is true that a spectacular publicity stunt gave Harry his next boost.

Houdini had often been dismayed by press indifference. His ability to escape mysteriously from handcuffs had not been found worthy of much space. A story did appear now and again, stories like those in the Holyoke and Springfield papers when Harry, three years before, had toured with the Gaiety Girls in Massachusetts. Almost always, however, it seemed to Harry that the police chief was mentioned five times more often than he.

When he arrived in Chicago, Harry immediately put his plan into action. The first man he should see was Detective-Lieutenant Andy Rohan, a classic character and an imposing figure: a genial, two-hundred-and-sixty-pound Irish cop with a carroty-red handle-bar mustache. The underworld said that Big Andy carried a little black bag when he paid friendly calls to gambling halls and red-light houses. It was supposed that as the bag got heavier with cash, police pressure grew lighter. Andy obviously was the man who ran things. No nod from Andy, no stunt.

In the past, Harry often had tried to arrange a police challenge simply by walking into headquarters and announcing, "I'm Harry Houdini, the Handcuff King. I'm playing over at the Bijou Theater. I thought mebbe you'd like to see a coupla tricks with handcuffs. Go ahead. Put any pair of cuffs you got on me. I'll show you how I can get out of 'em." In small New England cities, where the law men were polite and cooperative, this sometimes worked. But it was not the approach to take in Chicago.

Harry set up his challenge by first having the manager of Kohl & Middleton's introduce him to reporters. He showed them his press books—still very slim—as an indication of what he wanted to do in their fair city and they, in turn, took Harry to the great Andy Rohan.

In Houdini's previous jail stunts, police had fastened handcuffs and leg irons on him, then put him in an empty cell. In privacy he disposed of cuffs and irons. No one saw anything; no one bothered to wonder how it was done; no one was surprised; no one cared.

But this time Harry was shrewd enough to apply one of the basic rules of magic—"never tell the audience ahead of time what you are going to do." He merely chatted with Rohan, got his permission to "use" one of the cells, and cordially said good-by.

Several days later he called on Rohan again. While Bess entertained Big Andy with stories of their adventures as circus and road-show performers, Harry disappeared to study the locks of the cell doors.

To anyone unfamiliar with the construction of locks, and this includes virtually everyone, Andy's locks would have looked formidable. Harry knew, however, that locks in themselves don't make a jail secure; a jail is only as strong as its weakest warder. Few jail breaks, in fact, have been accomplished by prisoners picking locks.

But a large lock of old design (and the locks Harry saw were ancient) is very likely to be simply constructed, however intricate the pattern of notches on the "bit" of the key. Notches merely prevent another key of the same size from passing the wards—the raised obstructions inside the lock—where it can push back the bolt. As simple a tool as a piece of strong wire that has been bent into a right-angle shape will often bypass the wards and shoot the bolt!

Houdini got a good look at the cell locks, then returned to Bess and Rohan. After chatting for a few minutes more, they bade Rohan good day and departed for home. That evening Harry proceeded to make himself a pick that would open the cell doors.

The next day they were back and this time Harry needed only a moment with a door to test his pick. It worked! He was almost ready to leave when Rohan, smelling a rat, chased him out.

Soon, newspapermen were "alerted" to the fact that something was afoot. Houdini, they learned, was challenging the Police Department of the great city of Chicago to manacle him and confine him in a jail cell. He was to escape—if he could.

The challenge specified "regulation handcuffs and leg irons." Harry, of course, had keys which would fit those in use in Chicago.

Perhaps Big Andy was in a better mood on the day of the challenge. Houdini looked doubtful and apprehensive when Rohan put three pairs of cuffs on his wrists and locked him up in a cell. With Harry tucked away, the reporters repaired to Rohan's office to partake of liquid refreshments provided by the Houdinis—another important item in press relations of the times, which Houdini had learned.

In a short time, a very short time, Houdini strode triumphantly unfettered into the room!

The cynical gentlemen of the press were not thunderstruck.

"Andy Rohan was just telling us," they informed Houdini, "that you've been nosing around the jail for a couple of days. You probably have a pocketful of keys—you could have taken an impression of the lock with a key blank covered with paraffin or something."

Houdini spoke softly, but there could be no doubt as to what he meant. "Okay, if you think I'm using some cheap trickery or fraud, strip me stark naked and search me. Get a doctor to search me. Then lock me up again."

This was something new, even for Chicago in the year 1898. And Houdini was speaking, perhaps for the first time, with the authority of a great showman.

He may have given the reporters something more than his

new challenge to puzzle about. For the very word *naked* was disturbing enough. It was sometimes printed *n - - - d* in that spectacularly squeamish age of pretentious prudery.

Bess modestly left the room and Harry was duly stripped and searched.

It is all but impossible to tell exactly what Houdini did on any particular occasion. Given the effect, one can only speculate on the causes and rely on a knowledge of Houdini's methods. In this instance it would seem obvious that after using the key that unlocked the handcuffs and leg irons and the pick that unlocked the cell door, Houdini hid these minute objects somewhere within easy reach before returning to Rohan's office. One excellent place to hide them would have been *under* the lock casing of the door, where they could be stuck with a bit of conjuror's wax.

In any event, his clothes were put in another cell and Houdini was given a chance to perform the feat again. This time, he freed himself even more quickly than before.

Houdini's attempt to win publicity was an astounding success. A photographer had loaded his pan with flash powder and taken a picture of the manacled escape artist as he posed behind bars. When the story was featured on a page near the theatrical ads, Houdini rushed to buy up copies of the paper. He and Bess clipped and sent the stories to agents and theater managers.

With several dollars that he could not easily spare, Harry also wired an ad to one of New York's theatrical papers, a copy of which he duly pasted in the front cover of his scrapbook:

HOUDINI

the undisputed King of Handcuffs was stripped

STARK NAKED

thoroughly searched by 3 physicians and his mouth sealed up. He escaped out of all their handcuffs, leg irons, insane restraints, belts, and strait jacket.

He had exaggerated slightly, but the truth was that he could probably have overcome all those restraints had they been imposed.

As a result of this publicity break, the manager of the Hopkins Theater in Chicago telephoned Harry at his rooming house and offered him the coveted next-to-closing spot for the remainder of the week. Death had taken the headliner off the bill.

This was Houdini's second chance to break into big-time vaudeville. But Bess had come down with influenza the day before. Without her there was no trunk trick; without that, no closer. Houdini knew the act would be thin.

Yet he could not bear to beg off for so mundane a reason. He concocted another excuse. "I couldn't afford to play the rest of the week without star billing," he told the manager. The manager, however, agreed—star billing at eighty-five dollars a week.

Houdini was desperate. He tried still another excuse. "Sorry, but I couldn't play for that money." The manager came up to one hundred dollars.

At this price, relayed hurriedly to her by Houdini in whispers, Bess leaped out of bed. "Just get me over there, Harry— for that money I'd work if I was dying!"

Harry took her to the theater in a hansom cab, the first time she had ever traveled by such splendid means. But splendor had only begun. The Houdinis had the star dressing room with its imposing full-length mirror. In this atmosphere, Bess recovered rapidly from her illness. Fame and fortune, here we come. They had never worked better in their lives.

Harry spent all they earned advertising the triumph in theatrical papers. But agents remained unimpressed. So a small-time act got a little publicity and, in an emergency, was spotted into a big-time bill. That didn't make it a star act.

It was a cold winter with a below-zero wind cutting off the lake. The Houdinis went back to their perennial meal-ticket, Kohl & Middleton's Museum, where Hedges assured them of a couple of weeks. But after the glories of the Hopkins Theater, Houdini had a humiliating experience in store.

As was his custom, he defied anyone to restrain him with regulation handcuffs or leg irons. At one performance a burly character stepped up with a pair of handcuffs of a regulation type. Harry readily allowed the stranger to snap them on his wrists. In his cabinet he went to work on them with his duplicate key. Nothing happened! The bolt would not budge! Harry struggled and sweated, while his audience drifted away.

Finally he came out, damp and disheveled. The house was almost empty. But the beefy stranger, who turned out to be sergeant of detectives on the Evanston force, was philosophically chewing his cigar stump.

"Better give up, kid," he rasped. "This'll learn ye not to be so brash in defying the dooly constituted agents o' law an' order. Them cuffs won't open a-tall. On account of I dumped a pinch o' bird shot into 'em. Kid, you just got to get sawed loose!"

The incident got brief notice. The Chicago *Journal* of January 13, 1899, carried the story. Its headline read: WAS AN UNFAIR TEST; MAGICIAN HOUDINI SAYS SERGT. WALDRON PLAYED A JOKE ON HIM. The article said that the "Wizard of Shackles," currently appearing at a Clark Street Museum, had been faced with an impossible task in getting out of the tricked cuffs.

Harry's reaction to the fiasco was utter and bleak despair. He was convinced that show business was forever closed to him, that his career was ruined and that he was the laughingstock of Chicago, nay more—of the entire country. He tended, then, as later, to overestimate his importance. He slunk back to the Museum to collect his props and was bawled out soundly by Manager Hedges for being two minutes late.

"You mean I'm still working here?"

"I ain't fired you, kid. What's eating you?"

"I . . . I mean, after that business yesterday, having to be sawed loose. I didn't think you'd want my act. . . ."

Hedges guffawed. "Think nothing of it, kid. Could happen to anybody. Now hop to it and get up there. We're due to open. Can't have acts showing up late. Maybe in the future you'd better make them fellers lock and unlock their cuffs first."

It had never occurred to Houdini that anybody would have so little respect for handcuffs, obviously precious objects to him. It was beyond his understanding that anyone could deliberately ruin a pair. But Harry rarely failed to learn. Never again did he permit handcuffs to be locked on him before he had satisfied himself that they were in good working order.

The relief of not being black-listed in show business because of his failure now began to rankle in reverse—he was too insignificant for anyone to notice whether he failed or not. "You wait, Bess. The time's coming when I can't fail or I'd be ruined. I'll be so famous I can't afford to fail." The time was closer at hand than even Harry, with his conviction of his own greatness burning within him, could realize.

In his frantic and restless search for keys to open all the doors between him and permanent fame, Harry copied the man who so elaborately patronized him, the "lightning illusionist" Horace Goldin. Houdini was trying to cram a half-hour's act of magic into a ten-minute museum turn. Harry had the needle trick, a watch trick, his card flourishes, his silk production ending in the materialization of two live pigeons. It was a hectic turn and he was exhausting himself with it. The closing, his trunk trick with Bess, was almost a relief from the hard-driving work with the other effects.

One evening just at quitting time in a Minneapolis *musée*, a polished stranger, obviously a man of importance, engaged the Houdinis in conversation, complimented their art, and—wonder of wonders—asked them to have supper with him.

When they were settled, Houdini expanded in the presence of this cultured admirer. "Howd'ja like that trick with the silks and pigeons? Pretty good, eh? Nobody ever catches wise where I get the pigeons from. It kills 'em."

"I would say," remarked the stranger, "that you are securing the pigeons from standard loading pockets."

Houdini bristled in spite of himself. "Hey, wait a minute . . ."

The gentleman continued, "And as for your act—it's terrible."

The Handcuff King was almost speechless with rage.

"Not that you don't work hard at it," the debonair stranger continued. "But your act has no routine, one trick does not lead into another. You are just doing a lot of miscellaneous stuff. There were two things I did like—your challenge to the audience to confine you with their own cuffs . . . if any. And the trunk escape you do with your wife. That was very expertly done. I liked it. I'd like to see you work for me, doing just those effects. . . ."

"Work for you?" Houdini had the scalding realization that the well-mannered stranger was a showman. His brash defensiveness melted.

"I . . . I didn't get the name," Houdini faltered.

"Naturally, son. I didn't give it. I'm Martin Beck. Orpheum Circuit."

For once Houdini was speechless.

10. *In Handcuffs and Chains*

BECK WAS Mr. Show Business in the western cities. His Orpheum chain had quality houses all the way to the coast and his policy was "pay for what you get." He was a refreshing change from the grinding penny-pinching of the small-timers Harry and Bess had been dealing with for years. Furthermore, Mr. Beck had constructive ideas about the act.

"When I said your act was terrible," he explained kindly, "I was just being frank. It is terrible—as it stands. There's too much of it crowded into the time allowed. What I want you to do is confine yourself to just two tricks—your handcuff challenge and the trunk escape."

He outlined to the young magician the technique of building an effect. In the museums it wasn't considered necessary to build an effect. But in the big-time, Martin Beck told them, an audience liked to believe that it was getting the best and it was up to the performer to convince them of it.

"I'll try you out at sixty dollars," he concluded. "If they like you, I'll raise it."

They were to open at the Orpheum Theater in San Francisco the first week in June. When the Houdinis boarded the train they were down to their last five dollars. In view of the cost of meals along the way, Houdini loaded a hamper with food and he and Bess shared an upper berth.

The second day of the journey the food began to spoil. For passengers traveling on a modest budget the porter would prepare snacks on a small portable stove and provide coffee. But this was not always sufficient, and the Houdinis fared meagerly until they got to Albuquerque. There they had a couple of hours' wait and Houdini, always restless, got off the train to stretch his legs. Bess remained aboard, prostrated by the heat.

The train had started to roll and Bess was in a panic when Houdini appeared, lugging a large package. He had come across a crap game, gone in with three dollars and come out with eighty-five. In the package was a container of ice cream, with which he proceeded to treat the passengers. It was the upturn of his fortunes. He was never to hit the dime museums again.

Martin Beck's instructions that Houdini was to put away his cards, silks, and pigeons and concentrate on handcuffs—closing with the trunk which Beck insisted on calling an "escape"— had surprised Houdini as much as the offer of sixty dollars a week. To him a magician was not a magician without cards, silks, and doves.

What Beck was gambling on was an entirely new type of novelty act. In the eastern cities the theater chains were dubious about acts which were drastically new—unless the acts had acquired fame abroad. Eastern theaters were geared to a family audience that came every week and liked the old favorites done in familiar ways with just enough new material to give the bill spice. But westerners were traditionally a breezy, adventurous crowd and—even if they had never seen an act before, or anything remotely like it—they would applaud what they liked and boo what they didn't. Martin Beck was betting they would like the intense, tough young man with the winning smile and the proud challenge to confine him so that he could not escape.

Houdini, preparing for his stint with Beck, realized that he was likely to come up against some unforeseen implements of confinement. (The memory of Sergeant Waldron's perfidy with the jammed cuffs in Chicago could still send him into a fit of rage.)

In western cities there might even be makes of handcuffs lying around which Harry had never heard of and for which he would not have keys or picks that would work. So he would have to be wary of everything brought onstage; he would have to be two men—escape artist and escape-artist's assistant, for Bess was much too timid to handle obstreperous challengers.

Harry had already discovered one way of securing handcuffs —by asking, with his most winning smile, "If I get out of these may I keep them as a souvenir?" The audience generally decided in the affirmative and the owner, to keep from appearing a poor sport, usually had to say yes. In this way Harry had acquired numerous pairs of standard cuffs—some of which he had taken apart and reworked with a file so that, while the rachet would seem to hold firm, a strong tug, in the privacy of his cabinet, would pull the handcuffs open. This simplified matters considerably, for in an emergency he could always be sure of one pair which he could conquer under any conditions and with no difficulties at all.

Houdini had found that his challenge to the audience to place their own cuffs on him seldom resulted in anyone coming forward. People in ordinary walks of life simply don't go around carrying handcuffs in their pockets or hooked to their belts. He usually had to "plant" a few pairs in the audience to make the act run smooth. And if you are going to plant cuffs, why not plant gimmicked cuffs that won't give you any trouble? He was ready, willing, and able, of course, to handle any regulation manacles that came along.

The keys Harry used he carried in various places, trying out one spot after another. He found by experiment that some keys could be filed down or otherwise altered so that they would open several makes of cuffs and leg irons. This reduced the number of keys he had to carry.

The secret of a successful handcuff act lay in keeping the audience from suspecting the existence of the keys and gimmicks used to spring the bolts back and release the hands or feet. The "stripped stark naked" stunt was persuasive, but it was good only as a publicity setup. Nonetheless, it was a stunt he would not neglect. While playing the Orpheum Circuit he would have to set up a police jail-break challenge in every town!

In his first police tie-in in San Francisco, Houdini was introduced to the men of the detective bureau by a representative
of the Beck circuit. The cops laid out all the cuffs and leg irons
they had, and Houdini added to them from his own satchel.
He explained that these were for the benefit of the newspaper
photographers, to make the stunt look good. He was fast learning one important fact about the form of showmanship he was
making his specialty: it is not what you actually do that counts,
but what the public—including the audience in the theater or
the reporters at police headquarters—thinks you do.

It was, for instance, not necessary for the reporters to know
that most of the heavy manacles belonged to Houdini. The
detectives who put them on him tested them by locking and
unlocking them, as Houdini always required. The newsmen
were simply after a good story and good pictures, and Houdini
was fast learning to give them both. Nor was he above insuring
friendly relations with the press by providing a few refreshments. Whiskey was the most important ingredient, but thick
sandwiches were much appreciated too, newspaper salaries
being what they were.

His smile went a long way to make his path smooth with
press and police. Houdini learned the way to handle cops—to
infer that the boys from the papers were sterling good fellows
but inclined to be a little know-it-all. "Let's us fool the boys
from the papers," had a certain appeal to the members of the
police force.

The idea of tipping a cop is not as prevalent in this country
as in some others. Many officers would be insulted at the idea.
But jail turnkeys are different—or *were* different in the year
1899. And Harrry Houdini found that most of them were un-
cooperative unless first treated to a "turkey dinner for you and
the wife" by the tactful presentation of a five-dollar bill folded
small. "Here's a little candy for your kids," accompanied by a
five and the winning Houdini smile, could do wonders in getting Houdini a good look at the key to a prison cell where he
was soon to be incarcerated under the vigilant eyes of the

gentlemen of the press. In one hand he would hold a tiny slab of kneaded rubber such as was used in art schools to erase charcoal strokes in sketch class. (Today the same substance is used to clean the type faces of typewriters.) It was the ideal substance for making a perfect impression of a key.

In Sidney Radner's collection in Holyoke there is a small dark-red metal trunk on which, stenciled in white, is Houdini's name. Inside the trunk are mystery and wonder, a collection of picks and keys of the most tantalizing kind.

There is a tiny vise which can be strapped to a leg and used for filing out a new key or making alterations on an old one. There are keys with the tips padded with cloth—to be manipulated with the teeth. One gimmick is equipped with a tiny wooden cogwheel which could be revolved by rolling it against the carpet on the floor of the cabinet and so used for unscrewing the plug of an English "Plug Eight" cuff. Another, typical of Houdini's collection, is a double-end skeleton key possibly made to unlock both a jail-cell door and the corridor door of the same building.

Some sets of keys are held by safety pins. Others are kept in small change purses. Very few of the picks, keys, or gimmicks bear tags or labels—Houdini knew them by sight and touch.

The question arises unavoidably—how did Houdini, in the cabinet, and loaded down with leg irons snapped on his upper arms, irons on his ankles, the two connected by a couple of pairs of handcuffs joined together, ever find the right keys? And how did he use them?

Sometimes, we may be sure, Houdini had his keys hidden under the carpet or in the draperies of the cabinet. Later, when he was prosperous enough to have a trusted full-time assistant, they may well have been introduced into the cabinet through a tube that extended from the backdrop and that was, of course, invisible to the audience.

It was one of Houdini's early discoveries that the more cumbersome and impressive an escape looks from "the front," the easier it is likely to be on stage. As an example, audiences found among the most dramatic stunts in his repertory Houdini's escape from handcuffs, leg irons, and a mass of chains fastened tightly about him with padlocks. The obvious strength and weight of chain, glinting evilly in the stage lights, gave the routine its stunning effect. How, the audience wondered, did the chained man get free?

It was not, as Harry Houdini rated effort, a very difficult job. Unlike handcuffs, chains can often be slipped off. If the performer swells his chest and spreads his shoulders before being wound around and around with a single long chain, he can gain enough slack to wriggle out with the aid of hooks placed inside the cabinet in which he works.

There is an alternative method, simple but very ingenious. Harry learned it from side-show strongmen who, with indispensable advance help, break chains by chest expansion. Before the performance, the end link of the chain is put in a vise and bent back and forth with a wrench. The metal "tires" until one more heavy strain will snap it.

Perhaps because padlocks are familiar and forbidding objects, escape routines involving them almost always get across well. A huge lock on the chain seemed to the audience to make more hopeless Harry's plight. But it did not much complicate his job. Magic dealers had for a long time sold what the trade called "spirit locks"—padlocks of standard make that have been taken apart and rebuilt. They can be opened by a sharp rap, even by the insertion of a thin piece of wire in an inconspicuous hole.

In spite of such devices, Houdini's mastery of handcuff escape was an imposingly difficult undertaking. It required years of study and practice, complete familiarity with all makes of regulation manacles, a brilliant natural ability to handle unforeseen circumstances—and an exceptional degree of dexterity, determination, and nerve, as well as just plain strength and stamina.

When Harry and Bess came to San Francisco with an act including nothing but escapes, Bess worked with him only in the trunk trick. With no other help than her comfort and faith, Harry began the arduous trial-and-error effort to create a new kind of act.

Perhaps one burden weighed on him more heavily than any other. As before, he himself arranged the necessary publicity, setting up the stunts, the challenges, and the "news breaks" that had to be planned far in advance. He took care of it all—publicity, planning, creating.

As always, new enterprises completely absorbed Houdini. Totally different from the traditional vaudeville artist who relishes his brief leisure between shows, Houdini worked night and day. He slept no more than five hours out of twenty-four when he was trying to solve some particularly knotty problem. Bess always woke with him, often to hear at daybreak the most recent product of his ingenious mind.

Through the years Bess became more and more a sounding board for his new ideas. More and more, her personality became submerged in her husband's. Although deep within her she came to long for a cottage, some children, and a settled way of life, she enjoyed the excitement of show business and gloried in her husband's career.

Harry kept assuring her that some day they would have the little house and that they would adopt kids—dozens of them. But he also kept unfolding plans and projects that led far from a little house, through decades of time and around the world. And Bess abetted his plans.

She provided food at odd hours. (Harry would go for ten or twelve hours without eating, his attention absorbed by some project, then drink two quarts of milk with a dozen eggs stirred into them.) She saw to it that he washed his face; she stole away his underwear and shirts when they were soiled and she laid out clean ones. (Harry never noticed what he wore.) She took care of feeding and walking the dog. (In a way, dogs were a problem in their lives, for when Harry found one, friendless and shivering in the alley, he seldom resisted bringing it back to their lodging under his coat.)

And, although she worked hard, she knew long stretches of idleness, which could scarcely be called leisure since she never knew when Harry would want her for something: an errand, a sympathetic ear, comfort for his ego (as tender as a diva's)— or just plain companionship when loneliness struck him.

She did not resent the hours (or days!) he spent pursuing an idea with the singleness of attention of a yogi meditating on the all-pervading Brahm. She managed to forgive him when, as occasionally happened, he made a date to take Bess to dinner and showed up five hours late, a treasure—perhaps a scrapbook he had bought from some veteran magician whose tale of old times had held him—under his arm. And she forgave his temper, which could ignite like guncotton. For she knew his essential kindness; she had stood by when, for example, the sight of an old woman begging had reduced him to choked silence, moved him to empty into her grimy hands what money they had.

She never knew what her strange husband would do from one moment to the next. There was only one thing of which she could be absolutely sure: he was not interested in other women. (His enemies were to claim that he had a lifelong love affair with himself—or, more charitably, with a legendary deity whose name was in his own mind and was spelled in capital letters: HOUDINI.)

Bess had married an eccentric, but a genius. If she admitted to herself some disparity in their individual dreams, she said nothing. She filled in the gaps of her life by collecting dolls and designing and sewing their fancy costumes.

11. *The Way to Get Dough Is to Ask for It*

MARTIN BECK had started Harry and Bess at sixty dollars a week. True to his word, he had raised them to ninety dollars after he received reports from his managers that the act was catching on. Other acts encouraged the Houdinis to ask for more money—Harry and Bess were so naïve that they refused to lie about what they were making. Now they debated with themselves about asking the boss for a raise. Ambition conquered prudence—and they wired Beck, asking for one hundred and twenty-five.

A wire from Beck agreed to this demand, much to Harry's surprise and jubilation. After buying Bess a fur "neckpiece," the first she had ever owned, Harry increased the sum he sent home weekly to Mother Weiss.

Money interested Harry for only two reasons—it was a barometer of his success in show business and it gave him the means to buy books on magic.

On June 23, the Los Angeles *Evening Express* gave him a good write-up under the heading, KING OF HANDCUFFS AT THE POLICE STATION. He worked his way east, setting up his police department challenge in Nashville, Memphis, and Kansas City.

On September 14, 1899, an interesting item appeared in the St. Louis *Post Dispatch*, an announcement that a young variety artist, then performing in that city, was planning to jump from the Eads Bridge while in irons. There was no follow-up of this attempted bridge jump in Houdini's scrapbooks, so it is likely that at the last minute the police interfered. It was in a way a rehearsal for his first manacled dive from a bridge, which was also forbidden by the minions of the law. But that was to occur far away and in another country when Houdini, law-abiding by choice and training, did actually defy the forces of the state.

The Beck Orpheum tour ended in the fall of 1899 and Harry and Bess were again at loose ends. He had thought that after his "triumph" out west the eastern chains would be eager to book him. But he found that they were as cold to an escape act as they had been to his magic. Again, it was something too new for the long-established houses and their tradition-bound managers to appreciate. Or so it seemed to Houdini.

The year which had started so ignominiously in Chicago with his being sawed out of the gaffed cuffs at Kohl & Middleton's ended on a note of defeat, not as dramatic but almost as galling. He found that the best he could do was to pick up a week here and a week there, all of them in small-time theaters and with short pay.

The new century, he hoped, would be a turning point. Early in 1900, however, Houdini had another humiliating defeat— something which, to anyone else, would have been nothing but a practical joke, a conversation piece for a time, but no more. To a man of Houdini's tender ego, it was an unbearable attack on his dignity.

In the lobby of the Savoy Hotel in Kansas City, a commercial traveler, by name E. P. Wilkins, allowed as how he'd fix the feller as gets out of handcuffs. Houdini had entered a telephone booth, one that amounted to little more than a closet with a lock on the door. To make a call you first gave your nickel to the desk clerk, who would fetch the key and unlock the door.

While the escape artist was telephoning, the drummer sneaked the key from the desk and locked him in.

The hammering, kicking, and screaming which followed when Houdini found himself a prisoner were terrifying to hear. The waggish Mr. Wilkins made himself very scarce before a confederate finally "found" the key and let Harry out. Houdini went looking for the malefactor and would probably have wreaked most grievous mayhem upon him had he caught him.

When his rage had subsided a little under Bessie's sympathy, Houdini fell into a pit of the blackest gloom. Again, as in Chicago, he was convinced that his career was ruined, that he was the laughingstock of the country and would never dare to show his face in public again. Bess was much too tactful to hint at the truth—no harm had been done. Who cares if a traveling salesman locked a vaudeville actor up in a phone booth?

It was years before anyone ever caught Houdini in the same trap again. Then it was a group of fellow magicians, at a magician's banquet, who shut the World-Famous Self-Liberator up in a pay toilet with identical results—a titanic rage which frightened them all.

A man who builds a legend that it is impossible to confine him need be ready to have his legend tested by practical jokers at every turn. Houdini remained cagey and watchful. And he quietly let it be known that people who played practical jokes on him, or tried to, were in for trouble—not just a verbal dressing-down or punch in the nose, but long, continued, bitter revenge. In a way, he could hardly do otherwise; vaudeville actors were inveterate pranksters.

Houdini also took care to carry a little gimmick which resembled, at first glance, a pocket knife. It contained no blades —nothing but steel lock picks which would open most doors.

Through the dark days that saw in the new century, Harry kept hammering at himself with his constant barrage of autosuggestions: "I am Houdini. I am great. I am famous. I am on my way to riches and world renown." It was at this point, apparently, that what had been ambition before, became an obsession. The obsession was never to leave him, even after he was rich and famous and known the world over. It would haunt him until the day he died.

12. *Young Samson*

THE COMING of spring puts new hope into the most discouraged hearts—even those of vaudeville actors. As Chaucer observed, spring is the time when folks long to go on pilgrimages. The spring of 1900 was no exception: several young Americans set their faces toward the Old World in their quest of fame. Howard Thurston, an obscure card manipulator, set sail for Europe to play the music halls. And Harry and Bess, talking late into the spring nights, decided to make the plunge.

It was an age when European acts had tremendous prestige on the home market, so much so that theatrical papers carried discreet advertisements of "Foreign Baggage Labels—fool your friends, acquire that traveled look." But friends were not the ones the vaudevillians wanted to impress. Managers of theaters were the targets.

The first announcement of the trip was made to Bess: "We're going abroad! They never seen nothing like Houdini over there. Never *saw*, that is." To Bess' unspoken fears he answered, "What difference does it make, we got no bookings? We'll line 'em up once we get there. We'll slaughter 'em."

Bess had her doubts at first, but Harry's driving self-confidence was contagious. Mother Weiss took a dim view of the proceeding, fearing that her Ehrich would starve to death in a strange land, but was pacified by the thought that Ehrich could look up relatives in the Old World. She set about making a list of aunts, uncles, and cousins.

Houdini was now twenty-six. He and Bess had scraped up just enough money for their passage and a week's board. Their only other asset was hope—unbounded hope—and the conviction, shared by both of them, that Harry Houdini was a genius whom nothing could stop.

On May 30th the Weiss clan, Mamma in tears, the others desperately waving handkerchiefs, saw the couple off on their great adventure. When the ship got past Sandy Hook, Houdini's troubles began. As he had learned on the trip from St. John to Boston, seasickness turned ocean travel into a nightmare for him. At one point he grew so delirious that Bess had to tie him to the bunk! And when he declared that he wanted to jump overboard and end his agony, she fastened a life jacket on him.

In London at last, he quickly recovered and assaulted the booking agents with his press book containing stories of police-station stunts. The Britishers were not impressed. They had been badly stung on some American acts and were not tantalized by clippings from American papers, being of the opinion that Yankee papers would print anything for a bribe. When Harry brought out letters signed by the police chiefs of American cities, British booking agents fell back on the "well-known venality of American police."

Harry got off on the wrong foot in one respect; he claimed, in giving English agents his typically American "hard sell," that he possessed a "strange power over manacles and restraints of every description." The agents had not forgotten the Davenport brothers, brash Yankees of a generation previous, who had also claimed supernatural powers.

Houdini was in need of a manager. He had never had one, his act being too small to afford such an expense. But he needed someone now to do his selling for him—Britishers being temperamentally averse to people who blew their own horns. Especially Americans.

True to the old vaudeville slogan, every bad break brought Houdini just that much closer to the good one waiting for him. This time the break was in the person of a young Englishman named Harry Day.

In addition to being very young, even younger than Houdini, Day was not prejudiced against Americans. He was quite new to the world of show business and hence did not suffer from that atrophy of the imagination which is said to beset people in the booking business. Furthermore, he admired pluck and the man who had it. In the hard-breathing, cheeky young Yank, he sensed potential greatness. Day was never to regret playing his hunch—only a few years later he and Houdini were partners in the Crouch End Empire Theatre and other ventures.

At the turn of the century the Alhambra of London was the mecca for variety artists. Its manager, Dundas Slater, to humor young Harry Day, gave the unknown American act one week as a tryout.

The handcuff trick was not new to English audiences—the "White Mahatma," Samri Baldwin, had performed it as far back as 1871. What caught Slater's attention, however, was Houdini's challenge to members of the audience to bring manacles up on the stage. Slater made the escapist a proposition: "If you could get out of the cuffs down at Scotland Yard, young fellow, I might be interested in signing you on for a fortnight."

This was a challenge, Houdini's meat. "Come with me to Scotland Yard right now," he replied. Slater agreed.

At the Yard, the superintendent in charge told them that "Naturally, the Yard can't possibly be party to any sort of cheap publicity scheme. If we put handcuffs on you, young fellow, they'll be the real thing and we'll not give you the key."

Houdini frowned intently and demanded, "Go on, handcuff me. Put on three pairs, four pairs. Put a pair of leg irons on me, too."

Melville, the superintendent, took a pair of regulation "darbies" from his desk and led the way into the corridor.

"Here," he announced, while pulling Houdini's arms around a pillar, "is the way we handle Yankees who come over here and get into trouble." He turned to Slater with a smile. "Let's leave him here for a time. We'll come back in an hour and release this young Samson from the pillar of the Philistines."

"If you're going back to the office, I'll go with you," Harry said, handing Melville the handcuffs. Then he smiled.

Houdini knew, by experiments he had made before he ever crossed the Atlantic, that as beautifully designed as English cuffs were, they could be opened by rapping them in a particular way against a hard surface. When making challenges, he wore—strapped to his thigh beneath his trousers—a strip of lead on which to rap open such cuffs as these. In this case, however, he did not need the concealed strip of lead. The "pillar of the Philistines" had given him a solid surface that was ideal for the purpose.

Congratulated by Superintendent Melville, who admired pluck and ingenuity, Houdini was duly signed by Slater for a fortnight at the Alhambra.

The story that he had "slipped the darbies" of Scotland Yard spread all over London.

Harry Day, as Houdini's manager, began burning up the wires with telegrams to European theater managers and bookers. The young American escapist was an overnight sensation in London, and news of a hit travels fast in the world of the theater.

The fortnight was extended to six months—at £60 a week, equivalent in those days to $300. A dozen sandwich men, carrying signs advertising "HOUDINI" fore and aft, paraded the London streets. At the end of August, Houdini was still playing to capacity houses at the Alhambra, but Day had booked him into the Central Theater in Dresden, Germany, with an option for a holdover.

Such phenomenal success would have been too much for almost anyone's composure, let alone Houdini's. For years he had fought desperately to keep his head above water; Bess had gone on when she was ill, stumbling through her part in the trunk trick just so they could eat; he had continually sent his mother every spare cent, denying himself food. Hardship had hammered him into steel; he was like a tightly coiled clock spring. Now, with the economic pressures suddenly removed, his ego responded like a spring suddenly released. Houdini's vanity uncoiled at an alarming rate.

As his own press agent, Harry had never been bashful about blowing his own horn; newspapermen, resenting this, had failed to give him much space. But when Harry Day, in the best possible taste, sang the praises of his client in language which implied that the American *ausbrecher* was a superman whose feats bordered on the supernatural, the coverage was extensive. Harry clipped and pasted the stories, read them over and over, and believed every word.

Toward the end of summer, Houdini gave Mr. C. Dundas Slater a renewal for the month of December, and made his first visit to the continent. By the end of September, the management of the Central was trying to get the Berlin Wintergarten to release the young American for another month, but this the famous variety theater refused to do. They, too, wanted Houdini. Almost overnight, from an act nobody would buy at home, his had become an act in great demand.

Germany was a fortunate spot for his first date on the Continent. At home, Mother Weiss spoke the comfortable, colorful Yiddish of kitchen and market. Rabbi Weiss spoke beautiful German and insisted on his children learning it. So when Harry stepped out of the wings before his first audience at Dresden, he greeted them in good German; the crowd was his. By the time he got to the Wintergarten the house was sold out six days in advance.

Much has been written about Houdini's distinctive act and its implications—the buried wish of Everyman to cast off the shackles of obscurity, poverty, and oppressive restrictions. Perhaps nowhere was this deep appeal more evident than in the Germany of the Kaiser, where almost everything not compulsory was *verboten*. When Harry Houdini, the American "outbreaker," stepped quietly from his cabinet, holding aloft in triumph the leg irons and handcuffs with which he had been bound only a few moments before, the audience went wild.

13. *Underwater*

WHILE THE German populace cheered him to the rafters, German police officials and newspaper editors were of a different breed. With them, Houdini had several strikes against him from the start—he had come to Germany after gaining sudden fame in England (a procedure that was considered suspect among men who were already looking forward to *Der Tag*); he was an American (which was pardonable), but he was also a Jew.

Harry needed an assistant to help him handle the spectators invited onto the stage, to help arrange for police "demonstrations of escapery," and to make contacts for newspaper publicity. He found his man early on the German tour—a former officer of the Austrian army, Franz Kukol.

Kukol was tall, of good family; his mustache was ferociously waxed and up-turned like the Kaiser's. He was able not only to browbeat underlings but also to go through the bowing and scraping due the various "excellencies" of authority. He was, in short, an enigmatic figure—a "gentleman" who had also a circus background and who loved show business, an accomplished pianist who could do the basic musical arrangements needed for the act. And he had a way with German cops and German editors. Kukol became Houdini's assistant during those first hectic months and stayed with Harry for many years thereafter.

Houdini realized now that his new popularity depended on publicity and the first thing he tried to set up in Dresden was a stunt that would make all other performers with handcuffs look small. As a kid, swimming in the East River, he had always excelled at staying underwater. Why not jump into a river,

carefully manacled so that escape would make for sure-fire
publicity, and come up free?

When Houdini asked permission to leap from a bridge, the
police naturally informed him that such behavior was forbidden. Kukol, however, gained the ear of a high official in the
secret police, the ancestors of the Gestapo who rode herd on
German cops. The official passed the word along for Houdini
to go ahead and do his publicity jump—they couldn't put him
in jail for it.

Accordingly, Harry had himself loaded down with handcuffs, irons, and chains. He plunged into the river and stayed
down until the watching crowd was convinced he had drowned.
Then he bobbed up, tossing the long hair out of his eyes and
shaking his head so he could get the water out of his ears and
hear the crowd's cheers. When he got ashore, the *Schutzmann*
whose duty it was to keep people from walking on the grass immediately arrested the escapist and hustled him off to the police
court—where he was duly convicted of walking on the grass
and fined about fifty cents!

Herr Direktor Gustave Kammsetzer, of the Central Theater,
wavered between admiration and dismay: admiration for the
tough little American gold mine who had made the jump and
set tongues wagging all over Germany, and dismay that for
publicity purposes he had flaunted the sacred law of the *Reich*
—even in so small a matter as walking on the grass.

Leaping into a river just to escape from handcuffs and chains
underwater was one circumstance not covered by national laws,
provincial statutes, or municipal ordinances; still it was vaguely
frightening. But it was only a starter. With Harry Day pulling
wires from one end and Franz Kukol working from another,
Houdini cooked up challenges the German papers could not
ignore.

The unbeatable trio finagled Houdini into a "test" before the
Royal Saxon Police and got a statement—signed by the chief
of this august body—to the effect that the American showman
had, in very truth, managed through methods of skill, dexterity,

and technical knowledge to unlock, unfasten, or slip off the official cuffs and irons placed upon him by duly accredited upholders of law and order in the *Reich*! The local papers printed the story, and Houdini now had an official precedent which other cities in Germany would not be afraid to follow. In other words, he was "in."

A lively battle began, Herr Waldmann of Vienna trying to get the Wintergarten to release Houdini; then pleading with the Alhambra to let him start a month later than his contract called for.

With managers fighting over him, Houdini gleefully clipped newspaper stories from the papers and mailed them to friends back home in lieu of letters. Nothing he could have said about his triumphs could speak his fame as convincingly as the press.

Imitators were springing up in even greater numbers and the acts which had featured rope ties and cuff and chain releases suddenly found themselves in demand and booked solid. Europe was going escape-crazy and Houdini grew frantic at the thought of how much he could make if he were only twins.

So why not be twins? Had not Dash always worked with him well in the old days? Dash was even better at getting out of ropes than Harry, and he could teach Dash all he had learned about German locks.

Accordingly, Harry sent for Dash to share some of the gravy that was spilling over.

Dash came on the jump and with him he brought the one thing which could make Ehrich's triumph complete, its savor sweeter than honey: Mamma.

Mrs. Weiss got to Hamburg, where her suddenly famous son was playing, just in time to witness the presentation to Harry of a solid-silver bowl ornamented with five-mark pieces and surmounted with an eagle with wings triumphantly spread. This was success—and that Mamma should see it, too!

Queen Victoria had died in January of that year—1901— and Harry discovered a dress in a London shop that had been made for Her Majesty. He persuaded the shopmen to sell it to him—his mother and the late queen were identical in size.

Meanwhile, the managers continued to battle for his services. The theaters Harry Day had booked long in advance, at regular introductory salaries, fought ferociously to keep the fantastic headline act which they had signed on for a third of what it was now worth. Never one to quibble about money, Houdini plunged ahead, intoxicated with the sight of people in the street rioting to get in to see the products of his genius.

When he took Mamma back to Budapest to show her off to hordes of envying relatives, he had sunk so much money in special advertising schemes that he and Mamma arrived in the old home town practically broke. But Harry rallied and got the flossiest hall in Budapest—a glass-roofed palm garden—on the cuff, for a royal reception with Mamma on a throne. It was just the sort of triumph a boy might have planned, in dreams, for his mother. And in things like this, Houdini was never to grow up; or, at least, not while Mamma was alive.

His progress from one top spot to another across Germany, back to England, back to Germany again, with record crowds everywhere, finally took him to Paris, where he opened in December of 1901. Here, at last, was his chance to pay fitting tribute to his boyhood idol, the "Father of Modern Magic," Jean Eugène Robert-Houdin.

Harry had decided to invest all his spare cash in buying up old playbills, programs, letters, autographs—everything and anything that touched on the life story of his hero. When he started on this collecting spree he discovered, to his amazement, that the great man's widow was still living. Harry had gone to the cemetery with an enormous wreath which he placed on the tomb of the French conjuror. There was no gravestone for the wife and inquiries soon turned up the fact that *La Veuve* Robert-Houdin was living quietly in one of the suburbs. Harry bustled around, clad in his new finery—striped pants, morning coat, and silk topper, with a carefully knotted ascot (tied by

Bess) and a pearl pin to hold it in place—and with a flourish
handed his card to the elderly housemaid. The card carried the
single word, HOUDINI.

In a few moments the housemaid returned with the disturbing news that Madame knew no one by the name of Houdini
and had no wish to know him.

She slammed the door unceremoniously in the young man's
face.

That was enough for Harry. He drove back to his hotel in a
simmering rage which came to a boil when he was alone with
Bess and Franz Kukol. "The nerve of those stuck-up fakers!
Flowers I take out to the old man's grave; when I get to the
house they act like I'm a bum trying to ding a meal. Who'd get
such treatment in America; a dog wouldn't get it! Fakers!
Frauds! Held over a month the first spot I play over here;
Houdini is turning them away in Hamburg, in Berlin, in Dresden. In the Ruhr they knock out one wall of the theater, seats
on the stage they're fighting for—the stage so crowded I hardly
got room enough to turn around, standing room selling at eight
marks a ducat; I'm the greatest thing they ever saw over here.
And these Houdin people, they slam the door! What am I, a
leper or something all of a sudden? I'll fix 'em. I'll do 'em
something; they won't forget Houdini. They want to play dirty,
so I'll play dirty."

When he stopped for breath, his face scarlet, his chest heaving, Kukol ventured the remark that old Mme Robert-Houdin
lived a secluded life and was not aware of whom she was
refusing to see. The protocol, it seemed, would be for Houdini
to make contact with some highly-placed figure in Parisian
society who was also financially in modest circumstances and
would not mind, for a tactfully presented consideration, inquir-
ing who the friends of *La Veuve* Robert-Houdin were. Then,
on conveying the word that a young American magician was
desirous of meeting the widow of his boyhood idol, and paying
his respects, out of his veneration for the reputation of the
Master . . .

"Respects, nothing," Harry had caught his breath. "I'll write a book exposing the old fraud, the old *mumzer*. His book is full of lies. I've got the playbills to prove it—inventions he claims he invented. He stole other men's inventions. The great Robert-Houdin! He was nothing more than a common thief! The old *gonif* never invented nothing and I can prove it. I'll write a book! I'll give him the worst write-up he ever got in his whole life!"

It was no use interrupting or contradicting him or trying to bring sweet reason to bear. Bess kept still and waited for the tirade to cease. Kukol excused himself, bowing sharply from the waist to Frau Houdini, and made his exit.

Finally Harry retrieved his topper from the corner where he had flung it and began smoothing the nap with his sleeve. Bessie's heart went out to him. He was a boy; the rich kids down the block had told him he couldn't play in their yard. . . .

Seven years later, Houdini published at his own expense a book called *The Unmasking of Robert-Houdin*. In assembling material for it, he had raided the collections of Europe, bought up the magical items of dealers in autographs and holograph letters, sent out a call for old playbills, programs, and clippings, and founded one of the greatest collections of magical books and clippings in the world, doing a great service to magicians everywhere in his facsimile reproductions of old prints and playbills. Robert-Houdin was "unmasked" only inasmuch as it was shown that he had *adapted* rather than invented from scratch and that his life story had been written by a professional writer. Houdini, who at the start wanted to pattern his own life after his idol, managed to do so right down the line.

14. *In the Name of the Kaiser*

AFTER PLAYING the Paris date to record houses, Houdini hurried back to Germany. He was suing a German police official for slander.

In Cologne the *Schutzmann* Werner Graff had accused the American escapist of being a "fraud." The accusation was made in an article that appeared in the popular *Rheinische Zeitung* of July 25, 1901.

The general drift of Graff's article was that Houdini was "misrepresenting his talents" and the German people needed to be protected from him. According to the *Schutzmann,* nobody could get out of *everything* and Houdini was, therefore, guilty of "misrepresentation" in his advertising. It was a pretty weak claim, but so powerful were the police in the Kaiser's *Reich* that they could inflate almost any claim and make it stick.

Houdini scurried around until he found a lawyer, Herr Rechtsantwalt Dr. Schreiber, who was brave enough to sue a German official in a German court, and the fight was on.

Houdini's case against Werner Graff for slander was brought to trial in the Schöffengericht Köln on February 19, 1902. Graff duly took the stand and explained to the judge and jury that Houdini was a vaudeville illusionist capable only of releasing himself from his own handcuffs, leg irons, and chains— whereas the advertising matter claimed that he could get out of *any* handcuffs, leg irons, and chains. This, he explained, was an obvious misrepresentation, since everyone knew that it was impossible for criminals to escape from handcuffs, leg irons, and chains placed upon them by the duly appointed officers of the *Reich* who were experts at such things.

Houdini's counsel maneuvered it so that Graff's explanation

became a challenge. As a result, Graff consented to having Transport Policeman Lott confine Houdini in a regulation wrist chain with padlock.

The worthy Herren Graff and Lott did not realize that this chain, or a variation thereof, was one of the standard fixtures of American vaudeville and *musée* performers and that Houdini had started his act with it in the dime museums. Long before Harry had reached the *Reich* he knew a dozen ways of getting slack in the chain and dropping it from his wrists—which he now proceeded to do in the courtroom, much to the chagrin of Werner Graff.

The court found for the plaintiff, and *Schutzmann* Graff was ordered to apologize publicly to Houdini "In the Name of the Kaiser."

Graff and his colleagues took the case to a higher court, meanwhile ordering a locksmith to make a lock which, once it had been closed, could not be opened even by a key! The designer of this lock, Mastermechanic Kroch, indeed created such a lock—although he went to the trouble to make an effectual key to fit it.

This time it was Houdini *v.* the lock—no confining devices being imposed. The American requested privacy. He was allowed to take the lock into a room designated by the court. He emerged, in four minutes, with the trick lock open!

If this is an accurate account of what happened, we may suspect that Houdini had on his person a drill which he applied to the lock case, later pushing back the bolt through a tiny hole and filling in the hole with solder. There was no stipulation in the challenge of Herr Graff as to *how* the lock was to be opened. The court was sufficiently impressed to give Houdini the verdict again.

Graff and his colleagues now took the case to the highest court in the land, the Oberlandesgericht. The Handcuff King again won and the five august judges handed down a weighty decision in which they stated: "Being found guilty of the above charge [slander], Werner Graff is fined thirty marks in money, and should he fail to pay the sum fine, he will serve a day in prison for every five marks; and he is also fined to pay all costs of the three trials. Houdini has the right to publish the verdict one time in the Cologne newspapers at the cost of *Schutzmann* Werner Graff."

The results of this rumpus, in which the American beat the hated *Polizei,* served to make the public's attitude change from mere enthusiasm for Houdini to positive hysteria. And it gave Harry one of his best "interview" stories. As he kept telling it, he kept elaborating. Eventually he claimed that after securing his victory in the highest German court he also opened a massive iron safe, at the request of the judges. In recounting this adventure, Houdini would describe in dramatic style the fear and trembling with which he approached the steel monster, only to find that by some oversight the vault was unlocked and would open by a simple twist of the handle.

The final verdict had been handed down on October 24, 1902. But during "the law's delay" Harry had been as active as ever. In the autumn of 1901 he had been fastened into a police strait jacket by Count Schwerin, Chief of Police of Hanover. Harry "beat" the jacket in one hour and twenty-nine minutes but, according to the German papers, he was badly bruised and skinned, his clothes in tatters.

It is impossible to know, at this date, whether or not this tussel with the Hanover jacket was legitimate—that is, whether the long and painful struggle was simply showmanship or whether somebody had crossed him at the last minute, in which case Houdini would really have had a fight on his hands if the jacket's straps had been locked in the back. In any event the *Herr Direktor* of the theater, Herr Mellini, thought enough of the event to give a special benefit for his dynamic headline act and to present Harry with five hundred marks and a silver laurel wreath. Those prewar days were an era of naïveté compared to the half-century which followed. Today, any presentation of such a trophy would be found suspect by the newspaper scribes, who would assume that the artist had paid for the trophy himself.

In April of 1902 Houdini made a quick trip to the United States to visit his mother. In all, he stayed eleven days. Then he hurried back to fill an engagement touring with the Circus Corty-Althoff through Holland.

He was slowly, and sometimes painfully, working out his own methods of publicity. In Holland he had an extraordinary idea—being chained to one of the arms of a windmill. But the wooden frame gave way and dumped him from a height of nearly fifteen feet. Houdini was badly shaken up but not injured.

His exploits in the German courts further confirmed in his mind that the only kind of challenge which could be profitably and safely publicized was one he had already tested. A failure in public, he realized, could prove disastrous to his carefully-established reputation as the man whom nothing could confine. A challenger might have very little to lose by Houdini's beating his device, but Houdini could lose everything.

Along the way, Houdini had also discovered that it is possible to convey an idea which differs from the truth without telling an out-and-out lie—merely by not telling *all* of the truth. In publicity stunts and press stories this is fair procedure—the accounts of performers are not expected to be of a nature to stand up under oath in a court of law. For instance, on his first appearance in England in 1900, his handcuff escape, hidden by his portable cabinet of frame and drapes, lacked "punch" and he soon found out why when a reviewer suggested that the trap door, as an aid to the stage illusionist, was not an unknown device and that the handcuff king might well employ a concealed assistant in the cabinet or one who made his entrance through a trap in the floor to aid the artist in extricating himself from his bonds.

In the circus side shows and the dime museums there had been no suspicion of trap doors and concealed assistants for the acts played on platforms, sometimes simply braced on wooden horses. Houdini had never foreseen this explanation of his feats and hastened to forestall it by using a special cabinet for his handcuff efforts—this was a small frame, surrounded by drapes, but low enough so that when he knelt upon the stage his head was visible as he worked away on the cuffs. Then he realized that he could advertise his exploits as performed "in view of the audience," which was perfectly true—his head was in full view but not his hands and feet.

Houdini kept this small half-cabinet in the act as long as he worked with handcuffs. The cuffs, as each was conquered, would come sliding out from under the cabinet while the audience watched the magician, with sweat rolling down his forehead, master one restraint after another until he finally stood up and swept through the front curtains to take his bow.

Houdini had found, at last, the way to "sell" the handcuff trick. He made this principle a way of life ever afterward. A less courageous—and less egocentric—performer would have let Werner Graff's "slander" in a newspaper go unnoticed, changed his billing slightly, and been more cautious in his claims while in Germany, to avoid trouble. Houdini met trouble in head-on collision, and made it pay off in coin of the realm. From the excitement kicked up by his legal tussle with the German *Schutzmann* he learned his secret in its most highly developed form, complete with nuances: "Give 'em a battle to watch." In the end he was always triumphant though his other challengers did not have to issue public apologies to Houdini "In the Name of the Kaiser." No one ever dared "slander" Houdini in the public prints again, knowing full well that if he did, the Handcuff King would most assuredly "do him something." That is—outside of Russia nobody dared. He had yet to invade the sinister realm of the Czar where, down the ages, Jews had been murdered wholesale.

15. *The Impregnable Box*

DURING HIS German tour, Houdini developed a challenge gimmick which was to help determine the course of his professional life—the box escape. It doesn't sound very dramatic in bald outline, but Houdini brought to it all the know-how of challenge and suspense which he had perfected while doing his handcuff and leg-iron act.

When he opened at the Berlin Wintergarten his program was highlighted by the new feat. A packing box, built by a local firm of carpenters, was displayed for several nights in the lobby of the theater. Then, later in the week, at the close of the evening show, Houdini entered the box onstage while carpenters from the manufacturer took great pains in nailing the lid on the box, which was then concealed by a full-size cabinet.

While the orchestra played a loud, fast number, the audience waited, breathless with empathy for the *ausbrecher*. When Houdini emerged from the cabinet after the tension had mounted to the breaking point, the spotlight picked up, behind him, the box, standing unchanged and unopened, just as the carpenters had left it. Or so it seemed to the carefully inspecting eyes of the committeemen on the stage.

We must not forget that Houdini's first large piece of magical apparatus, acquired when he and Dash were working the *musées* and beer halls, was a box. The first one was a pretty crude affair with a trick panel opening inward to enable the boys to make their transposition. This box in time gave way to the substitution trunk, working on a different principle.

Houdini's first challenge box in Germany was probably a very simple device. In ordering the box, he gave the carpenters a rough sketch and specified the quality and size of the lumber

and the size of the nails. That the box should be in Houdini's
possession at the beginning of the week for display in the lobby
or in the window of a shop near the theater was obviously a
piece of good showmanship to which no one could object. But
while it was in his dressing room, just before the big challenge
performance, Houdini had time to knock out the nails holding
one of the side boards at one end and replace them with nails
that had been snipped off short. They would hold well enough
to pass a quick inspection by the committee, but once inside
with the drapes of his cabinet protecting him from profane
gaze, one good smash with his elbow could rip out the short
nails, giving the escapologist room enough to snake his way
through. It took but a moment to draw out the dummy nails
and replace them with the original long nails of the builders.
The hammering was covered up by the orchestra which was
crashing its way through "The Chariot Race," one of Houdini's
favorite numbers whenever sounds within the "canopy" needed
to be drowned out.

In performing this trick, Houdini's reputation as a Handcuff
King stood him in good stead—for escape from cuffs and release from a nailed packing case depended on entirely different principles. Houdini had been doing magic, with or without
an audience, since his teens, and he had learned painfully the
one supreme secret of the art, misdirection of the audience's
attention. There are many ways of accomplishing this and a
contributing factor is apparently to do the same trick several
times but each time by a different method.

Houdini began, with the first of his packing-box escapes, to
imply craftily in both his newspaper interviews and in his advertising matter that he had a "secret"—not a bag of magicians'
tricks but one, all-encompassing, dominating, hyper-mysterious
"secret" by which he worked his wonders. This was the most artistic kind of misdirection, for almost everything he did depended
on a different principle.

When the crowd began to suspect that he hammered out
boards and replaced the nails, Houdini varied his technique.

He had the box constructed onstage, plank by plank, with nails that were unusually long. Then he used a piece of equipment which had been used with great success in escapes from jails—not by vaudeville performers but by prisoners in dead earnest. This device is known as a "bar spreader," the component parts of which—a piece of steel pipe, a stout bolt, a nut to fit it, and a wrench—can be slipped to a prisoner one by one.

When the nut has been screwed on the bolt and is up snug with the bolt head, the shank of the bolt is inserted into the pipe. The whole assembly must be short enough to fit easily between two of the bars that "want spreading." It can readily be seen that when the nut is turned with the wrench, forcing bolt head in one direction and the nut and pipe in the other, something's got to give.

In the case of piano boxes (always a favorite Houdini challenge device, since he could make a tie-in with piano companies, music stores, and department stores in place of carpenters' unions, he would be duly manacled and leg-ironed, sometimes strait-jacketed, then placed inside the case which had been rapidly built onstage. By the time the last nail was driven home and the cabinet placed around the structure, Houdini was already well on his way out. The manacles were quickly overcome and so was the jacket, since for such a combination escape he used a "gaffed" jacket which would give him no trouble—the people were chiefly interested in the box anyway. Once the subsidiary restraints were disposed of, he began to fit together a small steel jack consisting of two T-shaped pieces of steel and a center piece which revolved, forcing the ends outward. With this in place against the side of the box on which it lay, the twisting motion forced out the boards of the other side no matter how firmly nailed or how long the nails. Once outside, with the orchestra blasting away at "The Storm King" (as many repeats as Houdini needed), he lost no time in disassembling the jack and hammering back the boards, leaving all shipshape.

A steel-banded box, according to Houdini's notes as edited by Walter Gibson, offered no difficulties: "Wire or steel-banded box. Have the end work. The band iron is put on with staples and the board that is the 'gag' falls in as usual, the staples being faked." While the notes do not mention it, since they were for Houdini's own use, the staples in the steel band which encircled the box lengthways and would have held the trick board fast without some previous forethought on the escapists' part, could easily be faked.

A confederate, supposedly a committeeman or carpenter, did his bit in fastening the steel straps around the box, hammering in very short staples which Houdini could pull loose by tugging in on the secret panel which had been previously "gaffed" while the box was in his possession prior to the challenge. In this case the box could not be reclaimed directly from the stage by the builders in an attempt to figure out the method of escape. But no matter. Houdini would not offer it to them until he and his assistants had time to replace the trick board with an "honest" one, and the staples with some of standard length.

When this had been done, the box would again be displayed in a shop window with a placard reading: "This is the box that the world-famed escape artist, handcuff king, and self-liberator, HOUDINI, got out of at the Palace Theater. . . ."

When word began to get around that Houdini opened challenge piano boxes with a secret jack, he blithely caused a box to be inserted in a canvas cover made to his specifications, which was duly laced up outside. Here the audience's attention was on the canvas cover. The box was inspected briefly by the committee which spent most of its time and energy making sure the lacing was tight and the canvas firm, with no "secret panels or trap doors." They could have saved their energy. There was no trick about the canvas bag at all.

In this escape, which was one of Houdini's early triumphs, the trick board in one end of the box was held by screws which seemed to go through from each side. Actually, the board was held by short, dummy screws outside and long screws inside.

When Houdini was inside, having the canvas cover laced on by the committeemen, he was already at work with his screwdriver and a pocket flashlight, taking out the long screws. The tying finished and the cabinet in place, Houdini pulled in the trick board and began untying the lacing from inside. This was at times a bit tedious but in those days people would consider it an event of a Sunday afternoon to stroll out to the park and listen to the local band playing in a kiosk. So here, with Houdini in the box and bag, they got a concert while they waited. Once outside the bag, the self-liberator quickly replaced the inside screws with short dummies, put the board in place and fastened it firmly with the long screws outside, then laced up the case, tying it with identical knots, and stepped out to take his applause.

But when it came to tricks, that spring of 1903, Houdini did not limit himself to the box escape. In London he had dusted off his Hindu needle trick and tried it out on audiences. They loved it and he "kept it in." And wherever he played, he opened the week by escaping from the local jail or, if the locals would not play ball, a jail in a near-by town where the warders were more cooperative. Houdini played it up big, always insisting that they confine him in the very cell which had successfully held a famous murderer or notorious jail-breaker.

A signed statement of the warden, jailer, chief constable, or whoever was in charge, was always part of a successful Houdini jail break. Such officials more than once were astonished to see the escape artist's assistants on the street, busily passing out handbills with the "testimonial" from the warden, when Houdini had made good his escape only minutes before. The handbills had been printed ahead of time, and Houdini delighted, on occasions when his escape led him outside the building, in taking a hand at distributing the handbills before revealing himself to the assembled officials and reporters in the jail office. On at least one occasion he came inside and presented one to the warden with his compliments.

Harry Day had booked Houdini into the Establishment Yard of Moscow, so in May the doughty American set out for the land of ikons, vodka, and the knout.

Unlike Germany, where the locks were among the best in the world, Russian locks—whether of trunk or prison cell—were pretty crude. Houdini needed a worthier challenge. He decided on a bold stroke as his introductory publicity stunt and he chose the *carette,* the dreaded Siberian prison van, a portable steel cell mounted on a wagon body and drawn by horses.

The *carette* was designed to prevent the rescue of political prisoners on its long, three-week journey to Siberia. It was made of sheet steel, and was entered through a door in the rear. The lock of the door was welded on, outside. The only ventilation in the *carette* was a tiny window, eight inches square and crossed by four steel bars. This window was a good three feet above the lock which, according to Houdini, was built so that the key locking it in Moscow would not *un*lock it—the unlocking key was in Siberia, the van's destination. This bit of added terrorism sounds farfetched, but it was just the sort of detail reporters would want to scribble down when talking to Houdini.

Of one thing we can be sure, since it is so typical of Houdini's known methods: in making his preliminary "casing" of the van, Harry concentrated all his attention on the lock at the rear. The faithful Franz Kukol, meanwhile, by dropping a match box to the ground, had taken the opportunity, while recovering it, to get a good look at the underside of the *carette*.

The notorious van, once its prisoner was locked in, was never opened and it contained no sanitary facilities. When it reached the Siberian destination, the prisoner was removed and the van was sluiced out with buckets of water, much as you would clean out the cage of a wild beast in a circus. Accordingly, the cell was lined with sheet zinc. But while the walls and door were formidable steel, the thing had a soft underbelly. It was here that Harry planned to make his attack.

The escape violated one cardinal rule of the successful challenge—"never publicize any escape that you have not tried out first and are dead-sure of being able to beat."

To get out of the *carette* as described, Harry needed two separate tools. Apparently, Kukol was supposed either to pass them to him after Houdini had been searched or leave them lying where he would pass over them. With conjuror's wax on their surfaces, Harry could pick them up with his feet as he walked. But at the last minute Chief Lebedev, of the Secret Police, crossed him up: he had prison doctors grab the impertinent American and give him a thorough search which included his hair, his ears, his nasal cavities, his pubic hair, and his rectum. They didn't miss the soles of his feet either and paid particular attention to his mouth.

Meanwhile, Kukol had managed to slip the tools to Bess, since he anticipated what was going to happen a moment later—a different set of guards and a doctor seized Franz and took him to another room where they gave him as careful a going-over as the Boss was getting.

When the Russians were satisfied that Houdini had no gimmicks concealed on him anywhere, they kept a tight hold on his wrists and marched him out into the courtyard of the prison where the *carette* stood. They allowed him one concession—the van was backed into a corner of the yard where the door was hidden from view. This, again, was misdirection on the magician's part, for he didn't care a hang about the door.

Harry was fastened in and then two chains were wrapped around the van and secured with padlocks on the side nearest the driver's seat—an additional challenge to which he objected loudly from inside. Lebedev merely laughed and returned to the office.

Harry was in a tight spot but the trick had not even begun. After a half hour he called to a guard who was on sentry duty around an angle in the wall and asked that he be allowed to speak to Bess. Lebedev granted this favor, since the guard reported privately that the American seemed on the verge of hysteria. It was a touching scene—or would have been had the heart of the terrible Lebedev been open to touching scenes. Bess whispered to Harry through the tiny barred window and then gave him a long, lingering kiss. Lebedev growled and pulled her away but she burst free and threw herself at the window, giving Harry a final kiss. Then the guards hustled her back to the office. Bess was weeping copiously—out of relief, for her part of the business was done.

In her mouth had been hidden two tiny tools—one a miniature can-opener and the other a coil of clock-spring steel, its edge notched into saw teeth. (This last has been a favorite of jail-breakers since the invention of clocks but requires delicate handling. Victor Hugo knew of it, for in *Les Miserables* he has his ex-convict hero, Jean Valjean, use it to free himself from ropes with which he had been tied by the villainous Thenardiers. What Hugo didn't know is that the saw would hardly work on rope but is very effective against iron or hardwood.)

Once in possession of his two vital gimmicks, Harry set to work, attacking the zinc floor of the van with the can-opener at one corner and cutting it close to the wall, a couple of feet along both angles. Then he brought into play the clock-spring saw and went after the boards of the wagon frame on which the steel box rested.

When he had cut out a section big enough for him to wriggle through, he wormed his way out, reached back and bent down the zinc flooring, and pushed in the sawed section of board. He then placed the tools in his mouth and raced back across the prison yard through the freezing dusk of the May night, wearing only the regulation prison drawers with which Lebedev had equipped his voluntary prisoner.

When he got to the office, Lebedev's astonishment was not so great that it prevented him from having Houdini grabbed and searched.

No reporters had been present, but Houdini was nonetheless gleeful as he made his way back to the hotel by droshky. He had swallowed the gimmicks during the second search and "unswallowed" them after the examination, while he was putting on his clothes. The lessons of the old Japanese and the hours of practice with the potato on a string had paid off!

Anyhow, that is the story of the carette, as the elusive American told it to reporters—outside of Russia. If the carette was built as he described it we are forced to deduce the use of the two gimmicks mentioned here. But experts in the field of escapery have their doubts. One cynical brother of the craft told me: "Look, it was Holy Russia, wasn't it? Hell, the easiest way out of the prison van would be with a hundred ruble note, inserted in the right place—the pocket of the jailer."

16. Grave Matters and an Impatient Throng

HOUDINI HAD BEEN booked for four weeks at Establishment Yard in Moscow. After his application of a can-opener to the dreaded *carette* his salary was doubled and he was held over again and again. In all, he played four months in Moscow, at three different theaters. During a week when he appeared before the Grand Duke Sergius, his fee, together with his salary at the theater, totaled £350—about $1,750 at the exchange rate of 1903, when a dollar a day paid for a good room in a good theatrical hotel and a table d'hôte dinner, with wine, was fifty cents.

When he left Moscow, it was to play three weeks at the great Nischni-Novgorod fair. All his life Houdini had heard of this fair, then the largest and richest in the world. The area itself was situated about halfway between Moscow and the Ural mountains, six hundred miles southeast of Petrograd.

The earliest mention of the fair, in ancient manuscripts, goes back as far as 1366, but long before that the monks of the monastery of St. Macarius had shrewdly made the spot the site of religious meetings, the monks providing food and drink for the pilgrims. This great assemblage developed into a trade fair and grew to be the greatest in the world, strategically located at the junction of the Volga and Oka rivers, where merchants of Europe could come downstream to observe the caravans from Persia and Astrakhan.

By day, Harry and Bess wandered through the maze of booths which displayed silks from China and hides of the wild horses brought in by the Tartar tribes. By night the outlanders

105

marveled in their turn at a man who could slip off handcuffs and chains and miraculously escape, apparently by witchcraft, from a nailed packing box. Rabbi Weiss's little boy, Ehrich, was doing all right for himself, "packing 'em in" every night, as he gleefully reported in his letters home.

In September, Bess, Harry, and Kukol hurried to Holland and the Circus Carre. In Drodrecht Houdini escaped from an old prison. The director of the circus tried to sign him up for a tour of Italy, but Harry was booked solid for months in Germany and for a full half-year in England. While in London, Harry had his hands full with one challenge—a challenge which, there is good reason to suppose, provided him with serious trouble and not just an opportunity to display his canny showmanship.

The episode was written up in *The Daily Illustrated Mirror* of March 18, 1904:

HOW HE PICKED THE "MIRROR" HANDCUFFS IN ONE HOUR AND TEN MINUTES

TELEGRAM OF THANKS

Not a seat was vacant in the mighty Hippodrome yesterday afternoon when Harry Houdini, the "Handcuff King," stepped into the arena and received an ovation worthy of a monarch.

For days past all London has been aware that on Saturday night last a representative of the *Mirror* had stepped into the arena, in response to Houdini's challenge to anybody to come forward and successfully manacle him, and had there and then made a match with America's Mysteriarch for Thursday afternoon.

In his travels the journalist had encountered a Birmingham blacksmith who had spent five years of his life in devising a lock, which, he alleged, "no mortal man could pick." Promptly seeing he was in touch with a good thing, the press man had at once put an option upon the handcuffs containing this lock and brought it back to London with him.

It was submitted to London's best locksmiths, who were unanimous in their admiration of it, asserting that in all their experience they had never before seen such wonderful mechanism.

As a result, the editors of the *Mirror* determined to put the lock to the severest test possible by challenging Mr. Houdini to be manacled with the cuffs.

Like a true sportsman, Mr. Houdini accepted our challenge in the spirit in which it was given, although, on his own confession, he did not like the look of the lock.

MIGHTY AUDIENCE

Mr. Houdini's call was for three o'clock yesterday, but so intense was the excitement that the 4,000 spectators present could scarcely restrain their impatience whilst the six excellent turns which preceded him, cheered to the echo on other occasions, got through their "business."

Waiting quietly and unnoticed by the arena steps, the *Mirror* representative watched Mr. Houdini's entrance and joined in giving his opponent-to-be in the lists one of the finest ovations mortal man has ever received.

"I am ready," said Houdini, concluding his address to the audience, "to be manacled by the *Mirror* representative if he is present."

A hearty burst of applause greeted the journalist as he stepped into the arena and shook hands with the "Handcuff King."

Then, in the fewest possible words, the press man called for volunteers from the audience to act upon a committee to see fair play, and Mr. Houdini asked his friends also to step into the arena and watch his interests.

HOUDINI HANDCUFFED

This done, the journalist placed the handcuffs on Mr. Houdini's wrists and snapped them. Then, with an effort, he turned the key six times, thus securing the bolt as firmly as possible.

The committee being satisfied as to the security of the handcuff, Mr. Houdini said;— *"Ladies and Gentlemen:*—I am now locked up in a handcuff that has taken a British mechanic five years to make. I do not know whether I am going to get out of it or not, but I can assure you I am going to do my best."

Applauded to the echo, the Mysteriarch then retired within the cabinet that contains so many of his secrets.

All chronometers chronicled 3:15.

In a long line in front of the stage stood the committee. Before them, in the center of the arena, stood the little cabinet Houdini loves to call his "ghost house." Restlessly pacing to and fro, the *Mirror* representative kept an anxious eye on it.

FALSE HOPE OVERTHROWN

Those who have never stood in the position of a challenger can scarcely realize the sense of responsibility felt by one who has openly thrown down the gauntlet to a man who is popular with the public.

The *Mirror* had placed its reliance on the work of a British mechanic, and if Houdini succeeded in escaping in the first few minutes it was felt that the proceedings would develop into a mere farce.

But time went by; 5, 10, 15, 20 minutes sped. Still the band played on. Then, at 22 minutes, Mr. Houdini put his head out of the cabinet "ghost house" and this was the signal for a great outburst of cheering.

"He is free! He is free!" shouted several; and universal disappointment was felt when it was ascertained that he had only put his head outside the cabinet in order to get a good look at the lock in strong electric light.

The band broke into a dreamy waltz as Houdini once more disappeared within the canopy. The disappointed spectators looked at their watches, murmured, "What a shame!" gave Houdini an encouraging clap, and the journalist resumed his stride.

At 35 minutes Mr. Houdini again emerged. His collar was broken, water trickled in great channels down his face, and he looked generally warm and uncomfortable.

"My knees hurt," he explained to the audience. "I am not done yet."

The "house" went frantic with delight at their favorite's resolve, and this suggested an idea to the *Mirror* representative.

He spoke rapidly to Mr. Parker, the Hippodrome manager, who was at the side of the stalls. The gentleman looked thoughtful for a moment, then nodded his head and whispered something to an attendant.

A WELCOME CONCESSION

Presently the man appeared bearing a large cushion.

"The *Mirror* has no desire to submit Mr. Houdini to a torture test," said the representative, "and if Mr. Houdini will permit me, I shall have great pleasure in offering him the use of this cushion."

The "Handcuff King" was glad evidently of the rest for his knees, for he pulled it through into the "ghost house."

Ladies trembled with suppressed excitement, and, despite the weary wait, not a yawn was noticed throughout the vast audience. For 20 minutes more the band played on, and then Houdini was seen to emerge once more from the cabinet.

Still handcuffed!

Almost a moan broke over the vast assemblage as this was noticed. He looked in pitiful plight from his exertions and much exhausted.

He looked about for a moment, and then advanced to where his challenger stood.

"Will you remove the handcuffs for a moment," he said. "In order that I may take my coat off?"

For a few seconds the journalist considered. Then he replied: "I am indeed sorry to disoblige you, Mr. Houdini, but I cannot unlock those cuffs unless you admit you are defeated."

The reason was obvious. Mr. Houdini had seen the cuffs locked, but he had never seen them unlocked. Consequently the press man thought there might be more in the request than appeared on the surface.

FROCK COAT SACRIFICED

Houdini evidently does not stick at trifles. He maneuvered until he got a pen knife from his waistcoat pocket. This he opened with his teeth, and then, turning his coat inside out over his head, calmly proceeded to cut it to pieces.

The novelty of the proceeding delighted the audience, who yelled themselves frantic. The *Mirror* representative had a rather warm five minutes of it at this juncture. Many of the audience did not see the reason for his refusal, and expressed their disapproval of his action loudly.

Grimly, however, he looked on and watched Mr. Houdini once more re-enter the cabinet. Time sped on, and presently somebody recorded the fact that the Mysteriarch had been manacled just one hour. Ten minutes more of anxious waiting, and then a surprise was in store for everybody.

VICTORY

The band was just finishing a stirring march when, with a great shout of victory, Houdini bounded from the cabinet holding the shining handcuffs in his hand—free!

A mighty roar of gladness went up. Men waved their hats, shook hands one with the other. Ladies waved their handkerchiefs, and the committee, rushing forward as one man, shouldered Houdini, and bore him in triumph around the arena.

But the strain had been too much for the "Handcuff King." and he sobbed as though his heart would break.

With a mighty effort, however, he regained his composure, and received the congratulations of the *Mirror* in the true sportsmanlike spirit he had shown throughout the contest.

PRESENTATION MODEL

The journalist intimated to the audience that a beautiful solid silver model of the handcuffs would be made, and asked Mr. Houdini's permission to present this to him at no distant date.

Mr. Houdini told the audience that he had been challenged many times before, but he had never experienced such gentlemanly treatment and fair play in any contest he had been called upon to enter.

Mr. Houdini's wife was present at the performance, but just before he cut the coat from him was so overcome that she had to leave the Hippodrome.

Mr. Houdini called his charming wife his mascot. "Eleven years ago she brought me luck," says the Handcuff Marvel, "and it has been with me ever since. I never had any before I married her." Mrs. Houdini is a fair, cultured, beautiful American lady, petite, fascinating, and clever.

Last night Mr. Houdini sent us the following telegram:—

EDITORS *MIRROR,*
2 Carmelite Street, London, E. C.

"Allow me to thank you for the open and upright manner in which your representative treated me in today's contest. Must say that it was one of the hardest, but at the same time one of the fairest tests I ever had.

HARRY HOUDINI"

The full text of the *Mirror* account of this famous challenge has been given so that we may study Houdini's life as the newspapers of his day reported it. But much can be read between the lines.

Houdini's correspondence with the London magic dealer Will Goldston covered some twenty years; the Escape King wrote his friend at least once a week. Goldston, one of the few magicians ever to be converted to spiritualism, had some stormy times with his American friend but always professed his admiration of Houdini's good traits while refusing to whitewash his memory or deny his unpleasant characteristics.

In December of 1929, three years after Houdini's death, Goldston published a book, *Sensational Tales of Mystery Men,* containing a number of recollections of Houdini. In one chapter, titled "Did Houdini Fail?" Goldston brings up the famous *Mirror* case. He makes an addition to the newspaper story; after Houdini had taken the pillow for his knees into the cabinet, waited, then created a diversion by coming out and cutting off his coat with his pocket knife, there was another wait. Goldston says: "At the end of an hour he asked his wife to bring him a glass of water. This she did, placing it on the edge of the cabinet. Houdini took the glass between his hands and drained it. Ten minutes later, he emerged from the cabinet,

and flung the handcuffs on the stage." Goldston goes on to say
that a friend (unidentified) whose sources of information were
usually impeccable, informed him the following day that the
lock had, in fact, beaten the Mysteriarch and that after struggling with the cuffs for an hour Harry had called Bess to him
and whispered to her that he was beaten and that if she could
not get the original key his career was at an end. Then, according to the anonymous source, Bess went to the "press
man," tearfully explained what was the matter and pointed out
that while it would mean nothing but a story for his paper,
soon to be forgotten, it meant Houdini's professional life.
Then, the tale goes, the gallant Britisher, stirred by Bessie's
appeal, handed over the key which she hid in the glass of water
and took to her hard-pressed husband, enabling the Handcuff
King to retain his crown.

Some friends of the Houdinis have claimed, "It doesn't sound
like the sort of thing Bess could do. She was too nervous, too
timid." But we must not forget all the times in their early years
when Bess had to "put on her cry-baby act" to stall off the pro-
prietors of rooming houses and hotels, not to mention the time
she appealed to the sympathies of the skipper of the St. John
to Boston steamer. The record shows that Bess was quite good
at pathetic appeals—her frail physique, her wistful, little-girl
face and manner, and long practice all indicate that if there
was one way out of the *Mirror* cuffs it was just this way. Houdini's violent sobs, while the delighted spectators were carrying
him off the field on their shoulders, sound more like humiliation and rage than overpowering emotion from any other cause.

Certain elements in the *Mirror* account suggest that Goldston's version is correct. There is the gracious paragraph at the
end of the story, praising Bess as attractive and clever. And
there is Houdini's special telegram, which seems to be saying
"thanks" for something more than merely a "fair test."

However it happened, Houdini got out. And typically, a few
years later, he featured the great *Mirror* challenge in a well-
printed booklet of sixty-four pages, *Harry Houdini, the Adven-*

turous Life of a Versatile Artist, which young fellows on his staff sold in the theater lobbies.

So hectic was Houdini's life and so filled with the setting up of challenges, hunting out old magicians, buying old press books and collections of playbills and programs from the distant past, and combing secondhand bookstalls, that he must often have felt the need for a few hours of quiet meditation. His favorite spot for such relaxation was in cemeteries.

Harry was so fascinated by cemeteries that he made a point of visiting the graves of famous magicians. This hobby apparently began on October 23, 1903, when Harry was playing the Central Theater in Dresden and, on a visit to the cemetery, discovered the long forgotten and neglected grave of Bartolomeo Bosco, one of the greats of magic half a century before. The plot had been rented and the lease was up; it was for sale. If sold, the bodies of Bosco and his wife would have been removed to some anonymous pit in one corner of the grounds. But Houdini forestalled this by buying the plot and deeding it to the Society of American Magicians.

This society had been founded on the 10th of May, 1902, in the "little back shop" of Martinka's Palace of Magic on Sixth Avenue, New York City. Houdini at first held himself aloof from his brother magicians in any great numbers, fearing, perhaps, that if they knew him they might lose their fear of "imitating" him. He came, in time, to see that he could get along better in show business if he worked with his fellow artists rather than against them, and a few years later he spent much of his spare time on his transcontinental tours of the United States in bringing the magic clubs of small cities of the hinterland within the fold of the Society of American Magicians, serving as president of the organization for a number of years until his death.

Houdini's first grave-restoring efforts—in the Friederichstrasse cemetery in Dresden—he chronicled by means of a snapshot taken, probably, by Bess, showing Harry, silk topper in hand, standing by the grave. Placing flowers on the grave of some old-time great of magic was something Harry would have done anyhow, for in some ways he was highly sentimental. But it was always gratifying if he could squeeze a little newspaper space out of anything and in later years his ceremonial bestowing of wreaths on magicians' graves was always good for a picture in the local papers. An old-timer commented, concerning this trait of Harry's: "In time he came to associate with other magicians, but you know the kind of magicians Harry liked best? It was dead ones—he had nothing to fear from them in competition. He was an odd little guy, that Houdini. There was one sure-fire way to get along with him—always act like you believed his own ideas about himself. And towards the end of his life these got so high-flown you wondered if he hadn't convinced himself that he was second-cousin to God."

There were magicians whose egos were just as inflated as Houdini's and with these he had frequent and violent clashes. But no old and broken-down performer ever put the bite on Harry and came away empty-handed. When he died, it was learned that Houdini had been supporting over a score of people by pensions every month out of his own pocket. During his lifetime he never breathed a word of these charities to anyone. Many of Houdini's secrets were secrets of the heart.

17. *The House of Mystery*

A SAFE is designed to keep people from opening it—from the outside. A moment's reflection will show that the locking mechanism must be available for lubrication and repair. This is accomplished by means of a small disc, usually circular and held by two small screws, on the inside of the safe door. Anyone familiar with safes can, in a few seconds, take off this plate, revealing the lock, and operate the tumblers from inside.

The widespread ignorance about safes Houdini decided to exploit early in 1904. Here, again, much of what we know about the actual event—or the conditions previous to it—we must get from observation and deduction. The challenge, publicized by Houdini, was that he could escape from "any bank safe in London." This "defi" was immediately taken up by a safe-building firm which, by a strange coincidence, had just come out with a new model they were proud of and wished to publicize. Houdini specified that the safe, a mammoth affair, should be delivered to the theater—the Euston Palace of Varieties—a day before the challenge performance.

It took a crew of men to move this giant into the theater and a squad of carpenters to reinforce the stage to bear its weight. The other acts, for that day and evening, had to play around and in front of the vault.

When the big moment came, Harry milked it for all it was worth. After warming up with handcuff tricks, he excused himself and returned wearing a bathing suit under a bathrobe. He explained the challenge, complimented the safe-makers on the excellence of their latest model, spoke a few kind words about the length of time they had been in the business and some of their best-known products, and wound up by reminding the

115

audience that there was a very small quantity of air in the safe
and that he would be forced to make his escape in a few
minutes or die by suffocation. The manufacturer's men stood
by ready to open the door at the end of the estimated time.

Harry then invited a committee from the audience to come
onstage to inspect the safe and "make sure there could be no
trickery." Just how he proposed to get out of a safe without
trickery was left unspecified. Among the volunteers who filed
onstage was a well-known local doctor and a tall, crisp-looking
man with a bald head and horn-rimmed glasses who looked
every inch the prosperous London lawyer.

Harry invited the doctor to give him a "thorough medical
examination." This, he suggested, could well take place inside
the vault, the door to be half closed for privacy. A member of
the committee was also invited to accompany them inside.

When the three men emerged, the doctor, prodded by Houdini, told the audience that he would testify in any court that
it was impossible for the escapist to have anything concealed
about his person. The other spectator agreed.

Houdini then thanked the doctor and the "umpire" for their
cooperation and solemnly shook hands with them and the bald-
headed gentleman. Harry looked as somber as if he were going
to be taken out and shot.

Finally, he stepped inside, paused as if gathering his courage, and then said sharply, "Very well, gentlemen, you may
lock the door." When it was secured, screens were placed before it to conceal it from all eyes. The crowd settled down
to wait.

For fifteen minutes it remained silent. Then it grew uneasy.
The representative of the safe company informed them that
Houdini had agreed to knock on the safe wall if he was defeated and required them to let him out. They had heard no
such signal.

Somebody in the auditorium suggested that the Escape King
might have fainted. Tension mounted. Several women grew so
nervous they had to be escorted from the room. Still the agoniz-

From the Dunninger Collection

The earliest known professional photograph of Harry
Houdini, probably taken around 1893. On a pillow to
the extreme left is a pair of "Bean Giant" handcuffs.

From the Dunninger Collection

One of Houdini's favorite photographs, displaying his muscular development and some of his most formidable-looking manacles.

Courtesy of Brown Brothers

Hanging by his ankles from the cornice of a building, the
Escape King strips off a strait jacket while crowds below
cheer him on.

From the Rawson Collection

The famous underwater box escape: (above) the Self-Liberator, manacled, steps into the previously examined box. The lid is nailed on and then Jim Collins (below) supervises the descent of the box into New York harbor. Actually Jim is waiting for the "all clear" signal from Houdini, announcing that the secret catches holding the escape panel have been released and it is safe to lower away.

International News Photo

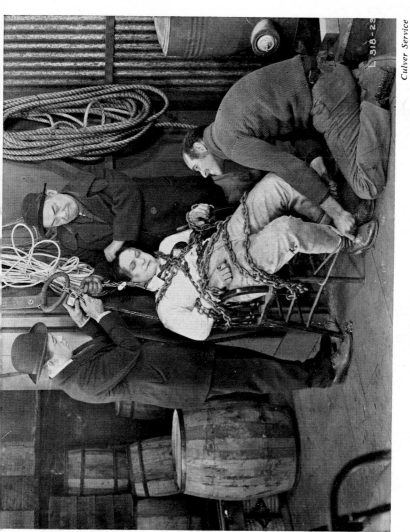

Culver Service

As the hero of a film melodrama, *Terror Island*, Houdini is bound with chains by the "bad guys" while they plot a heinous revenge.

International News Photo

In this crowded study of the house on West 113th Street Houdini planned his illusions and collected material for books of his own

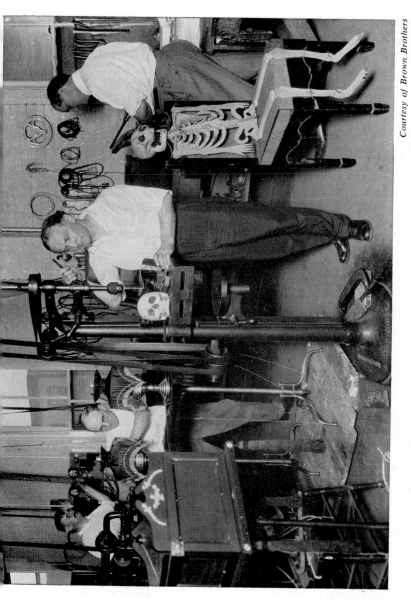

Courtesy of Brown Brothers

A dream come true: Houdini and Collins (second from left) build props for the big magic and spook show which played 1925-26.

Culver Servi

The Houdinis: a publicity photograph taken for the full-evening show of 1925 in which Bess worked with Harry for the first time in many years.

ing wait. After forty minutes one hysterical woman screamed that the theater manager should order the performance stopped; Houdini might already be dead.

By the forty-five-minute mark the whole crowd was whistling and shouting for them to open the safe. At the precise moment when the hysteria had reached its highest point, one of the screens moved. Then Houdini, his bathing suit plastered to him with sweat, calmly stepped out, looking pale and haggard, and took his ovation.

Next day the safe-builders' crew moved the safe back to the showroom and mechanics examined it. Nothing was altered; how the American had made his exit remained a mystery.*

The trick really begins with an idea in Houdini's mind, possibly gained in the middle of the night, when he would bounce out of bed, seize the nearest bit of paper and pencil, and scribble down notes before the idea was forgotten.

Having once conceived the notion of getting out of a safe, the elusive American starts to canvas the leading safe-manufacturers of London. He locates the latest and best model and has some talk with the sales manager, sounding him out on whether the firm is too old-fashioned and stodgy to go along with a vaudeville artist in a publicity tie-in. He finds that the safe company, like Barkis, is willin'. The first obstacle to the escape has been conquered.

Douglas Gilbert, in a volume called *American Vaudeville,* contributes this piece of Houdiniana:

"During his career Harry purchased or obtained the patent

* The author has had long and strenuous arguments with friends in magic about the advisability of revealing Houdini's secrets such as this one of the bank-vault escape. They argue, possibly correctly, that once the public knows how such an intriguing mystery is performed, it loses respect for (a) Houdini (b) all magicians. I do not agree. If magic were a closed trade, as in India, it would remain static, as Hindu magic has done for centuries, passed along from father to son with no developments or improvements. Magic grows by necessity—when the public learns how one trick is done it is up to magical inventors to develop something new. I cannot see any harm at this date in revealing the *modus operandi* of Houdini with the famous bank vault.

papers of every lock patented in the United States, Great Britain, France and Germany, and he knew more about locks than most locksmiths."

The master locksmith of New York, Charles Courtney, always insisted that Houdini was far from being a lock master. From Courtney's viewpoint this was perfectly true—there was an enormous amount of know-how concerning the installation, servicing, and repair of locks which Houdini did not know and didn't care about. His interest in locks was confined to getting them open in record time. But we may thus be sure that he studied the patent papers of a challenge safe with more than usual care.

When Houdini was sure of his way out of the vault, he went ahead and announced that he could get out of any safe or vault in London. The tie-in challenge was then announced as being taken up in response to the general challenge.

So far, so good. When the safe was delivered and installed at the theater, Houdini really got to work. He took off the plate of the lock-housing on the inner surface of the door and removed the springs which needed tools to draw them back, replacing them with weaker springs which could be operated by his fingers alone. The safe, when he left it, still operated perfectly. But all he needed to get out was a special three-pronged gimmick about two inches long, with which he could unscrew the plate and engage the weak springs.

This gimmick could easily be palmed by any magician but Harry was taking no chances. The forensic-looking gentleman with the bald head and glasses, who assisted in examining the vault, was none other than Harry's pal Will Goldston. The gimmick was fastened to Goldston's finger ring. When Houdini shook hands all around, Goldston's was the last hand he shook and from it he got the necessary "feke."

Getting out of the safe took only a moment. Once outside, while the audience slowly went mad with tension, Houdini was sitting on the stage behind the screens, quietly reading a book he had concealed under the carpet, pausing from time to time to peep out at the audience through one of the joints of the screen to see how the hysteria was progressing. At the very height of it he put his book away, rumpled his hair, and stepped out, simulating exhaustion.

It took more than a knowledge of safe construction to accomplish this sensation. It took a peculiar form of genius which was Houdini's alone. Once his secret became known there was a rash of magicians getting out of safes, but who can recall the name of one today?

In the spring of 1904, while "packing 'em in" in London, Houdini began to feel "seedy." His shirt was drenched with sweat before he had taken any exercise. True to his usual custom, he ignored his discomfort until Bess grew alarmed. She finally convinced him, with the help of the theater manager and various friends, that he had a high fever. A doctor, summoned over Harry's protests, declared that the magician had pneumonia and that if he did not get to bed and stay there he would die.

Houdini reluctantly went to bed; he must have been phenomenally weak, for he stayed there several days and when he had recovered enough to get about he set sail for home. He wanted to be near his mother.

Harry and Bess left England around the first of April. In some biographical notes written by Houdini he says that he spent the months of June, July, and August of that year in his "country home in Stamford, Connecticut." He may have visited in Stamford for a few days but he was soon stirring about.

The first thing he did was to call on the managers of vaudeville houses, spread out his press books, and tell them how he had played to standing room all over Great Britain and Germany. They were interested, since Harry had been bombarding them at regular intervals with clippings of his triumphs abroad. Also, he had written a European newsletter for *The New York*

Dramatic Mirror. His column was tightly packed with accounts of the leading European acts and Americans playing abroad. It was written in a combination of theater jargon and bombastic "literary" English but it had punch and was not overburdened with accounts of Harry's own triumphs. At least, after it got past the *Mirror's* editors it was not so overburdened. The home front knew Houdini had been playing to record houses. But still the big theater chains did not offer him money comparable to what he could make in Europe.

His was a novelty act and no one could tell whether a European novelty act—or one that had "killed 'em" in Europe—would go over in the States. In the bookers' offices Harry held his ego in check. Back home with Bess he let go with one of his typical rages. When he calmed down he cabled Harry Day to disregard their understanding, made when the couple left England, not to book him for the rest of the year. Now he instructed young Day to line up full time as far ahead as he could.

"So over here they never heard of Houdini yet, outside the trade papers!" he stormed at the air while Bess kept quiet, waiting. " 'How do we know you'll go over here?' In London they carry Houdini around the hall like a general, he just won a war! And here they don't know if Houdini will lay an egg! I'll fix 'em. I'll fix 'em good. I'm going back there and the next time I play in this country it's because the chains are begging for me. On their knees they got to come begging to get Houdini."

Harry had brought home a mountain of magical memorabilia, much of it purchased from the great magical collector Henry Evans Evanion, who had turned up, old, ill, and broke, at Houdini's hotel while the Escape King was recovering from his bout with pneumonia.

Much of this material he had never had time to sort out and he needed a place to store it. Also, he wanted to get his mother out of the railroad flat on 69th Street.

Harry solved both of these problems by purchasing a four-story, brownstone house with twenty-six rooms at 278 West 113th Street, Manhattan. Into it he moved his collection of magic books, playbills, old programs, letters, manuscripts, and odd pieces of magical apparatus acquired here and there on his travels, some of it from widows of famous magicians to whom it was nothing but a lot of dust-catching junk.

The 113th Street house, which Harry always referred to as "278," had plenty of space in the upstairs rooms and a capacious cellar.

The house also had an outsized bathtub in which Houdini later practiced staying underwater. It was not, as legend tells it, a swimming pool—it was just a big tub in which Houdini could stretch out completely submerged. That he practiced holding his breath underwater with chunks of ice floating around him is perfectly true. He was getting ready for some of his famous bridge jumps into rivers in midwinter.

On this voyage home Houdini also made a flying trip to the old home town of Appleton, visiting boyhood friends.

Before he sailed for England in August, Harry purchased a burial plot in the Macpelah Cemetery at Cypress Hills, Long Island. Thither he transferred the bodies of his father and his brother, Herman Weiss, entering a note in his journal that "Herman's teeth were in excellent condition."*

He opened in Glasgow on September 7th and in two days' time had set up a challenge with a harness and saddlery firm to get out of a special strait jacket designed for a private mental asylum. Houdini spent fifty-five minutes making his escape while the audience of anguished Scots suffered with him by empathy. The attendance at the Hippodrome that week broke all records with a gross of £1,400.

A rival escapologist had secured bookings in competition with Houdini by advertising his escape from "an unprepared coffin." The coffin was his own, but was given a cursory examination by a committee before he got into it.

* This family plot is now cared for by the Society of American Magicians.

Harry blew up at the audacity of his competitor and loudly proclaimed that he would, on a certain date specified, expose the chicanery of this impostor from the stage. On the 30th of September, before a jammed house, he had a coffin brought on stage and proceeded to demonstrate the foul means that had been used to deceive the public. It seems that his rival had caused the coffin to be put on display in the theater lobby until just before the performance, but between the time it left the lobby and the time it appeared on the stage certain under-hand procedures had been employed. The long screws holding the end of the coffin in place had been removed by the dastardly charlatan and short screws substituted. Houdini showed how it was done and then got into the coffin and pushed out the head after the lid had been secured firmly by clasps.

But he was only getting warmed up. After dwelling at length on the sinfulness of impostors who substituted short screws for long ones (Houdini's original method with packing cases), he invited the committee to examine the coffin now that the head panel had been securely fastened with long screws. Handing out screwdrivers, he encouraged the spectators to remove any screw they chose, even levering the coffin over on its side and inviting inspection of the screws holding the bottom to the sides. Several of these were taken out and found to be of satisfactory length. There was no doubt that they penetrated the wood of the coffin's sides.

Houdini then had all screws replaced and tightened, got in the coffin, and had the lid not only clasped firm but a few screws added anywhere the committee chose. When he was firmly screwed in he called out from his grisly chamber for the committee members to seal the screw heads in any manner they chose—some pasted postage stamps over the screws, on which they inscribed their initials. Others pasted stamps on the crack between the coffin lid and the sides.

Houdini was now hidden from view by his cabinet, which was lifted over the coffin. In a few minutes he parted the curtains and there was the coffin, apparently untouched but with Houdini outside it.

In reading accounts of wonders worked by mystagogues of the past, we are often left wishing we knew more of the circumstances. But I have told you everything you would have seen, had you been in the theater when Houdini did his coffin escape.

How did he get out?

It is the annoying practice of many exposers of mystery to refer to a secret as "childishly simple." It is a firm conviction of the author that nothing childish is ever simple. But be that as it may, the secret of Houdini's coffin was far from childish. It was diabolically simple.

While every screw in the bottom of the coffin could be taken out and examined for length, the escape was still made by raising the top and sides of the coffin from the bottom. The screws holding it fitted into dowels which in turn fitted into snug holes in the sides. All the screw heads could be sealed— even those of the bottom—yet when Houdini was inside and the curtains of the cabinet drawn, he turned over on his face, drew up his knees, and using the strength of his arms, legs, and back combined—the most powerful "lift" a man can make —pushed the coffin up off the bottom, slid out, placed it on the dowel posts and forced it down again by jumping on it.

He had taken a trick with which a rival was getting bookings and publicity and not only exposed it to the public but demonstrated his own vast superiority.

So great was his drawing power with British audiences that Harry began playing dates on percentage—a deal engineered by the shrewd Harry Day. One of his biggest weeks under this sort of agreement brought him $2,150. And there were no income taxes in 1904!

Part of these enormous sums were spent to good purpose— making sure that a few enthusiastic young fellows would stand outside the stage door of an evening to cheer the great man (or, in all fairness, to lead the cheering) and sometimes carry him back to his hotel in triumph and wait outside, keeping the excitement going, until Houdini had appeared and made a little speech from a balcony.

The master of this sort of engineered enthusiasm was old P. T. Barnum, whose *Struggles and Triumphs* and *Autobiography* had been closely studied by Houdini. Barnum, in giving Soprano Jenny Lind the big build-up in America, hired stooges to shriek in ecstasy as the demure Swedish nightingale descended from the packet ship. Two men, delirious with "love" for the famous coloratura, leaped into New York harbor and had to be fished out with great fanfare and consequent newspaper space.

It was during Houdini's long run in London that Bess, in a mood of impish mischief, decided to find out what Harry would do if his jealousy were aroused in a public place. Bess was never one to refuse a glass of champagne, especially if Harry was not around to forbid it. The occasion was a party in London where a retired colonel fell to joking with Bess. Harry was out of the room when Bess, with much giggling, settled herself on the colonel's knee. She was gaily sipping champagne with her arm around the gentleman's neck when Harry returned. He stopped upon the threshold of the room, his face suddenly ashen, his eyes wide with horror. He looked as if he were going to collapse, as though he had received a staggering blow to the midriff. Bess leaped from the obliging colonel's knee and hurried to his side but Harry couldn't speak. She tried to convince him that it had been a joke, conceived on the spur of the moment. Thoroughly frightened by this time, Bess explained to the hostess that her husband had been taken ill; she hurried him back to their hotel in a cab and put him to bed. He was inconsolable, sobbing tragically most of the night. It was days before Harry was himself again and for long afterward any chance mention of the word *colonel* would send him into the depths of despair.

In January of 1905 a cable from America arrived, offering the Escape King six weeks at leading theaters in the eastern states for $5,000. Triumphantly he cabled back that he was booked solid until fall!

18. *The Big Time at Last*

BY 1905 American vaudeville was entering its golden age. The genial Tony Pastor, who had given the Houdinis their first break, had pioneered in cleaning up the music hall, eliminating "blue material" from the acts, prohibiting smoking, and discouraging rowdy behavior among the patrons.

The American public responded with a whoop and a holler; a vaudeville show was something to bring the wife and kiddies to see. Its two-a-day policy made it a form of diversion to which ladies could even go unaccompanied without fear of insult or the wagging tongues of neighbors. The neighbors were there, too.

Into this gaudy bonanza Harry and Bess plunged when they returned home after the triumphal season of 1905 in Europe. Houdini opened in New York on October 2, 1905, as the headliner at Percy G. Williams' Colonial Theater, Broadway and 63rd Street.

In one way, it was the toughest spot in town. Although vaudeville, growing respectable, had lured the family trade, there were rough elements in Little Old New York who delighted in rattling the performers and, if antagonized, doing everything short of ripping up the seats. Monday matinee at the Colonial was a nightmare to vaudevillians, even those who could "josh" a music hall audience into a good humor. At this lush palace of entertainment was born a tactic of audience-displeasure which has persisted to the present day at ball parks and fight arenas—the "Colonial clap." This was applause designed to rattle and "break up" the actors onstage by its maddening, mocking rhythm: *clap, clap, clap-clap-clap.*

On that Monday afternoon in October, when the house lights dimmed and the cards on the annunciators at each side of the stage were shifted and bore the single word HOUDINI, the crowd stirred in anticipation; they had heard about the fabulous escape artist for years and here he was at last.

The orchestra struck up the stirring *Kaiser Frederic March,* footlights went up, and the curtain rose on a full stage with rich, maroon-colored backdrop. When the drapes parted, the Escape King stepped forward and marched downstage toward the audience, his chin held in, his gray-blue eyes staring directly ahead. There was something about this angle of the head, the tension of his body, and the implication of ferocity under iron control which reminded spectators of a charging bull. This was the man, if ever there was one, to hold the Monday audience of the Colonial—the young toughs of Broadway and their "skirts."

The music stopped. Houdini, with the faintest trace of a commanding smile at the corners of his mouth, threw back his head and started to speak. The crowd hung upon every word, enunciated in a sharp, incisive style which carried to the top row of the balcony:

"Good afternoon, ladies and gentlemen. Before introducing you to my latest inventions in the world of mystery, I would like to show you what can be accomplished with the aid of persistent practice by performing a feat which at one time was thought to be absolutely impossible—that of escaping from a regulation strait jacket. The attendants who have been selected have been instructed to put it on me as tight as possible. Before proceeding, I would like to say that there is nothing supernatural connected with my work. Everything I do is done by natural means. I invite a committee to step upon the stage and see that everything is just as represented. You will find the staircase on my left. Also at this time I shall invite any members of the audience who have brought handcuffs, leg irons, or other regulation police restraints to the theater in order to test my powers of self-liberation to kindly step forward and put me to the test. With your permission, I will now remove my coat."

By the very force of his personality, projected over the footlights like a bolt from a crossbow, he held them silent, absorbed in what was about to happen.

He wore, for this historic afternoon, his regulation matinee clothes—cutaway coat, striped trousers, gray vest, and gray ascot tie about a tall wing collar.

The assistants in livery who proceeded to buckle Houdini into the strait jacket of brown canvas were the faithful Kukol and a chirpy little Cockney whom Harry had acquired in London, Jim Vickery. Also, unknown to the audience, some of the spectators who came forward were friends of the Escape King. They were there as a safeguard "some wisenheimer shouldn't try to louse up the act."

The sight of Houdini, his long hair flying, throwing himself violently left and right, bent double, thrusting his elbows against his knees to force enough slack in the jacket to let him lift his arms above his head and bring their buckle within reach of his teeth—this was a new thrill for the famous Monday audience. They never gave out with any sound except enthusiastic cheers when Harry finally stripped the jacket from his arms and tossed it into the wings.

While Houdini was struggling with the jacket, the handcuff challengers were filing onstage. Kukol stood at the stairhead, apparently to assist the gentlemen to mount. Actually he kept a sharp eye out for strangers. Most of the challengers were quiet, well-mannered-looking men who had been selected before the show, from the crowd pressing in. They had been quietly approached by one of Houdini's boys and asked if they would like to assist in the performance by bringing handcuffs onstage. If a stranger came up—a genuine spontaneous challenger—he was immediately singled out and Houdini was warned.

The challengers were seated in chairs left and right of center stage. The first four or five men would be plants, bearing Houdini's own cuffs or leg irons. With five pairs of cuffs already on his wrists, Houdini could then afford to let a genuine challenger put any kind of cuffs—freak, antique, or specially made—on his forearms. His arms were so muscular that any restraint snapped on midway could not be closed so tightly that he could not slip it off over his hands, after a brief struggle. If the strange cuffs, so handled, scraped off a little skin and drew blood, so much the better.

On rare occasions some inventor or mechanic would fit a special pair of handcuffs with intricate locks and when such were brought up during a performance Houdini had his own system for handling them. First of all he would compliment the challenger, flash his most winning smile and step to the footlights announcing:

"Ladies and gentlemen—here are a pair of handcuffs like I have never seen before. They are the special invention of this gentleman here. I shall attempt to make good my escape from these manacles—which, by the way, are the most formidable I have ever tried—this coming Thursday evening on this stage when I invite you all to be present and witness my attempt to liberate myself."

This was not only a sure-fire device for getting many of the customers to come to the show a second time, but also would give Houdini and his boys a good chance to study the cuffs, their locks, and any difficulties they might present. Not many inventors in the United States ever brought their own special cuffs to test Houdini—that is, without his having quietly encouraged them beforehand, but there were quite a few in England and Germany whose challenge had to be met.

There are a number of things a hostile challenger can do to a handcuff king to embarrass him; Houdini knew them all. Cuffs jammed with shot were the usual weapon of the challenger against an escape artist. It had been found possible to fill cuffs with water and rust their action, so that they could be snapped on but could not be unlocked with their proper key or anything else. Hence, Houdini—and any other performer who was wise—always insisted that the cuffs be in good working order.

It was sometimes considered practical to take certain ex-

treme precautions. In Harry's youth, when Minnie Williams
was holding forth in her spook parlor on 46th Street, she got
occasional skeptics who came to scoff and remained to nurse
a lump on the head. Minnie would invite the skeptic to sit in
the cabinet with her to "insure against fraud," warning him
of the pranks sometimes played by malicious spirits on unbe-
lievers. The pranks, in such cases, were played but not by spirits. They were due to the application of a blackjack to the skull
of the troublemaker, a weapon effectively wielded by the medium's bodyguard, Bug MacDonald, or on occasion by the
formidable Minnie herself. This method of handling wisenheimers had made quite an impression on Ehrich Weiss and
it remained with Harry Houdini.

After Harry was rich enough to hire a staff of assistants,
they were carefully instructed in how to handle emergency
cases. When a stranger came onstage and loudly demanded
that Houdini submit himself to the challenger's cuffs or some
trick restraint—such as being tied up with surgical thread or
another form of ligature which Houdini could not match easily
if he had to cut himself loose and then bring out a duplicate
cord, untied—there was a standard procedure. The challenger
would see one of the Escape King's assistants beckoning him
from the wing. He would go over to see what was wanted and
thereupon the assistants would close in on him, suggesting that
he take his leave by way of the stage door. If he objected,
showed fight, or threatened to cause a disturbance, he was
quietly slugged and laid to rest out in the alley.

Houdini continued to play in and around New York and
was home on Election Day when he cast his first vote—for
William Randolph Hearst for Mayor of New York City. Harry
took little interest in politics. He voted for anybody who had
given him a kind word in conversation or in print, and his
choice of a future mayor for the home town was probably due
to favorable reviews he had received in Mr. Hearst's newspapers.

Harry had not forgotten nor forgiven the hesitancy of the

big-chain bookers to give him top money the previous year. He was still burning with this "insult" and when Christmas of 1905 arrived he let go with a blast in a half-page ad in a theatrical paper at a time when other acts were smiling their widest in print to convey Christmas greetings to all and sundry, especially to agents and bookers who might dig them up some work.

Houdini's Christmas ad began with the typical statement:

I TOLD YOU SO !!!

WHEN IT WAS DISCOVERED THAT HOUDINI, "THE PRISON
DEFIER," HAD BEEN BROUGHT BACK TO AMERICA AT A SALARY
OF $1,000 WEEKLY,

ALL THE WISE-ENHEIMERS AND SOCIETY OF KNOW-IT-ALL FEL-
LOWS POLISHED UP THEIR HAMMERS, SAYING "GOLD BRICK!"

IT HAS NOW BEEN POSITIVELY PROVEN BEYOND ANY CONTRA-
DICTION THAT HOUDINI IS THE HARDEST WORKING ARTIST THAT
HAS EVER TRODDEN THE VAUDEVILLE STAGE !!

HE IS WORTH MORE THAN THE SALARY HE IS BOOKED FOR !!!

The ad went on, in more restrained type, to list European jails from which he had escaped, theaters he had played abroad with record-breaking attendance, and quotes from wildly enthusiastic reviewers. The announcement wound up, as a concession to the season, with the words: "Merry Xmas and a Happy New Year to All."

The year 1905 closed with another triumph for Houdini, but of a much more personal nature than telling off the "wisenheimers."

Bessie's mother, a Roman Catholic, had never grown reconciled to her daughter's marrying a Jew. Early in the winter Bess had fallen ill and wanted her mother, so Harry had taken himself to Mrs. Rahner's house, planted himself in the living room, and refused to move until the mother came back with him to repair the long estrangement with her daughter. The lady finally relented, overpowered by Harry's entreaties and perhaps more than a little frightened by his intensity. There was a tearful reunion of mother and daughter, and Mrs. Rahner and Harry became fast friends.

Harry also had plans for getting back at one of his most virulent enemies. This was Dr. A. M. Wilson who, from his home in Kansas City, Missouri, published and edited the leading magical journal of the day, *The Sphinx*. Harry had sent Dr. Wilson several pieces about his European triumphs, none of which the good doctor had seen fit to use in his magazine. When Harry objected by mail, Wilson informed him that if he wanted an ad in the *Sphinx* he could pay for it at the usual rates. Harry exploded and vowed he would get even with the unspeakable doctor if he had to publish his own magic magazine to do it. This seemed like a splendid idea, the more he thought about it, and the following year he brought out his *Conjuror's Monthly*.

Wilson was no mean hand at colorful invective himself and for years the Houdini-Wilson feud raged, much to the amusement of everyone except Houdini. It was fifteen years before the two storm centers of magic ever met face to face and when they did they burst out laughing delightedly, shook hands, and realized that they had great admiration for each other. Dr. Wilson used to claim, jokingly, that he almost regretted that they had made up their quarrel: "There never was a man as good at a fight as Houdini."

When Harry hated he hated all the way; he never did anything moderately. And when he patched up his quarrel with Dr. Wilson, he took the doctor into his very small circle of intimate friends. Harry would have been deeply hurt if Wilson, on his visits to New York, had gone to a hotel. He had a key to the Houdini house on 113th Street and whenever he was in New York, that was his home.

The end of the year saw Houdini jubilant. He was up to $1,200 a week—doing the strait jacket, the handcuffs, and the substitution trunk with Bess—the identical act for which they had been paid twelve dollars a week in the *musées* ten years before.

19. *Jail Cells and an Icy River*

UNITED STATES JAIL

Washington, D. C., January 6, 1906

This is to certify that Mr. Harry Houdini, at the United States Jail today, was stripped stark naked, thoroughly searched, and locked up in Cell No. 2 of the South Wing—the Cell in which Charles J. Guiteau, the assassinator of President Garfield, was confined during his incarceration, from the date of his commitment, July 2nd, 1881, until the day on which he was executed, June 30th, 1882. Mr. Houdini, in about two minutes, managed to escape from the cell, and then broke into the cell in which his clothing was locked up. He then proceeded to release from their cells all the prisoners on the ground floor. There was positively no chance for any confederacy or collusion.

Mr. Houdini accomplished all the above-mentioned facts in addition to putting on all his clothing, in twenty-one minutes.

(signed) J. H. Harris
Warden, United States Jail, D-C

Whenever Harry made a jail break he got a "testimonial" like the one above.

The Washington Post of Sunday, January 7, gleefully recounted the stunt, and gave a clue as to how it had been performed:

"All these cells are brick structures with their doors sunk into the walls fully three feet from the face of the outer corridor wall. When the heavily barred door is closed, an arm-like bar runs out to the corridor wall and then angles to the right and slips over a steel catch which sets a spring that fastens the lock. The latter is only opened by a key, and there are no less

133

than five tumblers in the lock. One key opens all the doors in the corridor."

In the collection of Sidney Radner there are several sections of a slender steel rod which join to form an extension arm. These jointed sections can be screwed together in various combinations, to make a right angle. There is also a rachet action taken from an early model of a rachet screwdriver. A set screw holds a key firm at the end of the rachet device.

The duplicate key to the cells, the rachet, and the steel sections hardly thicker than large knitting needles, must have been hidden either in the famed Guiteau cell itself or somewhere outside of it within reach of Houdini when he was incarcerated. It would be a delicate task, when the extension right-angle was assembled, to reach around and fit the key into the lock, but once this had been done, a raising and lowering motion of the steel arm would slowly revolve the key until the bolt slid back.

When Harry finally won fame and success at home, he had to work harder than ever before in his life to stay on top. Among other things, he had to invent a "novelty act" which was constantly new. Up to his time this had never been done, and only the great ad-lib comedians have ever done it since. It was a task to make the stoutest heart quail but Harry plunged at it and kept the public's attention focused on him season after season.

The year 1906 was jail-break year. When this stunt lost its pulling power he worked out something else. For the next twenty years he kept himself in the headlines. When it seemed as if he had reached the limits of his audacity he went on to top his previous exploits.

The jail break became in time almost routine. The warden, the guards, and the newspapermen were facing an unusual situation, one which they had never encountered before, while Houdini was perfectly at home.

Houdini and his company would arrive in the new city on Sunday. Monday was a day of frenzied activity. First of all there was rehearsal at the theater. Then a visit to the jail or prison to set up the break. When this had been agreed upon with the warden, and passes to the theater generously distributed, the next job was to go to a printer with the copy for a handbill describing the successful break. The break itself took place Monday morning, or, when necessary, Tuesday morning.

The breaks seldom offered any danger once Houdini had learned to have all the angles covered. We must remember that Houdini always gave the impression that what he did he did all by himself, without the slightest help from anyone. But this was not true. Somebody—better if it was not Houdini—had to examine the lock of the cell door and, while doing so, get an impression of the key or find out what sort of lock it was. From this information Harry could decide which pick or tool he needed. Then, depending on the setup of the jail, he would decide where to hide the picks and keys.

In later years this was done by Houdini's trusted assistant, Jim Collins. Sometimes a bit of wire was all that was needed; it could be dropped to the floor in a convenient crack or placed outside the cell door within reach, lying close to the wall. At other times the handcuff key or feke and the pick or key for the cell door could simply be dropped to the corridor floor by an assistant—or by Houdini himself—concealed in a bit of scrap paper. Houdini's foot, planted firmly on the bundle on his way into the cell, acquired it, due to the presence of adhesive wax on one surface. In the more modern jails, equipped with a toilet in the cell, the committee would see, if it took the trouble to notice, a harmless-looking cork floating in the toilet bowl. But underneath the cork were stuck the picks and keys, acting like the keel of a vessel to keep the innocent side of the cork uppermost.

One of the most ingenious devices Harry Houdini ever used was developed on his first jail-breaking tour of Europe. He had noticed that the prison doctors who examined him always wore black frock coats of broadcloth. He therefore had a tiny bag made of this material equipped with a hook. His tools went into the bag, which was hooked brazenly on the back of the

doctor before the examination and secured afterward when
giving the doctor a friendly clap on the back.

To find anything as small as a lock pick or a handcuff key
on Houdini would have required special knowledge—of where
to look, when and what to look for—which his investigators,
however intelligent or well-trained in ordinary observation,
simply did not have.

So successful was his vaudeville season that Houdini was
encouraged to do something he had long wanted to do—have
his own full-evening show of straight magic as well as escapes.
He organized this in the early spring of 1906 but it did not
prosper. Running such an elaborate production was more of a
headache than Houdini cared for and at the end of the season
he gave up the idea, not to resume it for two decades.

The year also saw the publication of Houdini's first book, *The
Right Way to Do Wrong,* a ninety-four-page pamphlet designed
to inform the public on the tricks of counterfeiters, coiners,
smugglers, swindlers and con men, sneak thieves, and pick-
pockets.

This pamphlet was sold at a book stand in the lobby, a
profitable source of income. The book concession with the
Thurston show was valued at $10,000 a year.

In September of 1906 Houdini published the first issue of
The Conjuror's Monthly Magazine, which continued to appear
until August of 1908, when booking abroad forced Houdini to
suspend publication. In this thirty-two-page monthly his two
chief enemies—Dr. A. M. Wilson and Horace Goldin, the
"Lightning Illusionist" who had snubbed young Harry at Kohl
& Middleton's—came in for a regular roasting.

Hardeen, who was going strong in England with his own act,
contributed a column of vaudeville news similar to the one
Harry had written for the New York *Dramatic Mirror.* Jacob
Hayman, Harry's boyhood friend and magic partner whose
suggestion had resulted in the name *Houdini,* was now a professional playing the music halls and vaudeville theaters and

he contributed frequent newsletters. It was in the *Conjuror's Monthly* that Harry began to publish a series of articles which he headed *Unknown Facts Concerning Robert Houdin*. This was the first blast against his former idol whose widow had so humiliated him—in his own eyes—by refusing to see him. Yet while Houdini the editor was ripping into Robert-Houdin's famous memoirs, showing that the illusions the great Frenchman claimed to have invented were known before his time, Houdini the magician was trying to emulate his boyhod ideal still.

In 1906, at a special magic performance given for a social organization of which he was a member, Houdini caused three borrowed handkerchiefs to vanish; they were to appear at any spot in the city of New York selected by a member of the audience. The spectators each chose a spot and wrote it on a card; the cards, on being collected and one having been chosen, gave as the spot the top step of the pediment of the Statue of Liberty. A delegation was chosen from the guests to go immediately to the Statue of Liberty on Bedloe's Island in New York Harbor to search for the handkerchiefs. Sure enough, when they got there via elevated train and ferry boat, there was a tin box soldered shut which they brought back to the banquet hall and opened. It contained, naturally, the borrowed handkerchiefs.

The trick was well done and created a sensation in the ranks of the fraternal order, among which were some influential men. The working of the trick depended on careful timing and Houdini's willingness to go to considerable trouble. In the course of the performance, the handkerchiefs were vanished and passed to Franz Kukol who set off with them posthaste for the Statue of Liberty, picking up a tinsmith along the way. The committee got there a few minutes later and secured the box containing the handkerchiefs. The mystery lay in the choice of place—and there Houdini had recourse to a well-known magic principle. Suffice it to say that he knew that the island statue in the harbor would be the designated place of concealment, "chosen at random."

But the trick was one which Jean Eugène Robert-Houdin had used to good advantage when performing before the bourgeois King of France, Louis Philippe, at the Chateau St. Cloud.

On that long-ago and memorable occasion, Robert-Houdin, after borrowing and vanishing the handkerchiefs, gave his king a choice of three places where they could be made to reappear —a vase on the mantelpiece, a nook under the dome of the Hotel des Invalides where lies the sarcophagus of the great Napoleon, or a spot at the root of an orange tree in the conservatory.

The father of modern magic was using what is known in the art as a "psychological force." As the magician had anticipated, Louis Philippe ran the three choices over in his mind, deeming the vase too easy a place for the magician to reach, the historic tomb too far away, and the orange tree just right. When a footman had been instructed to fetch a spade, the party adjourned to the orangery, and there, sure enough, among the roots of the orange tree was uncovered a rusty iron box. When opened, it was found to contain the borrowed handkerchiefs and a stained parchment on which was written in faded ink the following message:

This day, the 6th June, 1786,
This iron box, containing six handkerchiefs, was placed among
the roots of an orange tree by me, Balsamo, Count de
Cagliostro, to serve in performing an act of magic, which will
be executed on the same day, sixty years hence, before Louis
Philippe of Orleans and his family.

Verily, that was magic. Robert-Houdin had had dummy handkerchiefs planted in the vase and a bundle hidden under the famous dome, just in case, but he knew his man, and Louis Philippe, the crafty monarch, reacted true to form. The trick was a good one, but what raises it to the heights of artistry was the "old" parchment letter of Cagliostro. This whiff of "real" magic, this startling projection of ancient mysteries into the present, this essentially poetic treatment was what made Robert-

Houdin great. This kind of poetic imagination applied to magic Houdini lacked. But Harry didn't need delicacy. In doing a combined strait jacket and packing box, who needed elegance? A dog wouldn't need it!

In the fall of 1906 Houdini was playing in Detroit, Michigan, and there, in the dead of winter, he determined to do a bridge jump.

He had been training for this at home in the large bathtub filled with chunks of ice, and it was a prospect so terrifying to the average comfort-loving citizen as to make headlines in the boldest type the papers could find.

In after years the story of this famous jump grew and grew, as Houdini retold it to newspaper feature writers. It appeared in its full legendary form in Kellock's "biography," told in stirring, if fictitious, detail. The traditional story goes like this:

Houdini had two weeks in Detroit and, wishing to give the public a free thrill, told the manager of the theater that he planned to make a manacled bridge jump in spite of the season. When informed that the Detroit river was frozen solid, he replied nonchalantly, "Well, what of it? Can't we get somebody to saw a hole in the ice? I am Houdini—that will be good enough for me."

Accordingly (so the tale runs) the hole was chopped and Houdini leaped—handcuffed, chained, and leg-ironed—into the swift-running river, through the gaping hole. Shivering thousands, watching from the Belle Isle Bridge and the river bank, shivered even harder in empathy. One minute, two minutes, three minues—the hero did not emerge, unmanacled or otehwise. After four minutes police were of the opinion that the Grim Reaper had finally cut down the escape artist. After five minutes the half-frozen reporters hurried back to their papers with the news that Houdini had perished. At this point one of the performer's aides threw a rope into the hole and prepared to swim down to look for the illusionist. But when eight minutes had passed, an arm dramatically broke the surface of the black water, quickly followed by Houdini's head, gasping for breath. He was helped out and wrapped in blankets. Later he told his friends of the press that the current had swept him downstream after he had escaped from the handcuffs and irons and that when he surfaced it was to find a ceiling of ice over his head. With superhuman presence of mind he lay still and floated, then noticed silvery bubbles of air between ice and water. By maintaining tremendous calm he managed to tap the air in these bubbles and subsist upon it until, seeing the rope splash into the water, he swam toward it and to safety. Next time, he told them, he would carry a tiny brass tube hidden in his bathing suit for just that purpose—to breathe the air in the bubbles.

The story sounds plausible. Newspapermen believed it, as did all the world. It became Houdini's most famous single outdoor exploit.

But in time doubt was cast on the veracity of the Mysteriarch's account of his eight-minute submersion in the frigid river. It was possible—people have saved their lives, after falling through ice and being swept downstream, by breathing the air between ice and water.* But somehow, it seemed unlike Houdini to take as uncalculated a risk as jumping into a swift-flowing river through a hole in the ice without proper safeguards. The date always given by Houdini for this exploit was Sunday, December 2, 1906.

The following excerpts from newspapers I owe to the diligence of Mr. Robert Lund of Detroit, an able magician and a devoted magical historian. Unable to find in the city any files of Detroit papers going back as far as 1906, he kept on sleuthing until he ran down a set of microfilm records in Ann Arbor. This story appeared on the front page of the Detroit *News,* November 27, 1906:

---

* On December 14, 1954 the New York *Herald Tribune* carried a story from Fort Dodge, Iowa, of a six-year-old boy who was rescued under such conditions when a bystander, summoned by the child's playmates, spotted his bright-red skating cap under the ice and chopped him out, none the worse for his ordeal.

"HANDCUFF KING" JUMPS MANACLED
FROM BRIDGE

Handcuff King Houdini Performs Remarkable
Feat and Comes Out Safely

Had a Rope Tied Around His Waist and Tied
to Bridge to Safeguard against Accidents

Tied by a lifeline a hundred and thirteen feet long, handcuffed with two of the best and latest model handcuffs in the possession of the Detroit police department, nerved by the confidence of a lion in his own powers . . . Houdini, the wonder worker at the Temple theater, leaped from the draw span of the Belle Isle Bridge at 1 o'clock this afternoon, freed himself from the handcuffs while under water, then swam to a waiting lifeboat, passed over the unlocked and open cuffs and clambered aboard.

In other words, the river was not frozen over, Houdini had a rope tied around him all the time, he got out of two pairs of cuffs and was picked up by a boat! As for escaping from under the ice—as Tom Sawyer would say, "He just let on he done it."

20. *Challenge and Response*

THE SEASON of 1907 found Broadway cheering the first edition of the Ziegfeld Follies. And at the hub of the theatrical universe, 42nd Street and Broadway, Willie Hammerstein presented vaudeville that was enlivened by special appearances of young ladies who had ventilated their husbands and/or lovers with firearms or ice picks. The irrepressible Willie added to the sensations of the year by getting one of his female stars arrested for her abdominal gyrations in Salome's *Dance of the Seven Veils,* forerunner of the strip. This was tough competition.

It was obvious to Houdini that, if he was to remain on top, he would have to devise new effects to keep the spotlight focused on himself. And one of his sure-fire ways to get attention was with the challenge.

He had already learned that public apathy and inertia was responsible for the lamentable lack of genuine challengers coming forward to "put him to the test." If he was to get any attention, he would have to furnish the challenges himself. This he proceeded to do, always presenting the trick "challenges" as originating with others.

Genuine challenges, by this time, were highly suspect by the Self-Liberator lest the cloven hoof of Cunning, Brindemour, Kilby, or other "imitators" appear beneath the lower hem of his cabinet.

His Boston date—five consecutive weeks early in 1907— was spectacular and historic.

In his notes for a book on the art of escapery, Houdini later wrote, regarding a "challenge" in the form of a wicker basket: "Be sure and always try the basket first before having it an-

142

nounced as a challenge. Make conditions to suit yourself. When you have the basket in your dressing-room, you can change the locks or cut off the hinges to suit yourself. But make it dead certain of not holding you."*

At Keith's Boston theater, his first publicized "challenge" was from a cardboard box! The point here, of course, was to get out without tearing the box.

This box had a deep cover, reaching nearly to the floor. After Houdini was inside it, ropes were tied around it and knotted on top where it was obviously impossible for him to reach them. It was not impossible, however, for him to pull in the side of the box and reach down with a sharp blade on an extension handle to cut the cord near the bottom. Duplicate cord he carried, wrapped around his waist inside his trousers and with this he retied the box, duplicating the knots of the challenger's men on top. The box was covered, by Harry's specifications, with dark glazed paper and in case he tore it getting out, he carried in his pocket a sheet of matching paper and a tube of library paste for making repairs.

Houdini followed the paper box with a number of ingeniously contrived wooden boxes variously strapped with metal and bound with ropes.

Then he made a tie-in with the Riverside Boiler Works and after due publicity, he was incarcerated in one of their most solid products on Monday evening, the 11th of February. This boiler was fairly riveted together and was fitted with an end like a lid. When Houdini was inside, two steel bars were thrust through corresponding holes in the edges of the lid and the top edges of the boiler. The bars had holes drilled in the tips and through these, padlocks were snapped by the challenger's workmen. The boiler had, of course, been built according to plans furnished by Houdini ahead of time, with the thickness of the

* This proposed book on his unique art was finally issued in 1930, edited by Walter B. Gibson, as *Houdini's Escapes,* under the *imprimatur* of Beatrice Houdini and the *nihil obstat* of Bernard M. L. Ernst, president of the Parent Assembly, Society of American Magicians.

iron specified, the size of the rivets and the dimensions of the locking bars. The security of the boiler itself did not concern the Escape King—what he wanted was a pair of steel bars cut to his order so that he could duplicate them before the performance with bars of his own. The challenger's bars of hard steel were hidden in the cabinet which concealed the escape. Once inside Houdini set to work on the duplicate bars which were of exceedingly soft metal. After sawing through these bars, he pushed them out, wiped up tell-tale metal dust, opened the padlocks with duplicate keys, got out the original bars and relocked the boiler, leaving the boilermakers to puzzle their wits in vain, and possibly to repair to one of the local bistros to drown their confusion in a few glasses of lager, accompanied by rye chasers.

Next day, at the afternoon performance, Houdini introduced a giant football cover constructed by a sporting goods manufacturer. This escape was noteworthy only as an ingenious publicity tie-in for the *modus operandi* was fairly obvious: the lacing of the football could be untied by patiently pulling the knotted section of cord inside by a hook. Another way, when the knots were elaborately sealed, would be for Houdini to cut the cord near the knots, make his escape, replace the cord, and emerge triumphant. He could then *pretend* to cut the already severed cord and take the sealed knots to the challenger who would be standing by or sitting in a box, asking him to verify the fact that the seals had not been tampered with.

Next Houdini showed the Boston crowds how he could get out of a crazy crib in full view of the audience. This was psychologically a brilliant move since escapes done behind the curtains of the cabinet were getting monotonous. Also concealed assistants with crowbars and keys were beginning to be suspected as a solution to his mysteries.

Harry was quite capable of planting such rumors in the press, and following them up with his crazy crib in which the spectators suffered with him during an agonized forty-five minutes while he grappled with knots and straps, straining and puffing. Harry would instruct his assistants to tie him tight so that he really had to exert himself to get loose. Anything to give the crowd a good show.

After the crib he brought out a "challenge" which, he claimed, had been invented by some ingenious members of the Boston Athletic Association. It was a box of clear glass, made to his order by the Pittsburgh Plate Glass Company (double tie-in) and it was a beautiful piece of craftsmanship.*

The plate-glass box is important in this history for another reason—it was the first of Houdini's "prepared" escapes (though presented as a challenge), in which the performer could actually be seen by the audience inside before the curtains of the cabinet hid him from view. It led, in time, to the famous Water Torture Cell which had a glass front. The box was ingeniously constructed: the glass bottom, sides and top, all single pieces, fastened together at the corners by bolts secured with nuts and washers outside the box. The bolt heads were smooth and could obviously not be unscrewed even with tools. The box could be left in the theater lobby, unlocked, where a sign called attention to its construction and the apparent impossibility of escape. Just before the show, however, the bolts which fastened the hinges to the cover at the rear were taken out and replaced with bolts which carried on each side of the head, a minute indentation. That was all. Once in the box Houdini would produce a tool hardly larger than a dime, a tiny crescent of metal with which he could unscrew the hinge bolts from inside. Later, if desired, he could open the padlocks in front with keys, and replace the "gaffed" bolts with "innocent" ones—the heads entirely smooth. This was, from an artistic standpoint, one of Houdini's masterpieces.

Once he had mastered all the angles of the "planted challenge" he rode it hard. Any feat which did not get coverage on the wire services was good for another town, and Harry repeated the challenges as his tour of the Keith circuit took him across the country.

* It is now in the collection of Mr. Michael Miller of Hewlett, L. I.

He played his final week in Boston in mid-February, and the next jump was New York. He had made a particularly strenuous effort to squeeze out that fifth week in "Bean-Town." It made a good bragging point in the theatrical papers. When attendance at the theater had started to slacken off Harry had cut loose with a barrage of picturesque challenges, always informing one audience what he would attempt to do later in the week, which insured repeat business.

By the 13th of March he was in Toledo, Ohio, where he was tied up by a committee of high school boys using tarred ropes. After forty-one minutes he was loose but there is no record of his ever trying this stunt again. An easier, if laborious, challenge followed on the 15th when the Marine Boiler Works presented him with one of their stoutest boilers, duly fitted with cover and secured with crossing steel bars. Harry painstakingly sawed his way out but this time he apparently tried it with the challenger's own bars, for it took him an hour and twenty minutes. It was a triumph of endurance, for both performer and audience. But in the Middle West, audiences seemed limitless in their patience.

In May at Rochester, he made his first bridge jump of 1907. Two weeks later, in Pittsburgh, a crowd "estimated by the chief of police to number 40,000" saw Harry leap, duly manacled, from the Seventh Street Bridge.

By this time the publicity stunts had shaken down into an orderly routine—bridge jumps from spring to fall and jail breaks in winter.

Harry reached San Francisco in August where, on the 26th, he jumped into the Bay with his hands cuffed behind his back and a 75-pound iron ball fixed by a chain to one ankle. As was properly pointed out in the accompanying burst of headlines, had he failed to release himself the weight would have dragged him to the bottom of the Bay for keeps. This was one of his most dramatic water jumps, and as far as I have been able to learn, he never repeated it. But after he had made his splash, first in the Bay and then in the papers, he astonished the San Franciscans by escaping from a large paper bag, its mouth sealed by the committee and the bag carrying their autographs to prevent substitution. The point of this piece of mystification is, of course, to get out of the sealed bag without tearing it or leaving signs of the mode of egress.

By fall, Houdini had worked his way down to Los Angeles where he treated the Angelinos to one of his most talked-about escapes—from a U. S. Government mail bag.

There was an element of officialdom connected with the escape which Houdini played to the hilt—having the Superintendent of Mails lock him in the bag. In his publicity Harry claimed that the bag had been secured by "a rotary lock belonging to the U. S. Government." There is no reason why we should take this statement as the unvarnished truth, since in publicity as in love and war, all seems to be considered fair when it comes to the press agentry of a professional mystery man. His business is to entertain by legitimate deception, and a few embroideries of the truth in his talks to newspapermen is legitimate enough, by tradition.

The bags which carried registered mail in Harry's day were made of stout sail canvas with a leather flap at the top, and eyelets which fitted over hasps. A strap was passed through the hasps when the cover was closed and the end of the strap was secured by a padlock. The bag was so sturdily built and the cover flap of leather fitted so snugly that it seemed impossible for anyone enclosed in the sack to manipulate the lock, even if he had a key—a key which, incidentally, never left the post office. We can discount the Los Angeles challenge of the rotary lock as a special event for which Houdini was duly prepared, as always, but about which we have too few details to make a guess at his method. When Houdini had to deal with padlocks he either used one of his own, which could well be a "gaffed" or "spirit" lock made to open by the insertion of a pin in an inconspicuous hole, or else he had duplicate keys. Only in very unusual circumstances would he resort to actually picking the lock unless it were of extremely simple design and eminently pickable.

We have already seen how Houdini could get an impression

of a key—on a bit of kneaded rubber in a tiny, rectangular metal pan concealed in the palm of his hand. When the padlock of the challenge mail bag was to remain in possession of a postal official until the evening of the performance, Houdini would be forced to get a secret impression of the key ahead of time. He never left anything to chance.

Once inside the bag and padlocked securely, Houdini lost no time in getting out his duplicate key. This had a string tied to it and by pushing the key through the narrow crack of the leather flap, he could, with considerable patience, maneuver it out of the bag and into the key hole of the padlock, and so liberate himself, closing the lock after his escape and leaving all shipshape.

For added drama he would sometimes introduce a loud-mouthed heckler who would demand to be shut up in the bag in an effort to discover Houdini's secret, only to yell in frantic, if muffled, tones for Houdini to release him before he smothered. This was the old "Risey in the box" gag, which he and Dash had worked at Vacca's Bowery Theater in Coney Island.

For some reason, this mail bag escape caught the public's fancy. A university professor was so intrigued by the problem that he bought a mail bag of his own and had his friends shut him up therein, only to call for liberation when it began to get stuffy inside. The good man then approached the problem in a scientific way—measuring the bag and trying to devise a secret opening which would pass inspection. In this he failed. He was persistent though, and bought a new bag which he put up to his students as a problem in logic. For a time the faculty and students of the university talked of little else than Houdini and the mail sack but they never guessed the true solution. It was a perfect example of something Houdini kept harping on in his later years as an exposer of fraudulent spirit mediums—the scientific mind is usually helpless against a trained trickster; because a man has mastered the intricacies of chemistry or physics it is no qualification for him to deduce how the Chinese Linking Rings, for instance, seem to melt into each other, passing solid metal through solid metal. Only a knowledge of the rings themselves can reveal the secret.

The scientific mind is trained to search for truth which is hidden in the mysteries of nature—not by the ingenuity of another human brain.

But ingenuity, for a stage performer, is not enough. It was not enough for Houdini to rack his brains and ransack his notebooks and files, creating ever new challenge devices. By the end of the season of 1907 the public seemed suddenly to tire of his manifold escapes. It had settled back in its seat with the conviction that nothing could hold Houdini, and that was that. Its attitude: "All right, so you can get out of anything. Now show us something new."

Houdini began to play to houses where there were a few empty seats. Panic seized him, peering through the curtain before making his entrance. He was slipping and no one knew it quicker than Houdini. On January 20, 1908, in St. Louis the theater manager told him he was worthless as a drawing card. Harry steamed ahead, setting up ingenious challenges but the crowds didn't come out. In Cleveland he got the final, crushing blow—there was another name above his on the marquee of the theater. This, Harry told himself, is the End.

But the challenge drew from Houdini his characteristic response: get in there and fight harder. For some time an idea for a prepared escape had been taking shape in his mind; after the novelty of the public challenge gimmick wore a little thin, he realized that the people wanted to see him get out of some impervious-seeming contrivance. They really didn't care who built it, as long as a committee from their ranks could examine it. And to meet this requirement, and play it for the maximum drama, Houdini and his assistants, early in 1908, built a device which for sheer dramatic possibilities could hardly be beaten. It was a man-sized milk can, its cover secured by padlocks, once the self-liberator was inside. This did not vary too much from his other inventions with one exception: Houdini proposed to escape from the locked can while it was filled with water!

21. *The Miraculous Milk Can*

LADIES AND GENTLEMEN, my latest invention—the milk can. I will be placed in the can filled with water. The committee locks the padlocks and places the keys down in front by the footlights. I will attempt to escape. Should anything happen and should I fail to appear within a certain time, my assistants will open the curtains, rush in, smash the can, and do everything possible to save my life. Music, maestro, please."

The assistants, Kukol and Vickery, have brought the can on stage, carrying it by handles riveted to the sloping shoulder, one handle on each side. Houdini exits while they are filling the can with buckets of water. When he returns he is wearing a bathing suit.

Riveted to the lid of the can are six hasps which fit over staples riveted to the neck. Houdini is raised by the assistants and is lowered feet-first into the can. It seems to be a tight fit but he finally manages to wriggle in all but his head. The lid is made ready and then his head submerges, water running over onto a canvas tarpaulin spread on the stage. This is the signal for the assistants, hurrying the committeemen, to snap the six padlocks through the staples, securing the lid.

The cabinet is then lifted and placed over the can and, while the orchestra slowly and ominously plays "Asleep in the Deep," the audience waits. The spotlight is on the curtains of the cabinet. Unconsciously the spectators try to hold their breath but are forced to give up, after half a minute or so, with loud explosions and gasps. One minute. Ninety seconds. Two minutes. Two minutes and a half. Great agitation, apparently kept under rigid control by Houdini's assistants. Three minutes. The audience is almost breathless. A stir passes over the crowd.

150

The tension becomes unbearable. Three and a half minutes—and Houdini parts the curtains and steps out, streaming water. Behind him the can stands locked and apparently unchanged.

The sensation this produced quickly brought Houdini's name back on the theater marquees in larger letters than any other act on the bill. It bounced him into the top-money spots again and into headlines. The milk can had a miraculous effect, not only on the spectators but on Houdini's career.

He had given them something brand new in the way of thrills. As a result, there was only standing room where he appeared. As he continued to tour, Houdini worked out other angles and built the presentation until it took almost his full half hour of program time. He might, on occasion, warm up with his strait jacket—audiences never seemed to tire of it—but the can was what "brought 'em out."

Since many people in the audience insisted on trying to hold their breath as long as Houdini was presumably entrapped, he played this up. Before the lid was locked he would suggest an informal contest with the audience—he would stay under water for one minute; all those who cared to, and who had no physical condition such as a weak heart, were cheerfully challenged to try holding the breath as long as he did. One by one they gave in before Houdini again stood up, his barrel chest heaving, shaking the long hair out of his eyes.

Later he challenged swimming champions to get in the can first while a big clock at one side of the stage ticked off the seconds. Houdini could actually hold his breath for three minutes and he seldom found a swimmer, no matter how distinguished, who could beat him.

The structure of the "1908 can," as Houdini called it in his notes, was diabolically ingenious. Constructed in Chicago, according to Houdini's specifications, the can bore the general shape of an ordinary milk can with a flanged lid that fitted inside the neck—the type which children carried to the store to get milk. It stood about forty-two inches high, with a sloping shoulder and a cylindrical neck. From floor to shoulder it measured about thirty inches, the slope measured about five inches and the straight neck another seven. The seams were riveted and soldered water tight. There were two handles, one on each side, fixed to the sloping section of the "shoulder." The body of the can tapered in about an inch toward the floor. This was a stroke of genius for it killed the theory that the can was really two cans in one and that when Houdini was inside he had but to stand up and lift the outer can off the inner one.

The milk can really worked on a variation of this—the double principle was used but only the shoulder was of double thickness. The rivets which seemingly held it to the body were fakes. Inside the can were dummy ends of rivets so that any exploring committeeman could find them with his fingers. Yet when the cover was locked on, Houdini had but to stand up, pushing hard against the lid, and lid, neck, and false shoulder all came off together.

The handles which were fixed to this shoulder were a subtle bit of misdirection. The top section was attached to the bottom by two trick rivets. When the assistants carried the can on stage by the handles, these two rivets held the thing together. Once the can had been filled with water and Houdini stepped inside, he stayed only for a moment underwater while he unscrewed the two real catches. With these out of the way, the escape was foolproof.

But the lid of the can had to have a few tiny air holes in it so that atmospheric pressure would not hold the top on too tightly. Even if the shoulder had stuck, Houdini, by placing his lips near the top of the domed lid, could have sucked in enough air to sustain him while he signaled his assistants that something was wrong.

With the two real rivets tightened inside, the can could be placed for display in the lobby of the theater with perfect safety, though it was always carefully watched and tested before the performance.

But the year was an historic one in the Houdini saga for another reason than the milk can. In 1908 Harry gained a new assistant, a man who soon became his chief aide and on whom Houdini depended more and more as time proved his worth. This was an English mechanic with sandy-reddish hair, a man of medium height and of so average a cast of countenance that he could pass in a crowd—he would have made a first-class "tail" for any police department. His name was Jim Collins.

Collins was a Londoner, born in Highgate where, tradition has it, Dick Whittington was sitting on a stone by the roadside when he heard the distant bells of St. Mary le Bow ring out their heartening chime: "Turn again, Whittington, thrice Lord Mayor of London."

Although Franz Kukol was a master at staring down pompous European bureaucrats and police officials, and could do the music for the act and rehearse the orchestras for the cues, he was no mechanic. And Houdini very much needed a master mechanic—someone who could take a rough sketch, develop it into workable plans, order one part from one machine shop, a second part from another to preserve the secret, fit all parts together, and produce Houdini's basic idea in practical form. Such a man was Collins.

Collins was also a fine cabinetmaker. He soon learned as much about locks as he was likely to need as Houdini's chief assistant. He could go along on a prison break and hide the required picks or keys skillfully in the cell where his true role was often not suspected—he could pass as a member of the committee and so solidly respectable did he look that nobody took him for a showman. His hair was thin on top, he wore glasses, and his manner was unassuming and modest; few could guess that he was, in truth, the right arm of the great Self-Liberator.

The Houdini company now consisted of Collins, Kukol, Jim Vickery and, in Europe, George Brooks, with extra boys hired as needed. Bess functioned as wardrobe mistress, morale officer, and comptroller. She also acted as go-between with her stormy husband and the boys when this was necessary. When the boys needed extra money she played poker with them, betting wildly on weak hands.

The company traveled in two railroad cars (the tiny cars of England and the continent), one of which carried the baggage, props, and Houdini's special traveling library, designed by Jim Collins and built to hold a hundred books.

Being an assistant on the Houdini payroll was no sinecure. The boys supervised unloading the props and installing them at the theater. The act occupied three dressing rooms—one for Houdini, one for the boys, and a third for the apparatus—this one was always called "the shop" and in it Collins cut keys and built gimmicks to get out of special challenge devices which Houdini still featured even after the milk can.

The stage, during Houdini's act, was always blocked off— no other performers and no stagehands were permitted within the confines of special screens which Houdini's boys placed around the stage area while the act was on. As an antidote for this exclusiveness, on closing night—Saturday—Houdini would send out for sandwiches and beer, flats would be laid across wooden "horses" on the stage after the final performance, and Houdini would play host to the other acts, the musicians, and the stagehands. These last were not the arrogant emperors of the theater they have since become under the wing of a vigilant union. They were little more than laborers, and Houdini's including them in his farewell party was regarded as an act of great kindness.

Other acts on the bill held Houdini in awe for two reasons— the driving force of his personality and his openhanded generosity when one of them was ill or in trouble. To Harry a good deed was something to be done quietly: "So when you do a *mitzvah* you don't take along a brass band." This was Mother Weiss speaking.

When the equipment had been moved into the theater, it had to be inspected to see that everything was in working order and in readiness. If handcuffs were used or were brought up from the audience, Collins spotted them at once and could be trusted to provide the proper keys or picks.

Besides unpacking the baggage, the boys also were pressed into service as distributors of handbills commemorating the boss's latest jail break or bridge jump. Houdini would distribute a stack himself when business showed signs of slacking off.

When one of the boys made a mistake, Houdini fired him on the spot—and was highly offended if the boy took it seriously and threatened to stay "fired." Then Harry would thunder at him, rebuking him for his disloyalty. Collins was "fired" once a week just on general principles, for he seldom made a mistake.

He was a rare, rare bird, was Jim Collins—an absolutely dependable man. Like many Englishmen, he liked his beer and often something a lot stronger. The strain of working for Houdini required some form of quick relaxation, but although Jim was able to take on quite a load after the show, he was always bright and chipper the next morning. Houdini himself would drink his token glass of beer at the closing-night party and that was all.

It was an exciting, exhausting life. When Jim heard the Boss screaming, "Collins! Collins! Get in here quick!" he never knew whether he had mislaid a handcuff key, whether the theater was on fire, or whether Houdini had just had a revolutionary new idea, such as putting vaseline around the collar of the milk can to keep the water from seeping out. Jim Collins maintained a philosophical calm in the face of catastrophe.

Any successful trend in show business spawns a vast litter of imitators. Before long, "Handcuff acts, you could buy them off pushcarts." Many of the small-timers used gaffed cuffs and trick padlocks, and they were eating into the potential bookings of Houdini and making the handcuff trick commonplace. Harry decided to drop the handcuff part of the act entirely and when he opened in Berlin at the Circus Busch on the 10th of September, 1908, the cuffs were no longer part of the program.

He also devised a replacement for the much-imitated strait-jacket escape. One thing he tried, with fair success, was an "insane blanket." This restraint was employed in asylums in place of the jacket. Any blanket could be used and all that was needed were a number of straps.

As applied to violent mental patients, the victim was apprehended by the attendants, and held by them while he was rolled in a heavy blanket which was fastened about him by stout straps—one around the neck, another around the waist, a third around the knees, and the last one tightly confining his ankles. Trussed up in this manner, it would take him several hours to wriggle loose. The violent expenditure of effort as applied to reality—and a blanket strapped around the body is the impingement of reality in unmistakable form—served to help quiet the patient and keep him from hurting himself or anybody else.

As used on the stage by Houdini, this restraint was increased by having a belt fastened about his waist before the blanket. The hands were tightly strapped to this belt first, the ankles were bound together, then the blanket was applied in regulation fashion. It required a considerable struggle before Houdini could release his hands, unbuckle the straps under the blanket, and undo the other buckles through the cloth. But it had this advantage—he was out before the audience realized it and he would suddenly kick the blanket high into the air and leap to his feet triumphantly to take his bow.

Ever since the woebegone expedition to Nova Scotia and New Brunswick, when he had visited the hospital in St. John, Houdini had haunted mental institutions in his search for ideas for good escapes. Now, in the civilized madhouses of Germany, he found something new. This was the wet sheet pack, one of the most ingenious methods of immobilizing a man without hurting him that has ever been devised.

In the late William Seabrook's book *Asylum* there is a vivid description of the wet pack, how it is applied and the strange soothing action which it has on the patient. Sheets are wrapped around the body, tucked under-and-over arms and legs, then the whole body is turned back and forth as more sheets are wrapped around it; the patient, resembling a cocoon, is then soaked with buckets of warm water and left in a warm room on a rubber sheet. Here again, as actually applied to violent cases, the sheet pack is not designed to restrain a person permanently—it gives the patient a sense of soothing security, according to people who have experienced it during spells of mental disturbance. There are always some patients in any institution who can eventually wriggle out—but this is expected. It gives them several hours of wholesome exercise which they would not take otherwise.

When Houdini first saw a patient encased in a wet sheet pack his eyes lit up—this, verily, was something he might work into the act. He got a couple of the attendants from the asylum to come to his hotel and put him in the pack, and then spent two hours getting loose. They put him in again and this time he was ready for them; he had analyzed the restraint and had developed a method of getting precious slack. But when the warm water was doused over the cloth it increased the difficulty of the escape a hundredfold.

He tried out the wet pack in public, wearing a bathing suit, and found that it took him an hour and a quarter to get loose. It was an escape which could be a sensation before a certain type of audience and flop dismally before another. Finally Houdini made it more strenuous by having bandages secure his hands under the sheets and having the whole cocoon-like wrapping, with him inside it, bound fast to an iron cot with linen bandages across his body.

The escape was the most difficult, in terms of energy expended, that Houdini ever tried. And after using it both in Europe and at home, he eventually gave it up. The effect on the audience was simply not in proportion to the violence of the struggle.

On the 23rd of October, 1908, Harry celebrated his "twenty-fifth anniversary in show business." This was stretching a point, since he measured from his single appearance with the five-cent circus in Appleton when he was a boy, but it was good for a banquet tended him by the management of Circus Busch. At this affair there were a number of congratulatory speeches, after which the guest of honor got up and made a graceful speech, congratulating himself.

During this period Harry also worked out one of his most ingenious devices—a device that illustrates the difference between a talent for stage effects and true genius—his escape from a gallows.

The gallows was not of the inverted "L" type, commonly shown in illustrations. It was, instead, the kind with two uprights and a stout beam across them, the uprights fixed firmly to a platform at their base. Houdini began by having his wrists tied, his hands crossed on his chest. The ends of the ropes were then brought around his body and knotted tightly in back. Leather cuffs were strapped around his ankles and short chains were snapped into rings in the ankle cuffs. The chains held his feet firmly, since their other ends were snapped to rings in the side posts near the base. A leather collar was buckled about his neck and a rope was passed through a ring in this collar, then brought down and tied to an eye embedded in the wood of the platform between his feet. Finally a stout rope was wound three times around his neck—which was protected from abrasion by the leather collar—and the ends of the rope were then carried up and secured to the crosspiece of the gallows.

This gave the audience a pretty problem to think about while the curtains shielded Houdini and the gallows from view. In a very few minutes, however, the escapologist would appear, having freed himself from the gallows, and would busily attack the knots of his wrists with his teeth. When the last rope gave way, Houdini would triumphantly toss the ends of rope out into the audience as souvenirs and take his bow.

It was truly an impressive puzzle, yet in the hands of a less expert showman it would not have caused any sensation. As he performed it, there seemed to be no explanation—for how could he have bent down to unfasen his feet with the rope twisted tightly about his neck? And how could he have unwound the rope from his neck when his hands were tied at chest height? And how could he have released the ropes tied behind his back unless his wrists were freed first? The minds of the spectators went 'round and 'round and found no answer.

For an experienced rope-tie artist, the answer was simplicity itself. The solution is to be found in Houdini's old "bible," *The Revelations of a Spirit Medium*. There the anonymous author advises a would-be medium, if tied up too tightly, to have a knife blade concealed in his clothes, cut the rope, and then produce a duplicate, claiming that the spirits came to his aid and untied him!

Harry did not claim spirit aid then or ever but it was the same procedure—as soon as the cabinet was in place, Harry went to work on the rope confining his wrists. He had a sharp blade fixed to a stout harness which buckled around his chest under his shirt; it took but a moment to slice his hands free. Then he pulled two of the loops of rope around his neck, drawing them so tight that they momentarily cut off his breath. When he had enough slack to work one loop over his head, the other two followed easily. By bending down to unfasten his ankles, he was free.

Now came the stroke of genius—hiding the cut wrist ropes in his pockets, he drew out duplicate ropes in which slip knots had already been tied in an intricate pattern.

As Houdini stepped out of his cabinet, gnawing away at the wrist ropes and then flinging them off triumphantly, he was using misdirection of a high order, implying that the wrists were freed *last* instead of first.

In the opinion of many magicians, Houdini's handling of the finale of the gallows escape was one of his finest moves. As Houdini himself wrote, in the *Unmasking of Robert-Houdin*, "the secret of showmanship consists not of what you really do, but what the mystery-loving public thinks you do."

22. *Quick Study Connoisseur*

WHEN HOUDINI shifted his public challenges from packing boxes and iron boilers to official restraints used by insane asylums, he featured these, too, on handbills headed with the name of the theater where he was appearing:

THE OXFORD

Mgr. ....Mr. Blyth-Platt

London, November 6, 1908

Mr. Harry Houdini
Dear Sir:
Having heard that Steward Martin of the Bedlam Asylum, London, could not accommodate you with any form of restraint, allow us to inform you that we, the undersigned, qualified Lunatic attendants, do hereby challenge you to allow us to strap, lace and rope you in the regulation manner to a "Crazy Crib." That is, in the general way adopted by Asylum attendants for restraining patients suffering from *delirium tremens,* or murderously or suicidally insane. If you will make your attempt to release yourself in full view of the audience, we will attend the Oxford on Wednesday evening and put you to the test.

(signed) William Marshal
33 Thorngate Rd.
Paddington, W.

(10 years Male Nurse and 3 years Insane Attendant, Paddington Workhouse)

John Du Kean
299 Hampton St.
Newington, S. E.

160

(London Hospital Insane Attendant, 4 years, 9 years at North Dakota Asylum)

Albert Diadams
New Insane Attendant
Jewish Hospital
3, Tottenham

(3 years at Cane Hill Asylum)

———

Houdini has accepted the above challenge and will attempt to release himself in full view of the audience on Wednesday Evening, November 11, 1908.

This, as we readily recognize, was just the old crazy-crib escape—the one, in fact, that Houdini had tried to sell in his magic catalogue eleven years before in New York. But it had one all-important difference—this time it was presented as a challenge by "Lunatic Attendants."

The crazy crib, as an escape, took quite a lot of wriggling but was well received by audiences. The rest of the season Houdini carried his own "Lunatic Attendants" with him as a part of the company. They functioned expertly in buckling him into the strait jacket, fastening him to the crib and, doubtless, assisting in his private experiments with the wet sheets.

In late January of 1909, Harry got a long and interesting letter from Ira Erastus Davenport. The game old showman proposed a world tour for Houdini and himself, he to lecture on the growth of spiritualism and the part played by his late brother and himself in its popularity, while Houdini would tie it in with his own escapes, thereby "exposing" the cabinet phenomena as the product of natural causes without letting the public know how the tricks were done. They never put his plan into operation, for Davenport fell ill shortly after the letter and died in 1911.

In April a death occurred which caused Houdini mixed emotions. He pasted a brief notice of it in his scrapbook, clipped from the London *Daily Mail*:

"*Landshut, Bavaria.*—A so-called 'Handcuff King' named

Ricardo, who has been appearing at a music hall here, sprang this morning heavily manacled, from the Luitpold Bridge, purposing to take off his handcuffs under water. He failed in the attempt and was drowned."

During the summer, Houdini grew lonely for his mother. So he sent for her to come over for a visit, bringing Bess's mother with her. Mrs. Weiss and Mrs. Rahner had a luxurious visit, being wined and dined by Harry and Bess at every opportunity. Harry started them off each day with a pound-note apiece for spending money, which did not include, of course, purchases for relatives back home.

The mothers wound up their visit while Harry was playing in Plymouth, and he arranged a special treat for them in proper Houdini fashion. He set up, through Collins, a challenge with the employees of the Government Dock Yard who built a packing case on the stage, secured with nails two-and-a-half inches in length. This obviously called for the use of the little dismountable jack, but he made the escape in good form and in record time.

It is probable that the hysteria of the crowd awaiting Harry outside the stage door was not entirely spontaneous. In any event, they carried him to his hotel on their shoulders. While the two mothers watched from the window of their suite, the crowd cheered the Escape King for ten minutes. It is not every man who gets—or can arrange—such a chance to show off before his mother and his mother-in-law together.

But something always seemed to darken Houdini's greatest hours of triumph. During the visit of the mothers, Harry's pet dog Charlie grew ill, was taken to a veterinary and then brought home again to die. Houdini and Bess, having no children, were fiercely fond of the dog and the death of "little Charlie dog" threw a pall over their otherwise radiant summer. They had had the dog for eight years, since they first assaulted Fortress Europa.

Will Goldston used to tell of his first meeting with Houdini, whom he had known by correspondence several years before

Harry crossed the Atlantic. On a day in 1900, Goldston was walking down Lime Street in Liverpool during a heavy snowstorm when he saw, coming toward him, a short man wearing a shabby suit and a disreputable hat; the man's coat collar was turned up against the storm and as he drew closer Goldston saw that he was carrying a small dog inside his coat to shield it from the cold. Recognizing the man from photographs, Goldston went up to him, excusing himself and asking, "Are you Harry Houdini?"

The shabby man bristled slightly: "Yes—who are you?"

"Will Goldston."

The radiant smile broke over the American's face and he seized Goldston's hand, pumping it cordially. In almost the next breath he asked, "Tell me, Goldston, where can I get a pair of patent-leather shoes? I got to have 'em for the act. I can't find a shoestore that carries 'em."

Goldston told him that what he should ask for were patent-leather *boots* and took him to a shop where he was fitted with a pair. Houdini then turned to his English friend, demanding, "Take me to the American Bar. I've got to get there right away. It's urgent."

This Goldston did and then found out what the urgent matter was—other acts on the same bill had told Houdini that at this bar the proprietor was making up a purse for the widow of a magician who had just died, broke. Houdini made himself known to the publican and handed over two pounds, leaving himself broke. The salaries at which Harry Day had first booked him were, naturally, quite small. But Houdini never hesitated to empty his pockets in a charitable cause. On saying good-by to Goldston he set out again for the theater where he was playing, carrying little Charlie dog cosily under his coat.

In 1909 Goldston supervised the publication of Houdini's book, *Handcuff Secrets*. Regarding strait-jacket escapes, Houdini wrote somewhat acidly: "There is a peregrinating impostor in Germany who escapes from a strait jacket from which any child could make its escape. He has it made of pliable white canvas with very long sleeves and short body, though when strapped on him, it seems as if he were firmly secured. In making his escape, he goes through fantastic gyrations and eventually wriggles out of his fastenings."

This design of a jacket—with long sleeves and short body—was actually an excellent idea and Houdini later used such a jacket himself in doing the escape in which he hung by his feet, upside down, over a crowded street.

In the book of handcuff secrets there is also an interesting paragraph regarding skeleton keys. It begins: *"It is always possible to find the shape of the wards by putting in a blank key covered with wax . . ."* and ends, *". . . a small collection of skeleton keys, as they were called, of a few different patterns, were all the stock in trade that a lock picker required."* This paragraph is illustrated by two sketches, one of an elaborately cut key bit and the other of the skeleton bit which would open the same lock. The interesting thing about this paragraph is that it is copied, almost word for word, from the Encyclopaedia Britannica article on "Locks" and the two sketches of key bits are obvious tracings from the encyclopedia illustrations.

I mention this not to discredit Houdini—he may have copied out the text and the pictures several years before, then forgotten the source and mixed the copied notes in with his original jottings. Ultimately, Goldston simply picked them up and put them into the text of the book verbatim.

Profits from the sales of his pamphlets in the lobby of the theater were frequently donated to the disaster fund of any town he was playing where there had been a mine cave-in or a flood leaving victims in need of public help. While this charity was announced during his performance, to encourage the public to buy, it was never mentioned in the press. It was a *mitzvah* and, according to Houdini's code, must be done quietly.

In the autumn of 1909 Houdini was playing in Oldham, where there was no synagogue. On the anniversary of his father's death Harry journeyed to Manchester, borrowed a prayer shawl from another man, and said the *kaddish yosom,* the Hebrew prayer for the dead. He was not an orthodox Jew; just a dutiful son who knew that Mamma would be pleased when he wrote to her about it.

Houdini had never paid the slightest attention to current events. Spectator sports had no allure for him—anything athletic which appealed to him had to be something he could do himself and excel in doing. In music his taste ran to melodies he could whistle and numbers which would make a good background for a magic trick or escape. He was a passionate reader but only of books pertaining to the fields in which his interest lay—magic, early magicians, show business in general, spiritualism in its physical phenomena which utilized, so he claimed, magician's methods to deceive the public.

But Bess had learned long since that her Harry was unpredictable. She never knew what he would do next but even she was surprised when, in the early months of 1909, Harry's interests took a new and unexpected turn. He began to buy paintings, etchings, and sketches.

It is likely that his interest in the graphic arts had been stimulated by his purchases of paintings and drawings with magicians as subjects. This is a field of magical history which has usually been neglected by the dyed-in-the-wool collectors of magician's playbills and equipment.* But when he actually began to buy, there is no question but what he bought art for art's sake.

He was always a "quick study" in the days when he and Bessie played the "ten, twent', thirt' " melodramas, and now he did a quick study of art appreciation. He began haunting auctions and bringing home to their hotel room his newly acquired treasures. At first Bess went along with this new mania of her husband's. But it was one thing for him to bid for, and get, an

---

* It has been stimulated in the United States in recent years by the admirable collection of Milbourne Christopher.

old engraving of a mountebank doing the cups and balls; such a picture had no great artistic merit and hence the bidding was not brisk. It was something else again when he had his heart set on a Watteau landscape and he threw caution to the winds. Bess grew alarmed lest they return from this European tour art-poor. As it was, Harry was always flinging money away, either on worthy charities or on some rare magic book. Bess had to salt away what cash she could so they would not run short and have to borrow.

One evening during his "art period," Houdini was having dinner in the London home of Will Goldston when his host called his attention to a small but exquisite water color he had recently acquired. Houdini looked at it sharply; his face drew into lines of pain and he began biting his lower lip, a sure sign that he was deeply disturbed. Then he turned away and approached Goldston, his eyes burning. "Will—you've got my picture!"

"Impossible, old chap. I bought it at a reputable auction."

Houdini came closer, trembling with rage and frustration. "Will, I tell you, it's *mine*. It was offered to me. I said I would let them know. I've got to have it."

Goldston was piqued. "But my dear fellow—I *bought* it. I can show you the bill of sale. The picture was free and clear. There was no option on it. . . ."

The gray-blue eyes turned ice cold. "It's mine, Will. *I've got to have it!*"

The urbane Goldston smiled. "Harry—your friendship means more to me than any picture. Don't let's have words over it."

Houdini nodded decisively. "That's right. Nothing should come between friends. I'll take it now." He lifted it from the wall and walked out with it under his arm. Goldston later saw it, hanging on the bedroom wall, in the house on 113th Street in New York. Houdini never mentioned it again.

But art was soon on its way out of his affections. When he played Hamburg, Germany, in November of that year Harry paid a visit to the race track and there he first set eyes on a contrivance which drove all thoughts of art collecting out of his mind. Before a week was out he had one like it and had rented a building to keep it in.

His new love was a flying machine—a Voisin biplane, hardly more than a frail assembly of box kites. Before he learned to fly it he had the word HOUDINI painted proudly on the rudder and had his picture taken standing before it with his cap on backwards, aeronaut fashion. He was determined to fly if it killed him; only he *knew* it wasn't going to kill him. Which may well be the only reason it did not. Houdini was a true adept at the "magic of believing."

23. *The Aeronaut*

IF BESS had cast dubious eyes on the outflow of money during the art period, it was as nothing compared to what came next. When Houdini first saw the flying machine that day at the Hamburg race course, he knew he had to have it. Inquiries made of the pilot revealed that it was a model designed three years earlier by M. A. Santos Dumont, and was the product of Messrs. Voisin.

Harry paid 25,000 francs for the plane, rented a building to serve as a hangar and hired a mechanic, M. Brassac, to teach him how to fly it. The plane had an English E.N.V. 60.80 horsepower petrol engine, powerful for that day, but temperamental.

One of the essentials of flying in the year 1909 was good weather. Wind killed people. For two weeks Harry fumed on the ground, spending every available moment going over the working of this new device in which he proposed to make a brand new escape—an escape from gravity.

Finally the wind died and Harry took off, rose a few feet and dived, nose first, to earth, smashing the propeller and part of the frame. Another two weeks for repairs. Finally he did manage a successful take-off and landing—staying aloft a couple of minutes—and was jubilant.

By this time he had received a princely offer of four weeks in Australia at top money, his salary to include traveling time to Australia from France and then from Australia to Vancouver.

He set sail from Marseilles on the 7th of January, 1910, with the biplane dismantled and stowed safely in the hold. With him went his mechanic.

The trip took twenty-nine days and he was seasick all the way. When they reached Adelaide and his feet were firmly planted on the earth again he began stowing away huge meals, gaining back the twenty-five pounds he had lost on the voyage.

There is perhaps no period of Houdini's life about which there is so much controversy as the Australian tour. We know that he made a sensational bridge jump—there is a photograph of it. The papers reported that when he hit the water the force caused a sunken corpse to rise to the surface; when Houdini, having cast off his manacles, swam up and looked about for the rowboat which was to pick him up, he was so startled by the long-dead corpse that he "froze" and had to be hauled into the boat like a log.

Later, at a press conference, the American self-liberator told reporters, "Don't insult me by calling me a magician. I am an *escape artist*. In America if you shake any tree a dozen magicians will fall out."

There is a legend that during his first weeks "down under" a stranger called on him in the dressing room and told Houdini quietly that there was enough work in Australia for the "home guard" escape artists but none for an outsider; if he knew what was good for him he would bloody well cancel his bookings and head for home.

But Jean Hugard, master magician and native of Australia, who was there at the time, says this tale is fiction. "Houdini played the four weeks of his contract," he says, "but his renewal clause was not taken up. The Australians were too impatient to sit for half an hour while he worked away at some challenge device inside his cabinet. He did cancel further bookings in New Zealand and sailed for Vancouver. But if there had been any 'plot' among Australian performers to run Houdini out of the country I would have heard about it. I think the story is pure fiction. Also, I don't believe Houdini could have been scared away from a profitable tour—he would have fought back. I think his act just didn't go over very well."

One thing, however, is certain. He was the first man, officially, to make a successful airplane flight on the Australian continent and land without damage to the machine. He flew a measured mile.

The Aerial League of Australia, a rather hastily organized outfit, presented him with a trophy—a plaque on which was mounted in high relief a globe featuring the southern hemisphere with Australia in the center. From the plaque sprouted two wings holding between them a panel with Houdini's name and the date—March 16, 1910. Houdini later claimed that he made eighteen successful flights in the southern continent, one of six minutes, thirty-seven seconds.

In Sydney, Houdini hunted up the grave of William Henry Davenport of cabinet fame and found it sadly neglected and overgrown with weeds. He arranged for its proper care and had his picture taken standing beside it, a print of which he sent off to the surviving brother, Ira, in Maysville, New York.

In Australia he actually learned to drive a motor car in order to get to the flying field early in the morning. But no one except the iron-nerved Brassac would drive with him. After he left Australia in May, Houdini never flew a plane or drove a car again. His passion died down as quickly as it had arisen.

The story of Houdini's trip home, and of how he bested the Fiji Islanders at their own game of diving for coins, has been told many times but with a significant omission—the "gimmick" by which it is possible to catch coins thrown into the sea.

When the ship put in at Suva, Fiji Islands, the native boys canoed out, loudly calling for the passengers to throw coins and watch them dive through shark-infested waters to recover them. They would swim down after a coin and bob up with the coin in the mouth.

Houdini was in good shape, the sea having been calm, and he had been suffering from inactivity. True, he had won the passengers' rope-skipping championship by skipping rope 439 times without missing; but this held no element of cleverness and danger, which was his meat. The island boys with their coin-diving presented a challenge.

Harry started a discussion on board, claiming that the boys were deceiving the public—they really caught the coins in their hands and transferred them to their mouths. To settle the argument he challenged one of the Fiji lads to a coin-catching contest, both men to have their hands cuffed behind them. The islanders shied away from handcuffs, but Houdini found one who would let them tie his hands with rope. Houdini, naturally, was handcuffed. He dived along with the boy, two coins being thrown, and when the islander came up without his coin Houdini shot up feet first shortly after with both coins in his mouth. He explained to his fellow passengers that he had removed his hands from the cuffs, caught both coins as they plummeted through the sea toward the bottom, put them in his mouth and resumed the cuffs.

In such a situation he would have used "jump cuffs"— manacles worked over so that they could be released by a sharp tug. Catching the coins in the sea was no great task for a swimmer as expert as Houdini. Coins do not plummet toward the bottom, they "side slip" back and forth, zigzagging slowly in their descent.

The brief visit home in the summer of 1910 was timed to coincide with his mother's sixty-ninth birthday. Harry rejoiced with her. On the 5th of July he had gone up to Maysville and had his picture taken with old Ira Davenport who was dying of throat cancer. Ira spent his last strength demonstrating the famous rope-tie to Houdini, or so the Mysteriarch claimed.

Bookings in England were set for the fall and he left aboard the *Mauretania* on August 10th. Again the sea was his friend, and he treated the other passengers to a half hour of magic during the crossing. But the ship had hardly passed Sandy Hook before Houdini was hard at it with pencil and paper, figuring out new prepared escapes to take the place of the milk can when the fickle public grew tired of it.

To his delight, he found that while novel challenges soon tired the American public, the less blasé Britons were fascinated by them. Also, they were much less skeptical about what they read in the papers. At Chatham, Houdini set up a stunt which was a "stem winder"—he had himself tied over the mouth of an antique cannon with the fuse lit and made his escape before the fuse burned down to the powder pan, as spectators cheered. He neglected to inform them, via the press, that the cannon had no powder in it.

To do many of the things which became routine for him, Houdini had to play the part of a superman who could slither out of leg irons and slave collars and melt through walls. This was long before the days of "method" acting and inner-dynamics on the stage, but Houdini had already discovered that if you want "them" to believe you are a superman with strange powers you have to believe in it yourself. And it could be no little, halfhearted belief, either; "you got to put your back in it." Consequently he believed *hard*. And in time this thousand-volt charge of belief affected him off stage as well as on; the belief carried over and he was convinced in his own mind twenty-four hours a day that he was something comparable to Nietzsche's *öbermensch*.

Part of the superman myth was invulnerability to the common ills that flesh is heir to. Houdini drove himself hard and kept in good physical shape, but early in 1911 he was forced to undergo minor surgery for an abscess. This both humiliated and annoyed him, since it cast doubts on his invulnerability.

In April 1911, he came home laden with more treasures acquired from antique dealers and secondhand booksellers, but without the fortune in cash many other acts ascribed to him. Harry spent several fortunes on books and one of the mysterious places the money went when he was on tour was in freight for the mountain of literature he packed along with him. During the 1910-11 season he was using the strait jacket, the needle trick, challenge devices built locally, and the milk can as the closing trick. The whole of his necessary props didn't weigh one hundred pounds, yet his freight bills were enormous.

When he found, in some hole-in-the-wall curiosity shop, the

rusted remains of a writing- and drawing-automaton or an oil painting depicting a rope-walker at a fair, he brought his find home gleefully in a cab, had Collins invent some container for it to travel in, and carried it with him. Harry seemed to distrust warehouses, and the red tape and waiting involved in having stuff sent to him from abroad irked him. He took his treasures with him, where he could dig them out and look at them in the middle of the night if the spirit moved him. The house on 113th Street was getting jammed with crates of books and historical pieces of magical apparatus.

Houdini had yet to make newspaper headlines in his own home town of New York, but the golden rain was falling over show biz and he decided to catch his share. In a sense, he had been forced to wait for vaudeville in the States to grow up to him. But he knew well that constant variety was the key to big houses at home, and he began thinking of a sensational publicity feat which he could use when his famous underwater handcuff and leg-iron release had grown stale.

This new thriller was very simple in essence—it consisted of being buried alive. Harry kept extensive notes on this project, the earliest being notations on ship's stationery, in which he visualized the feat performed with a packing case or box. This would be buried in a large grave and his problem would be to make his escape from the box and then dig his way up to the surface of the ground through the loose earth.

His notes specify that the box was to be gaffed by two boards, hinged in the center and folding inward with special hidden catches to hold them while the box was being inspected by the committee. Once inside and buried, he could pull in these boards and start digging, placing the dirt in the box as he excavated his tunnel toward the light and air. In the collection of Sidney Radner there is a bundle of four hooks made of steel wire which carries a paper tag: "Buried Alive." These hooks were obviously to be used in wrenching inward the two hinged boards which formed one end of the underground box.

Houdini was always fascinated by cemeteries, graves, headstones, burial plots, and vaults. The heroic and persistent efforts he put into developing his "buried alive" stunt passes belief. When he did finally "coin his thrill in publicity" from the trick, it was a burial not in earth but in water, and it depended not on gimmicks but on courage and stamina. This he loved.

Meanwhile, through the summer of 1911, he worked on his wet-pack escape "in full view." He was practicing it in public, trying to learn the most effective way of "selling" it to audiences. There is good reason to suppose that he never did manage to get out of it a satisfying amount of audience response in return for the energy he poured into it. The wet sheets were a man-killer. And the fact that every large asylum had at least one inmate who could wriggle out seems to have galled Houdini no end. The truth was, of course, that the asylum patient had no audience waiting for him to make his escape so they could get home to supper or to bed. The inmate had all the time in the world.

On November 20, 1911, Houdini wrote from New York:

My dear Goldstone:

Just a line to let you know that I have met with a most peculiar accident, and am confined to my bed with strict instructions not to move. During a challenge in Detroit, Mich., I was strapped into a large bag with round straps with such force that my opponents burst a blood vessel in my kidney. I bled for two weeks before I thought of being examined, and immediately after examination I was forced to go to bed, so I am taking a vacation laying on the broad of my back and doing some thinking. I have cancelled a number of weeks, but I will be able to go to work, as the hemorrhage has already stopped, but must give the broken blood vessel a chance to heal. I am informed they heal very quickly, but you must remain very quiet. Am simply rushing this away to you as I will have very little time to do much writing.

With kindest regards and best wishes, I remain,

Sincerely yours,

Dictated "B"   (signed) Harry Houdini*

* A photostat of this letter was given to the author by Mr. George Pfisterer of Philadelphia and is printed here with his permission.

There was a time, as in the bout with pneumonia in London, when Houdini would go to bed and take care of himself. That time was passed by 1911. His refusal to give in and take it easy after the injury in Detroit indicates that, for him, the stoical treatment of injury had become a compulsion. Doing an escape act for two weeks with a hemorrhaging kidney was not courage—it was obsession. And as Houdini's fame increased and his competition grew tougher, his obsession with the "superman" image of himself grew more and more obvious.

The two weeks he spent laying-off in New York, when he dictated the letter to Goldston, were not passed in idleness although he would lie on a couch for as much as half an hour at a time. He used these weeks to supervise the unpacking of his treasures and some cataloguing of his playbills and holograph letters, not to mention the framing of old prints and dictating of notes for proposed books he was planning to write.

By the first of December he was back in harness, opening at Keith's in Columbus, Ohio. He was still in great pain and confided to friends: "I think I started to work too soon. Maybe I should have laid off another week."

The kidney always gave him trouble and forced him to sleep with a special pad; otherwise, the pain would wake him up. He also grew highly sensitive to light and slept with a blindfold of black silk about his eyes.

After a month he put the wet pack in the act again, using it as a special feature toward the close of the week. Early in the spring of 1912 he tore a ligament in his side doing this escape but never missed a performance even though the pain would leave him white-faced and shaking.

He was booked to open at Hammerstein's Roof Garden in New York in July and he swore that this season he would crash the New York papers which had always shied off from Houdini stunts. This time he and Collins cooked up a dilly. He would be shackled securely and make his escape from a packing case—after it had been thrown into New York harbor!

24. *Shower of Gold*

EARLY RISERS on the Upper East Side of Manhattan in the spring of 1912 could observe a most peculiar operation taking place in the Municipal Swimming Pool at 80th Street and the East River. It had to do with lowering a packing case down a chute and into the shallow end of the pool. The case was a formidable-looking box, and was weighted within by bars of pig iron and without by two heavy lengths of iron drainpipe fixed to the sides of the box at the bottom. When the box had submerged, with four men holding fast to the rope, and had remained under the surface for about thirty seconds, there came a splash beside it and a man appeared, shaking long hair out of his eyes. The men on the edge of the pool were, in order of their importance to this drama, Mr. James Collins, Mr. Franz Kukol, Mr. George Brooks, and Mr. James Vickery. The man in the water was the world-famed Self-Liberator, jail-breaker, aeronaut, world traveler, author, and self-made mystery man.

Every morning, just after daybreak, the same group assembled in this spot for a week. At first the packing case was only half submerged after the little man with muscles like a lightweight wrestler had got inside and the cover had been lightly fastened down with a couple of brads, just enough to keep it from floating away. Houdini was preparing his assault on the hitherto impregnable fortress of New York journalism.

Elsewhere his water jumps with handcuffs had been considered news enough to make front pages. Here, in his own home town, the papers were wary. So a great deal of thought and effort had gone into the experiments in the pool. The box was essentially the same as the one with which he and his

176

brother had made their break into show business. It had a board—forming part of one end—which was not what it seemed; it was apparently firmly secured to the posts of the box corners by screws, but these screws were deceptive—they had been cut off with nippers so that they were a scant half-inch long and had then been inserted and tightened. What really held the board in place were concealed hinges at the bottom of it and two secret catches installed in the board above it.

The box could stand any ordinary examination. Once inside it, the Escape King, by using a thin strip of steel, could operate the catches so the board would swing in. There was room for him to wriggle out, even though a rope passed around the box both ways. Once free he could hook his feet under the iron pipes fixed outside at the bottom and pull the board toward him until the catches engaged. He had then only to hang on until his breath was exhausted and then let go, bobbing up to the surface.

The stunt was timed with his opening at Hammerstein's Roof Garden, a theater high above the Broadway throng, with windows on all sides and a roof which could in part be rolled back on torrid summer nights to reveal the stars. The stage held a large tank of water built two years before to house the sensational Annette Kellerman, a swimming star who appeared in a one-piece bathing suit! She had received $1,500 a week.

It was an era of fabulous vaudeville salaries. Eva Tanguay, a carrot-topped bombshell, was drawing down $2,500 a week, doing a solo. In comparison, legit salaries lagged; Lionel Barrymore, playing leads on Broadway, got only $850 a week and that was tops for serious drama.

Houdini was offered eight weeks at Hammerstein's at $1,000 a week—not an inconsiderable sum for an escape artist in America!

Prior to the opening, the stunt of the underwater box was previewed at an East River pier and the press was duly notified. They came out to watch in a jovial "show us" mood. The public meanwhile had not exactly been kept in ignorance of what Houdini was planning to do. The docks near by were black with people. Then New York's "finest" elbowed their way through the throng with their traditional war cry: "Wade a minute, wade a minute! What's goin' on here? C'mon, break it up!"

Houdini expostulated eloquently. No dice. Nobody was allowed to jump off no New York piers, box or no box. The little Escape King rallied and signaled for a tug which was, by a somewhat contrived coincidence, standing close by. He invited the newsmen aboard, took his packing case, his manacles, and leg irons, and steamed for the open harbor. In the excitement, one newsboy jumped in the drink and tried to swim after the tug. It was stopped and he was taken aboard, dripping and triumphant. He was good for at least a paragraph all by himself. Houdini was missing no bets this time. It was a hot day and there was no chance of the boy catching cold.

When they got well away from the minions of the law, Houdini's brink-of-death intensity sobered the scribes. He had them examine the cuffs and irons, then lock them on him. He got into the box and had the cover placed in position. Collins provided hammers and nails, and the newspaper reporters nailed the cover fast themselves after having thumped the box to their hearts' content. The box was duly roped and started on its journey down a chute into the sea.

As one man the reporters took out their watches.

After an agonizing wait of fifty-seven seconds an arm broke the surface. The hardened and sophisticated New York reporters, the most cynical newsmen in the world, burst into a rousing cheer and fell over each other helping Houdini aboard.

The box was hauled in by the rope and the boys left off getting their story from Houdini long enough to give it a thorough going over. They ripped the cover off. Inside were the manacles.

How?

This time the editors could not ignore Houdini. It was a

publicity stunt, sure. But what a stunt! It forced its way into print. Houdini had won. The New York press was his.

Every night thereafter the Self-Liberator demonstrated the underwater packing-case escape in the tank of the roof garden.

When the excitement began to die down a little, he went to a construction firm which was putting up a midtown skyscraper and made one of his famous tie-ins. They had their riggers rope Houdini to a bare girder twenty stories above the Broadway pavement. It was a standard rope-tie escape, just as Houdini had done it a thousand times in the dime museums. The only rope he had to be careful about was the first one applied— which bound him firmly around the waist to the girder. When he had made good his escape he entertained the newsmen by a demonstration of exotic knots which had, supposedly, been used to confine him. No editor in the world could resist Houdini now.

At the end of his first week at Hammerstein's he demanded his pay in gold. Hammerstein growled in mock indignation, "What's the matter, Harry, good U.S. currency isn't good enough for you?"

"Never mind the gags. Just give me the dough in twenty-dollar gold pieces. I got a reason. It's personal."

He carried the canvas bag of gold back to his dressing room where Brooks and Vickery were waiting with rags and silver polish. They set to work, shining up the fifty "double eagles." When the hoard shone to Houdini's satisfaction he lugged it out to a cab and uptown, clutching it happily. When he strode into the house he ran in to where his mother was sitting by the window, watching the goings-on out on 113th Street.

"Mamma, Mamma—do you remember before Father died, he made me promise always to take care of you? Remember?"

"Ja, mein Sohn, Ich gedenk'."

"Well, Mamma—hold out your apron!"

And he poured the shower of gold into his mother's lap.

Houdini always claimed that it was the happiest moment of his life.

The underwater packing case now supplanted the bridge jump. Houdini referred to it as "My challenge to death." And he never, under any circumstances, announced that he would be lowered into the water. He always said, "I will be *thrown* in."

It is doubtful that he ever signaled to be lowered away before he had the catches slipped and the board already pulled in a fraction of an inch just to make sure. A professional daredevil never takes any chances.

It was Collins who had made the thing possible; he built the box, installed the secret panel designed for simplicity and sure action, supervised the nailing of the cover and, where it was used, the addition of a strip of band-iron around the box, making sure it did not interfere with the "working board." He superintended the roping and hoisting of the box, when it was swung over the water by a crane, and he waited for Houdini's signal from inside that all was well before ordering the box lowered away.

The presence of Collins gave Houdini a powerful psychological advantage—in Collins he had perfect trust, not to bungle, not to forget anything, not to let anybody interfere with the critical parts of the trick, and, most important of all, not to double-cross him, sell him out, blab his secrets, hold grudges, or show temperament. Jim was literally worth his weight in gold to Houdini and though the relationship was always "master and man," both of them wanted it that way. Collins liked nothing better than to serve a worthy master. As Brother Joseph had his Richelieu, and Will Chiffinch his King Charles, so Collins had Houdini. They were an unbeatable combination for eighteen years. Had Collins been in the dressing room that fateful day in 1926, Houdini might well be with us yet.

He closed at Hammerstein's the last week in August and hurried aboard the *Kaiser Wilhelm II* to meet his engagements in Britain. Houdini's embarkation was always a scene of excitement, heart-wrenching farewells to his mother who stood tearfully on the dock, last minute rushes by Houdini back again

to throw his arms around his mother one more time, Bess and
Collins finally pulling him loose as the gangplank was being
drawn in, protestations of love and devotion being shouted
back and forth as the ship left the dock, handkerchiefs waving
until the ship was down the bay and out of sight.

The voyage was calm, and Houdini and Collins got down to
work the first day out. They were trying to devise something
which would be an improvement on the "can."

They figured out a milk can which could be built (to specifications as to dimensions and materials but without any installed gimmicks) by a challenger. Escape would hark back to
the iron express box where he cut the soft metal rivets of the
hinges and, once out, opened the padlocks, hammered in soft
rivets to pass inspection, and relocked the box. A double can
in which the bottom of the inner can would be pushed free, the
inner can being put into position upside down, was another idea
which blossomed in Houdini's mind during this period.

The idea of being put into a milk can upside down now took
hold of him, and Collins was kept busy, consulting with tinsmiths in making cans of decreasing size, to see how small a
can could be and still enable Houdini, lowered into it head
first, to turn right side up after the lid had been secured.

But as he continued to devise plans for future escapes, Houdini's mind dwelt more and more on tanks filled with water,
from which escape seemed impossible. He worked out various
gimmicks for releasing the tops of such caskets but never found
one which was sufficiently simple, portable, foolproof and
which, at the same time, provided opportunities for drama.

He never found one, that is, until the following year when
he combined a number of effects to produce his greatest prepared escape. Once it had been designed, and after several
models had been built, he got one that functioned perfectly and
met all his demands. It was a glass-fronted tank of water; he
could be seen while inside it; he entered it upside down; and
the whole device presented an obvious impossibility. He called
it the Chinese Water Torture Cell.

25. *Darkness and the Deep*

HOUDINI CLOSED in Bucharest, Roumania, in the spring of 1913 and hurried back home to open his second season at Hammerstein's Victoria. This time he featured "The Double-fold Death Defying Mystery, in which Houdini is Locked into an Air-Tight Galvanized Can Filled with Water, which in turn is Securely Locked Up Inside of a Hermetically Sealed Iron-Bound Wooden Chest. Failure to Escape Means Death by Drowning."

At least two other performers by now were featuring milk cans, and in Houdini's opinion, even though these artists of evasion were playing in Europe, the field was getting crowded; he had to "give 'em something new." His answer, pending the perfection of the super escape which was occupying his spare time and Jim Collins' as well, was to encase the milk can in a chest, the top of which was secured by padlocks. It was an idea which had been germinating since the first can was built in 1908.

There is no record that the second receptacle was filled with water at the Victoria—the use of a wooden box seems to preclude this. Nor do we know whether or not it was an "upside-down" can—in which the bottom would be gaffed to release Houdini, who could turn right side up inside the water-filled can.

Houdini's Hammerstein booking was for two weeks only. He laid off three weeks more, staying with his mother who seemed to be feeling the oppressive weight of the years.

Houdini was to open at Copenhagen on the 18th of July. He waited until the last minute and set sail on the *Kronprinzes-*

sin Cecilie on the 8th. The leave-taking, recounted by Beatrice
Houdini, was a disturbing one:

> Persons at the pier beheld a curious sight. They saw
> Houdini clinging to a little old woman in black silk, embracing
> and kissing her, saying good-by and going up the gangplank,
> only to return to embrace her again. *"Ehrich, vielleicht wenn
> du zurück kommst bin ich nicht hier"* (Perhaps when you
> come home I shall not be here), his mother remarked as they
> reached the pier together. She was seventy-two and no longer
> felt any certainty about time. Houdini apparently could not
> leave off reassuring her and showing his affection for her.
> Finally she had to order him to go. Houdini, turning to the
> bystanders, said, "Look, my mother drives me away from her."
> "No, no," protested his mother, "but you must leave now.
> Go quickly, and come back safe to me."

He was the last person aboard, leaping up the gangplank
just before it was drawn up. The last he saw of his mother she
had caught one of the paper streamers he had thrown, and he
was leaning far over the rail holding the other end.

During their farewells Mrs. Weiss asked her Ehrich to bring
her a pair of woolen slippers (*"Nicht vergess' nummer sechs"*).
He did not forget them—Number 6—but she was never to
wear them.

Dash was home that season and was playing in Asbury
Park. His mother went down to see him and while there, suffered a stroke. Dash immediately cabled Houdini at Hamburg.
Houdini was still at sea when his mother died on July 17th.
He missed the cable at Hamburg and it was relayed to the
theater in Copenhagen. When he finally read it he seemed
stunned; he returned to the hotel where Bess found him. She
quickly packed two small bags and hustled him aboard a train
for the German port where they could board the ship on its
return voyage, leaving the faithful Collins to take the rap for
the broken contract, which in Denmark was a serious offense.
Jim stayed in jail until the situation was explained to the
theater manager.

On July 30th Houdini stood by the grave in Cypress Hills while his mother was laid to rest beside Rabbi Weiss. The warm, woolen slippers, Number 6, were placed in the coffin with her.

During the month of August, Houdini spent nearly every day at the grave, speaking to his mother as if she could still hear him. He was inconsolable, waking from fitful sleep at night, crying his mother's name. Along Broadway it was rumored that grief had driven him insane.

While Mrs. Weiss had lain paralyzed and dying, she had tried to speak. The family, grouped around her, knew that she was trying to leave a message for Ehrich. But they could not understand the words. Houdini, on hearing this account of his mother's death, could make a good guess at what she was trying to tell him. But he could never be sure. It had to do with Houdini's forgiving a relative in a situation which caused considerable dissension in the family.

Before he again sailed for Europe to pick up his interrupted tour, Houdini paid a final visit to his mother's grave. In the years that followed he seldom left New York without "saying good-by to Mamma." And his first act on setting foot in New York, even before going to his home, would be to have a cab take him to Cypress Hills.

By the middle of September he was in good enough shape to open in Nuremberg, after arranging to have his mother's letters to him, dating from 1900, typed in English script so that he could read them easily.

At the Nuremberg opening he presented, for the first time before an audience, his greatest prepared escape, the Water Torture Cell. Its reception was all any performer could ask, yet for once the cheers fell upon deaf ears. Houdini took his bow and hurried to the dressing room, where he had a fit of uncontrollable grief which paralyzed him for hours. Death had stolen the sweet fruits of triumph from his greatest "death-defying" feat.

On November 22nd he wrote Hardeen from the Alhambra Theater in Paris:

> My Dear Brother Dash,
>
> Received your letter from Boston; you certainly have worked there often enough.
>
> Save your money and then you will not care if you go back there or not.
>
> Re the Birthdays, I shall *celebrate mine*? always APRIL 6th. It hurts me to think I cant talk it over with Darling Mother and as SHE always wrote me on April 6th, that will be my adopted birthdate.
>
> Dash its TOUGH, and I cant seem to get *over it*. Some times I feel alright, but when a calm moment arrives I am as bad as ever.
>
> Time heals all Wounds, but a long time will have to pass before it will heal the terrible blow which MOTHER tried to save me from knowing. But to other things or else I cant finish this letter. Am working on a few new things in Illusion line and as soon as I accomplish anything will let you know.
>
> Have had a wonderful month, business however is dropping off. But am not worrying.
>
> Hope alls well with you and your family Bess joins me in sending love. Bess has not been well of late cant understand it. Maybe she is sick ??? Do you remember that story? I shall never forget it.
>
> Let me hear from you when ever convenient
> > as ever your brother
> > > (signed) Harry Houdini

This letter, now in the Radner Collection, is interesting to the student of Houdiniana for a number of reasons—it establishes that April 6th was not the true day of his birth, indicates that Houdini did not know the real date, and hints that Mrs. Weiss knew of the family discord before Houdini left for Denmark, but did not tell him the last time they were together, in order to spare his feelings in the matter. It also shows the warm, if bossy, big-brother relationship he had with Hardeen.

It is interesting that Houdini did not mention the Water

Torture Cell, which he always referred to in his notes as "Upside Down" or simply "U.S.D." It may be that he did not realize at this time the true importance of what he and Collins had wrought.

It became an escape of which audiences seemed never to tire. He used it year after year, as his closing trick. He would try other effects, only to return to it; and he included it in his last production, the three-act, full-evening show which was to be his swan song. No other escape of the World-Famous Self-Liberator caused as much talk among laymen or as much heated argument among magicians.

There were at least two models of Upside Down built. The first one had a crosspiece of metal covering the glass panel in front. The second version, now in the collection of Sidney Radner, has an unobstructed view into the interior of the tank. It is made of mahogany, the frame for the glass panel is of steel. The total shipping weight of all the sections with their special packing cases and trunks is between 1,600 and 1,700 pounds. There are five special cases, plush-lined like the cases designed to carry costly dueling pistols. In these are packed the two sides, the bottom, the back, and the special frame of the top with its sliding stocklike panels which held Houdini's ankles imprisoned as he was hoisted into the air, head down, and lowered into the water-filled cell. There is a special crate for the metal front with its glass window, another for a spare pane of heavy glass; a third crate packs the sheet metal lining of the cell and the slender metal bars which guard the glass in front. An ordinary trunk holds the blocks, tackle, and ropes for the hoist, the yards of rubber for the "seal," and the bolts with which the cell is assembled.

When Houdini had been lowered into it, bronze hasps were snapped up, locking on the cover. Padlocks, which could be loaned by spectators, were fastened through hasps for good measure.

The audience saw Houdini hanging head down in the water by his ankles. Curtains closed. For three minutes, while the orchestra played "The Diver," the crowd waited—and then Houdini appeared, streaming water, smiling as if exhausted.

How did he get out?

To this day, no one knows. Radner, in showing me the famous "cell" which he got from Hardeen in 1943, told me that he had never filled it with water. The rubber strips have deteriorated with age. If, in the future, he ever replaces the rubber, assembles the cell as it was put together for Houdini's performance, and fills it with water to within six inches of the top, I have an idea that he might discover something interesting about the Water Torture Cell.

I believe the stocks release only when the water in the cell reaches a certain level.

However, the cell was built for Houdini to the fraction of an inch; Radner himself, though an athlete and one of the few semiprofessional escape artists of the world, is much too tall to fit into it. It may be that the Water Torture Cell will keep its secret forever.

As Houdini presented it, after the curtains were closed, Collins appeared wearing a fireman's helmet and rubber coat and holding a red fire ax. He made a great show of peeping into the cabinet, restless, anxious, as if any second he would have to rush in and smash the glass window to save Houdini from drowning. The row of slender steel bars covering the window inside the tank could have been added to the cell as a safety measure, for if the window had been broken, the rush of water would have swept the escape artist into the jagged edges of glass. On the other hand, smashing the glass with a blow of the ax would be very dangerous for the occupant— the sudden increase in pressure caused by the blow might give him the equivalent of a diver's "squeeze" and prove fatal. Certainly it would break his eardrums.

At the bottom of the tank, within easy reach of Houdini's hands, were two circular valves which open with a half twist. If anything had gone wrong and if the mechanism which holds the stocks panel in place (and later releases it) had jammed,

Houdini had but to reach for these valves and twist them to let the water out.

The metal bars probably served another purpose—to give Houdini something to help him in turning right side up, for the cell is of a size for him to double his body in it, helped by the buoyancy of the water. The one thing a man hanging upside down can do in water more easily than in air is turn right side up!

Of one thing we can be certain; however the famous device works, it is quick, simple, and foolproof. Houdini devised a great many elaborate structures but when it came to getting them out of the drawing-board stage and into three dimensions, he always settled for something nonmechanical and simple. In a variation of the milk can, where escape depended on his cutting the rivets that held the hinged cover, he was careful to make the cover fit *outside* the neck with plenty of leeway so that by pressing up against it with his head, he could get all the air he needed. He could easily have held his breath while cutting the rivets but he was not one to leave anything to chance.

During the fall and early winter of 1913 Houdini went through the motions on stage but the old fire was gone. He spent most of his spare time writing prose poems to his mother; some he had printed; he sent them to friends.

Harry Day could have booked him solid through December but Houdini was too sick at heart to work. He took the month off and he and Bess went to Monte Carlo. Bess was hoping that it would take his mind off his grief, and for once she did not nag about his wasting money. But his heart was not in gambling, either. Their first evening at the casino ended with Houdini five hundred francs ahead. He was listless and distraught. The second night he won fifteen hundred francs and quit, still silent and morose. He only brightened the next day when he and Bess visited the graveyard where were buried the suicides of Monte Carlo. He wrote copious notes about this

visit and reported the grave of a man and his wife who died
in a suicide pact.

By the new year his hair was quite gray at the temples; Bess
thought it made him look more distinguished and Houdini
thoroughly agreed. He had a new set of professional photographs taken.

The coming year, 1914, was to set in motion a social up-
heaval which destroyed the old, leisurely way of life. When the
Kaiser's legions started their march through Belgium, the
world quickened its tempo. And along with the new march-
time came a demand for speed; audiences would no longer wait
for an hour and a quarter if Houdini found himself in difficulties behind the cabinet curtains. They got restless. The long,
painful challenge escapes, such as the wet pack, were on their
way out.

The times were ripe for the Water Torture Cell, but Houdini
had an even more startling illusion in store. Along the way
some journalist had tagged him "The Man Who Walks Through
Walls." And in the coming season he was to do precisely that—
or seem to!

26. *Through a Brick Wall*

THE DEATH of his mother worked deep changes in Harry Houdini. In April of 1914 he celebrated his fortieth birthday in Edinburgh, Scotland, lamenting that his Darling Mother was not there to give him her blessing.

Actually, Houdini had been a boy until that dark summer when he rushed home to find his mother lying in her coffin. He had been a brash, egocentric, sentimental boy. He was now a brash, egocentric and sentimental man. That he was a man at last is shown by his changed attitude toward other mystery men. He was no longer afraid that the bigger boys would take his toys away. He now began moving toward other performers in a tentative gesture of fraternal interest.

Houdini and Goldston founded the Magicians' Club of London, with Houdini as its perennial president. He had a specially carved chair to sit in when he presided at meetings—a chair raised high off the floor so that his head was well above the heads of the other members.

And he had finally become reconciled to not keeping all his "secrets" from the world of magic. There were brilliant men in the profession—men who could figure out everything he did. Or could at least invent their own methods for accomplishing the same effects. Also he was discovering that magicians are the greatest boosters of other magicians whom they admire. Magic-crazed boys whom he had encouraged with a few kind words and some coaching were now grown men, making a place for themselves in show business. Their sincere admiration for Houdini was sweet; in his bitter loneliness after his mother's death he drew closer to his fellow men. Providing, of course, they did not do escape tricks, and providing they never reminded him of anything which attacked his own picture of himself as a superman.

There was a story Goldston liked to tell of a Magicians' Club meeting at which Houdini was to preside. When the lights in the hall blew out, Houdini and Will went out to locate the fuse box in the cellar. The cellar was protected by a padlock of simple make but heavily rusted. Houdini worked and sweated away at the stubborn lock with his lock picks while Goldston held lighted matches. Finally the master of manacles blew up and admitted that he couldn't get the lock open. The magic meeting proceeded by candlelight—an ideal setting for magic tricks anyhow. But Houdini alternately boiled and simmered. Later, when some magus with more nerve than brains teased Houdini about his defeat by a cellar-door padlock, the Self-Liberator sailed into him with ten minutes of violent invective. The tactless one slunk away; no one else ever dared mention the incident to Houdini again.

To bolster his self-portrait, Harry always wanted to excel at other forms of magic besides self-liberation. The great name in legerdemain at home, since the retirement of Harry Kellar in 1908, was Howard Thurston who had taken over the Kellar show on his return from a tour of the Orient where he played before the Emperor of Japan and the Dowager Empress of China. Thurston was five years older than Houdini, had gone to the Dwight L. Moody Bible School, and had been planning to become a medical missionary when a performance of Alexander Herrmann changed his life course; ever afterward he was in love with magic.

From Kellar, Thurston bought many of the old master's most elaborate illusions, including his magnificent "Levitation of the Princess Karnac." This beautiful presentation of the floating lady was probably the high spot in American magic. And it was technically a masterpiece. The equipment for it was packed in eleven cases and, when it was set up, covered a good portion of the rear wall of the stage—all this to float one tiny girl. But it was the flawless timing and melodious voice of Howard Thurston which made the illusion true enchantment.

Houdini and Thurston eventually got to be friends, but Houdini always envied the illusionist. Both had started out as "Kings of Cards," but Thurston's polished manner gave his adroitness the extra touch which Houdini's hard-driving personality could never equal. Now, in 1914, Houdini determined to beat Thurston at his own game—the full-evening show.

Goldston put him in touch with the illusion builder Charles Morritt, who had created effects for Maskelyne and Devant at their Egyptian Hall theater of magic in London.

Harry called his show *The Magical Revue* and he included in it his old stand-by, the substitution-trunk trick, "Metamorphosis." This brought Bess back into the show, to her delight, and Harry expressed his opinion that she had never worked better.

One of the tricks, which Houdini gave a hard sell, was "The Rain of Gold," his own version of a coin-production effect in which he seemed to pluck gold pieces out of the air until they filled a bucket. On the program he called it "Money for Nothing." But he never got as much out of the trick as other performers—whereas the great "King of Koins," T. Nelson Downs, made it a miracle.

The most interesting item on this program, to magicians, was "De Kolta's Marvelous Cube," one of the legendary tricks of magic. Houdini apparently used it only once—and did this to establish his ownership of the famous illusion, which he had secured from the widow of the inventor, Buatier De Kolta.

The effect was a startling one, although not quite so mysterious as myth has made it. The magician comes on stage carrying a small satchel which, he informs the audience, contains his wife. From the bag he produces a six-inch cube marked with spots like a die which he places on a platform. At a signal or the firing of a pistol, the cube suddenly expands to a couple of feet square, whereupon a girl steps out.*

---

* The illusion disappeared for years, was discovered and bought by Milbourne Christopher, who put it into working order. He retains the secret of its operation.

Goldston stated in his memoirs of Houdini that the London show folded in a week, but Houdini played the provinces with it for several weeks before he finally gave in and went back to escapes. The name "Houdini" meant thrills and death-defying stunts to the audiences, and they were not content to watch him whisking agile girls in and out of boxes.

On the 4th of May an English inventor, S. E. Josolyne, had sold Houdini a trick:

> *I, Joslyne* [without the second "o"], *for £1 received from Harry Houdini have given him the right of doing the mystery of walking through a steel wall and if he does it I am to receive what he sees fit in any form and he can permit it to be shown.*
> (signed) S. E. Josolyne
>
> *Empire Newcross*
> *May 4th, 1914*

On the reverse side is written: *"Received from Harry Houdini £3 in all regarding my Walking through Wall of Steel Illusion. S. E. Josolyne."*

The idea which Houdini had bought, if presented as an illusion, would have been a puzzling one. But in a properly-staged illusion show, all the feats are puzzling. Houdini set about adding his own touches to the principle and he wound up with a sensation. He planned it for his opening at Hammerstein's in July.

On his way home aboard the *Imperator* Houdini was in top form. He had been told by a friendly purser that ex-president Theodore Roosevelt would be aboard and Harry got set for him. He knew that a magic show would be required, and he set up a mystery which, he hoped, would be so startling that news of it would travel ahead of him by wireless.

It did not take Harry long to make the acquaintance of Roosevelt, whom he greatly admired. He arranged it so the request for a show was put to him by an officer while he was accompanying T.R. on a brisk "constitutional" around the deck. They had been talking about spiritualism and the tricks of the fraudulent mediums. When the officer approached and asked Houdini if he could, as usual, be depended on for a few feats of legerdemain at the concert, T.R. declared that the idea was bully and asked Houdini to give them a mock séance. All was going according to plan.

During the show, Houdini called on the audience to write questions for the "spirits" to answer by a message written on a slate previously shown blank. These were collected in a basket and from them one was to be selected for the spooks to answer.

Roosevelt took great care in writing his question, being warned by Victor Herbert, also among the spectators, "Turn around. Don't let him see you write. He will read the words by the movement of the top of the pencil." T.R. accordingly turned his back, was given a book lying on a near-by table, rested the slip of paper on it, and wrote.

When the questions had been collected, Houdini suddenly changed the routine and put them aside, asking the ex-president to hold on to his question and place it between the "spirit" slates. This was done and when the slates were opened, Roosevelt was thunderstruck to see a map in colored chalk with a route clearly marked on it and an arrow pointing to a spot. It was of a section of South America where he had led an expedition a few months before to discover the sources of the River of Doubt. His question, when opened by T.R. and checked by the other spectators, read, "Where did I spend Christmas?"

This was news indeed and the "wireless" operator soon had it sparking its way to the news services in New York so that Houdini sailed into the harbor sharing the honors with Roosevelt.

It was a combination of showmanship, publicity sense, and luck. The real miracle lay in a lucky break, which explains many of the seemingly inexplicable wonders of famous mystery-mongers, from Daniel Dunglas Home to Houdini.

In his preliminary patter, Houdini had suggested the sort of questions that might be written: "What do I have in my left trousers pocket?" "When did my Aunt Kate die?" "Where was

I last Christmas?" He had fixed it so that a question written by himself, "Where was T.R. last Christmas?" would be the one apparently chosen at random. T.R.'s question he planned to answer in another fashion. On the saloon tables were a number of novels from the ship's library, bearing paper dust-jackets pasted inside the covers. Before the show Houdini had slipped a piece of writing paper, topped by carbon paper, under the cover of several books and when T.R. was looking for a hard writing surface, Houdini simply handed him the nearest book. On taking it back a moment later, he had only to pull out the carbon sheet to find out what Roosevelt had written. T.R. had swallowed the bait and written "Where was I last Christmas?"

This had a special meaning for Roosevelt, since the celebration of Christmas at a camp in the far Andes was the subject of one of a series of articles about his expedition which he had sold to the *London Telegraph*. At the time of the séance the installment about Christmas Day had not appeared. Houdini, on the other hand, had heard about the articles from newspaper friends and before he sailed had actually gone to the paper, taken a private look at the Christmas Day piece, and copied the map which was scheduled to appear with it.

The production of the map in colored chalk on the slate was just good magic. The lucky break of Roosevelt's question, which Houdini allowed him to place between the slates himself, made it a miracle.

On July 6th, when he opened at the Victoria (this time at $1,200 a week), most of the audience had read the story of the ghostly map and settled back to witness another miracle. They were not disappointed.

Houdini announced that he would present his latest invention. When he was gaining fame as a jail-breaker, he had often been called "the man who walks through walls"—and now he was going to give the audience a chance to see him do just this.

A wide rug was spread on the stage and over it an even

largest sheet of seamless muslin which was carefully examined by a committee. At one side of the stage a squad of bricklayers was hard at work, erecting a wall of bricks and mortar on a steel beam a foot wide and ten feet long, mounted on heavy casters which raised it three inches from the floor. They worked with amazing speed and got a nice hand from the crowd when they finished.

The wall was by this time eight feet high and as long as the beam—ten feet. It was rolled to the center of the stage at right angles to the audience. The committee was placed around the wall, being asked by Houdini to take care to stand on the muslin sheet "to prevent any suspicion of trickery." He called the attention of the audience to the fact that he could not, by means of trap doors, leave the stage on one side of the wall and come up through a trap door on the other—the rug and cloth made it impossible for him to leave the stage at all.

The committee was watching the far end of the wall, the audience the near end; everyone could see him if he tried to climb over. A couple of small three-wing screens were then brought out by Collins and Vickery and placed against the wall, one on each side. Several feet of wall was visible on each side of the screens. Houdini stepped behind one screen, waved his hands above the top, and shouted, "Here I am." There followed a drum roll from the orchestra. Cymbal. Houdini calls from the other screen, "And now I'm here!" and he steps out, having, as everyone could see, made his way from one side of the wall to the other!

The effect was so startling and the conditions so impossible that the audience was stunned.

"Through a Brick Wall" never got the volume of applause which it deserved—the people were struck dumb with wonder.

Houdini quickly followed this with his East Indian Needle Trick and closed with the milk can in a locked chest.

Hammerstein advertised "Complete change of bill every week" so Houdini changed his act or at least its main features. The week beginning with the Monday matinee, July

13th, he did the brick wall, the needles, and closed with can and box.

Next week the program promised, among other wonders, an Arabian Whirlwind Troupe, George N. Brown, World's Champion Walker on the 20th Century Walking Machine, and Houdini doing his underwater escape from a steel-bound box: "No coverings used, box in full view of the committee during the entire performance."

This last was one-third true—the *top* of the submerged box was in full view since it sank until the top was awash. The tank, however, was devoid of light and as far as the committee was concerned, Houdini might just as well have done his escape in a pool of ink.

During this stay at Hammerstein's, Houdini paid a visit to his old union—the Neckwear Makers. He had meticulously kept his dues paid up all these years. One of his former co-workers came up to him and advised, *"Nu,* Ehrich—you know the greatest escape you ever made? It was from the necked-wear business."

With so many acts on the same bill—some of them head-liners from "medium small time"—it was only natural that the jockeying for display in the ads and in the lights on the mar-quee was fierce. One young woman persuaded Houdini, who usually demanded the marquee all to himself, to allow them to put her name under his in letters only slightly smaller. This Harry agreed to do, though it went against his principles. The girl's agent had the theater front photographed, retouched to leave HOUDINI out and used the fake photograph in advertising his client in the trade papers, where she seemed to be heading the bill, with Houdini not mentioned. Harry stormed into the agent's office and smashed a good portion of the furniture.

After he closed at the Victoria, Houdini never used the Brick Wall again. Ordinarily, during his act, the stage was screened off and none of the stagehands was permitted to get a glimpse of Houdini's props. But this was impossible with the Wall. The trick had this defect, a deadly one in Houdini's opinion—

everybody else on the show knew how he did it! For he went *under* the wall.

The rug and floor cloth contained no secret openings, but a trap door was used nevertheless. When Houdini stepped behind one of the screens, an assistant below the stage opened a trap door on cue. This gave Houdini room, as the carpet sagged, to wriggle under the wall and come up on the opposite side, after which the trap door was quietly closed. That was all there was to it. The committeemen standing on the edges of the cloth kept it from sinking far enough to be noticeable.

When the talk of the stagehands soon spread the secret of the wall, Houdini dropped it like a hot *latka*.

After Hammerstein's, he went back to the Keith time, using the jacket, the needles, and the Water Torture.

By this time "bridge jumps while handcuffed" were in the repertory of any magician who was a good swimmer. Dash now did the underwater packing case; and others—without Houdini's "permission" or advice—were soon to follow. Notably, Harry Blackstone.

Houdini, casting about for a new and startling publicity gimmick, hit upon the strait jacket—only this time he was going to do it hanging head down from the cornice of a skyscraper! "The *mumzers*, let 'em try to imitate that!"

27. *Elephants and Eagles*

WITH EUROPE in the agony of World War I, Houdini began to mine the rich vein of the home territory, playing theaters he had never appeared in before.

His new publicity thrill had all the excitement of a "high act" at a carnival with, incidentally, none of the risk. In Kansas City, in September, he made a tie-in with the Kansas City *Post*. While a crowd of five thousand watched from the street below, Houdini was buckled into a strait jacket by members of the city's detective force. He was then lifted by the feet and swung out over the street by a crane mounted on the roof of the *Post* building. Making his escape from the jacket in two and a half minutes, he tossed the jacket triumphantly down into the crowd. Since the stunt also publicized the paper, he was sure of front-page coverage.

It was a perfect gimmick—the inverted position actually made it easier to get his arms above his head and strip off the jacket. Houdini was such a master of all variations of the strait jacket by this time that he had little to fear, even at the hands of wiseacre committeemen, though Collins was always standing by—self-effacing, resourceful, diplomatic and, when the occasion arose, a good man with his dukes. The fact that his hair was thin on top and that he wore glasses made him seem completely innocuous.

Starting in a small way in Kansas City, the upside-down jacket escape got more and more elaborate. The hot spot of the trick was the way the ankles were tied, and this Collins always supervised—for unless there was sufficient padding and the ropes were fixed in the right fashion, it would be easy to break a bone. Also, Houdini had once had an uncomfortable

time of it aloft when a high wind began slamming him into the
cornice of the building. Ever afterward, he made sure that a
guide line was also attached to his ankles, and one end held
by someone at a lower window, who could pull him inside in
the event of wind. There is no record of Houdini ever having
to give up a suspended jacket escape for this reason, but he
covered every safety angle.

The jacket escape, at high altitude, was an exciting thing to
watch, for Houdini's violent twistings and archings of his body
as he struggled always gained the sympathy and admiration of
the crowd.

Where it was not possible to set up the jacket escape, he
went back to other ideas and public challenges.

In Salt Lake City, in December, he had a casket company
put him in a coffin (whether it was his or theirs is unspecified),
screw down the lid, and then—for safekeeping—lock him up
in a burial vault. The casket, in this case, might well have been
his old stand-by from the British music hall days, its bottom
held on by tight-fitting plugs.

Once Houdini had his publicity snowball rolling, everything
he did had a way of turning into news. In 1916 he had an
unintentional news break which got him linage all over the
world. It had to do with a *beau geste* which had been fumbled.
In 1916, in a ceremony at the Metropolitan Opera House in
New York, Sarah Bernhardt was presented with a bronze statuette of herself. John Drew, one of the country's best-loved
legit stars, made the presentation speech; the bronze was supposedly given The Divine Sarah by the "actors and actresses of
America."

Bernhardt was one of Houdini's idols, not only for her heart-
wrenching portrayal of *Camille* but for her courage—at the
age of seventy-two, with one leg amputated, she was able to
"pack 'em in" at the Palace with a tab version of the famous
tear-jerker. Houdini was glad to hear of the bronze presentation.

But a news story soon appeared with the embarrassing fact
that when the bill arrived from the Gorham Company, which had

cast the statuette, no one could be found willing to fork over the $350. All the theater "greats" who had signed the presentation scroll avoided the vulgar matter of who was to put up the dough. In the end, the Gorham Company sent Bernhardt the bill. They got back the statuette and a blistering letter from the great diva.

When Houdini read the story he blew up, raged at the cheap-skates for fifteen minutes, then ripped off his own check for $350 to the Gorham Company, made out with penstrokes that gouged the paper. He wrote Bernhardt, begging her to accept the statue again in the name of America's *vaudeville* artists.

It was a typical Houdini gesture, impulsive, generous, and explosive. Within two weeks his clipping services had mailed him 3,756 clips about his Bernhardt statuette gift. They averaged fifteen lines of newspaper type which, at rate-card prices, would have cost him about $56,000.

Ever searching for new sensations, in 1916 Houdini began experiments in being "buried alive"—without a coffin! The idea was for him to stuff his nostrils and mouth with cotton (à la the yogis of India when doing one of their buried alive feats of self-induced catalepsy), then get in a hole in the ground, on his hands and knees with a hood over his head. Under cover of the hood, he would push the cotton from his mouth. As the hole was filled with loose earth, the air space made by the arch of his body was to give him enough oxygen to enable him to scratch his way up and out of the grave. Try-outs in private proved that the weight of the earth was so crushing that he might well find the grave a real one, so Houdini abandoned the trick, compromising with being buried in a box.

In the spring of 1917 the country which had elected Wood-row Wilson for a second term on the slogan "he kept us out of war" erupted with a skyrocket burst of patriotism on its entrance into the same war. On June 11, 1917, Houdini gleefully wrote to Goldston: "I register tomorrow for enlisting. HURRAH, now I am one of the boys."

The recruiting officers, however, gave him a bitter blow by insisting that a forty-three-year-old man was too old for their purposes, even though he could get out of strait jackets while hanging by his ankles.

Characteristically, Harry threw himself into bond rallies and camp shows. For the latter, he let himself go, doing the straight magic which he loved. His "Money for Nothing" got tremendous response from the doughboys. Their cheers, and the thought that these lads would soon be crawling across No Man's Land, raked by machine gun fire, and suffocated by poison gas, left Houdini choked with emotion. He began to produce five-dollar gold pieces from the air and toss them out to the boys as souvenirs of home. By the end of the war he had distributed $7,000 in this fashion, without cashing in on it for publicity; it was a *mitzvah,* out of his own pocket and gladly given.

By the Armistice he had sold $1,000,000 worth of Liberty Bonds, singlehanded. He and Collins had also invented a diving suit for the Navy, from which a diver, in trouble, could release himself quickly and float to the surface. The plans submerged in the files of the Navy and never surfaced again, but the boys had done their best.

Houdini, in 1917, entered his last phase in his relationship with his fellows of the mystery craft. In that year he was elected National President of the Society of American Magicians. His enemies claimed that he had sandbagged his way to the office by purchasing Martinka's Palace of Magic, the shop in New York where, in the back room, the parent assembly of the S.A.M. could meet rent free. Actually, Houdini and Thurston were the two names that spelled "magic" to America by this time, and Thurston was anything but the whirlwind organizer that Houdini was in bringing the magic clubs of the West and South under the banner of the S.A.M. Houdini was the man to build the society and if he was going to be in it, he had to be the head of it.

But all was not smooth sailing in the ranks of the magi.

Once, at a banquet, a magician of "dubious loyalty" to Houdini asked to be allowed to do a trick. He went to Houdini's table, saluted the great man, and placed a penny under one of his hands, a dime under the other. He then stood a full glass of water on the back of each hand, announcing that when he said the magic word, the penny and the dime would change places.

Houdini, always wary, suspected treachery and tried to slip off his shoe—in an emergency he could, for simple operations, use his toes like fingers—but the magus was too quick for him and imprisoned his hands beneath the water tumblers. He then moved to the opposite end of the room, said his magic words and, on cue, the lights all flicked off, leaving the banquet room in darkness. The voice of the magician cut through the murmur: "You're the greatest escape artist in the world, eh? Let's see you get out of this one!"

The childish "trick" is an old bar puzzle, probably well known in the wine shops of Pompeii; if Houdini had kept his head he might have turned the tables on the wisenheimer by having, when the lights were turned on again, changed the dime and penny into two of his beloved gold pieces. But Houdini reacted in exactly the way the practical joker knew he would—he sent the water flying with a great smashing of glass and roars of "That bastard! Lemme at him!" But the prankster had taken off for parts unknown.

Houdini, it has been observed, would never take an uncalculated risk. But on occasion, for a special event, he would set up escapes that involved some chance. One such occasion was a super-monster benefit which marked the 13th anniversary of the New York Hippodrome, "the largest theater in the world." Proceeds from this truly staggering array of talent went to the Stage Women's War Relief Fund. Leo Carrillo was master of ceremonies; the bill included drill displays by the Army, the Navy, the Marine Corps, and the Junior Police of the 15th Precinct. Of all the distinguished ladies of the theater who took part in a colossal pageant and tableau called The Battle Hymn of the Republic, only Josephine Hull's name would be recognized today. Preceding the grand tableau was an event chronicled in the souvenir program as follows:

Special Challenge Performance of

H O U D I N I

Having accepted a challenge from the Officers of the U. S. Tank Corps, Houdini will attempt to make his escape while submerged in the Hippodrome pool, after being strapped into a full-length "restraint suit," which is to enclose him from the neck down to, and including, his feet, after which he will be suspended over the Hippodrome tank, head down, and thrown into the water.

The test will be in charge of Captain Henry H. George, 3rd, of the Engineers Corps, who signed the challenge. Note: The Hippodrome tank will be opened and filled with water in full view of the audience.

This restraint suit, now in the Radner collection, was one of Houdini's own inventions. It is made of thin brown-and-white striped awning cloth and resembles a strait jacket which has been continued down into a sack. The leather cuffs are only an inch wide. Houdini was put into it in strait-jacket fashion and additional straps were added around waist, knees, and ankles. It was a spectacular escape, which gave him a splendid chance for picturesque contortions on the floor of the stage.

But getting out of it under water was something else again. It was one of those things which could be done in the famous Hippodrome tank and no where else. This enormous pool, revealed when the stage floor was removed, had been the scene of some lush water spectacles in which show girls trouped down ornate staircases and disappeared into the water. Presumably they came up again somewhere, but the audience was left to wonder where and how.

Actually, they came up by turning at the bottom of the stairs and swimming through underwater archways in the rear of the tank, which led up under the backdrop to the surface of the water and stairs coming out.

It was an ideal setup for a spectacular Houdini "one shot," for among Jim Collins' many talents was swimming. When the Escape King was lowered into the tank, head down and jacketed, Collins swam out from the secret exit, grabbed him, dragged him up and out, and unbuckled the suit, whereupon Houdini took it and swam back, emerging on the public side of the tank. Or, at least, that is what probably occurred—the exact details never have been revealed. Leaving aside the difficulties of getting out of the suit when it was soaking wet, it is unlike Houdini to have missed a bet like this in a tank so constructed. But it would have been equally unlike Houdini to have done such a stunt regularly—depending on anyone else completely for his escape, even Collins.

It was on this same Hippodrome stage, where Houdini appeared throughout the entire 1918 season, that he presented his most talked about feat of straight magic—his Vanishing Elephant.

The illusion had been suggested to the "Hipp" manager, R. H. Burnside, the previous year by the illusion inventor Guy Jarrett, who had built a four-foot model of his own version of the vanish. Like many geniuses, Jarrett was all craftsman, with no politician or businessman in his make-up. For one reason or another, Burnside at first nixed the elephant illusion in favor of a spectacle promised by Thurston. When this did not materialize, he got Houdini to vanish an elephant for him, which Houdini did.

It was not much of an illusion, since the elephant was led into a cabinet which had been pushed on stage by four assistants. A dozen more assistants were required to turn the cabinet sideways, whereupon two circular panels were dropped, giving the audience a view *through* the cabinet. Ingenious spectators surmised that the "bull" might very well be lying down inside, since an elephant lying down flattens out considerably. Houdini did not care whether anyone guessed the *modus operandi* or not. The "Hipp" could only hold a few thousand at each performance. Millions read of Houdini, the "man who made an elephant disappear," and that was what he wanted.

This same season at the Hippodrome saw a real "first" in magic; it was also a "last." On July 16, 1918, Houdini bought from the famous bird-importer George H. Holden, of lower Fifth Avenue, a tame eagle of unspecified species, for which he paid $200. Usually impetuous in his spending, Houdini in this transaction displayed one of his occasional bursts of business cageyness. He drew up an elaborate sales agreement, which Holden signed, whereby if the eagle proved unworkable in the show, Houdini could bring it back and Holden would keep it for sale on consignment, the price not to go below $150.

Harry the conjuror used the eagle in a typically startling Houdini fashion. In a magic routine in which a glass cylinder of water turned suddenly to ink, he proceeded to draw from the middle of the ink, unstained and dry, the "flags of all nations," climaxed, of course, by Old Glory four times the size of any of the others. That it was possible to "top" the American flag in a silk production during wartime no magician would believe, but Houdini did it—by producing the live eagle which sat on his shoulder! This really drove the audience wild.

It was, according to Houdini, the first tame eagle since historic "Old Abe," a mascot of the Union Army during the Civil War. Houdini named his eagle "Young Abe." There is no record of his ever having any trouble with this formidable bird except once. The eagle and Houdini's pet dog both traveled in similar boxes and on one occasion, when Houdini was setting up the show, he found that the box delivered to the theater contained not his audience-stunning eagle but the dog. This drove the Boss into one of his finest beserk rages; like most of his storms, next day it was forgotten and never referred to again.

It was rare for Houdini really to blow up at members of his own company. When one of them needed a "dressing down," the Boss gave it to him in private, always ending the session with calm directions for the future, and never again referring to the matter.

By the end of the war, Houdini had more serious competition to worry about than "frauds and cheapskates doing imitation handcuff acts." The nickelodeon before the war had been a penny arcade attraction, usually occupying premises that had formerly been a store. For a time they never seated more than 299 people—halls holding 300 or more required a theater license. But in 1914 a group of courageous pioneers sank a million into the Strand Theater, a Broadway house with a thirty-piece orchestra, which presented nothing but motion pictures, "admission two bits." The Vitagraph Company followed by converting the Criterion Theater for screen entertainment only. The enterprising Marcus Loew took the industry another jump forward in welding the new attraction to live talent when he inaugurated the personal appearance of the star with the first run of the picture.

In 1915 D. W. Griffith had shown the way with his controversial epic *The Birth of a Nation,* in which he invented several motion-picture techniques—the close shot, the long shot, the angle shot, shooting "day for night." It tore open the healing wounds of the Civil War, put the Ku Klux Klan back in business, and opened on Broadway at a two-dollar top for a run of forty-four weeks before going on the road.

To transport a legit company, complete with scenery, props, and costumes, was a major undertaking in logistics. Now the same drama could be shipped cheaply by express in a few flat cans. In the flickering shadows of the new art, Houdini could read the death sentence of big-time vaudeville. His response to this challenge was typical Houdini.

28. *A Grim Game*

It was unlike Houdini to go for long without some all-consuming enthusiasm. Once he had made a stab at being an art collector. Art had given way to flying. Now he fell in love with moving pictures.

The new industry was starting to turn out a few serious films of merit, and innovations were on the way even in 1919. Color films had already been tried out; there were still many problems to be solved but the idea, once planted, had taken root among the chemists and technicians. And experiments had long been underway to make the movies talk. Not only would they talk—they would also sing. And when elaborate musical revues in gorgeous color—with singing stars backed by a full orchestra—were available to every crossroads hamlet in the land, then vaudeville would be a thing of the past.

Many variety stars refused to see this inevitable development and spent their declining years in bitterness, waiting for vaudeville to "come back." Such was not Houdini's way. Something had to be found to replace his vaudeville act not only as a money-maker but also to keep his torch of fame burning bright. And in 1919 the answer was obvious—he should become a movie star.

His first effort was a serial, *The Master Mystery,* which played for thirteen successive Saturday afternoons at neighborhood theaters throughout the land.

One of Houdini's collaborators on the script was Arthur B. Reeve, a precise, scholarly little man best known for his fictional character Craig Kennedy, Scientific Detective. This American version of Sherlock Holmes had made its appearance in *Cosmopolitan Magazine* in 1910. Reeve was a pioneer in

208

science fiction. Like the great Jules Verne before him, he did not "extrapolate" very far in his science. He kept up with developments in criminology and new discoveries and inventions which might, by a stretch of the imagination, be applied to crime detection.

In *The Master Mystery,* Reeve was working against a great handicap—he had Houdini as a collaborator and Houdini had his own ideas about what he wanted to do.

The story, such as it was, began with a mysterious company called International Patents, Incorporated, controlled by a ruthless tycoon from his castle home which, by a happy circumstance, was built on a cliff overlooking the sea—or occasionally, as the story progressed, a river. Below this cliff dwelling was a secret storeroom, hewn from the living rock, called The Graveyard of Genius—where were kept models of inventions which the company had purchased from inventors and had then shelved to keep progress from interfering with the dividends of the vested interests. (Teddy Roosevelt had waged strenuous war against trusts which stood in the way of progress and were suspected of buying up inventions and killing them; Houdini was a great admirer of T.R. The ideology seems of clear derivation.)

Houdini played the part of the hero, Quentin Locke, a secret agent of the Department of Justice investigating the nefarious actions of this criminal company. The tycoon who battened on the genius of betrayed inventors happened to have a beautiful daughter, Eva. . . .

The plot was considerably thickened by one of the suppressed inventions which moved under its own power—a giant man-shaped creature of steel called, simply, The Automaton, which lumbered out of its secret den carved from more living rock at least once in every installment. It was constantly defying bullets and crashing through doors like matchwood to place the fair Eva and the intrepid Locke in double jeopardy.

In some unexplained manner, this metal monster with electric light bulbs for eyes had at its beck and call a motley crew of ruffians identified on the film's titles as "the emissaries of the Automaton." They were a patient and persevering lot, worthy of better things, for week after week they did their best to eliminate Houdini, only to have him come back slugging the following week. In a dank subcellar below a Chinese opium den Houdini is bound by the emissaries with barbed wire; the Automaton kicks over several carboys of acid; close shot: Houdini struggling madly. Subtitle: *"Like writhing snakes the rivers of seething acid creep closer, closer. . . ."* At the beginning of the next installment our hero wriggles out of the barbed wire just in time to keep from getting seethed only to wind up at the end of the chapter tied with ropes and rolled under a freight elevator which is slowly descending to crush him. . . .

Next, Houdini—or Quentin Locke—is nailed in a packing case and tossed into the drink while, on the dock above, the Automaton directs its emissaries to capture and, presumably, rape the shrinking Eva, though the second objective may have been the emissaries' own idea; it would hardly occur to a man made of iron.

As a change from its constant use of brute force, the Monster occasionally used subtlety, such as infecting its victims with the "Madagascan Madness," a delirium characterized by uncontrollable laughter and conveyed by inhaling the smoke from candles with poisoned wicks.

It was the era of the "vamp," a siren-stereotype originally created by Theda Bara, and inevitably *The Master Mystery* had one; her name was De Luxe Dora and she held forth in a low dive called the Black Tom Café, frequented by "flotsam and jetsam in human guise."

In the end, after getting loose from everything, including a garrote applied by the Madagascar Strangler, a dark-skinned gentleman wearing a turban and a Prince Albert coat, Locke invents an explosive gas bullet which penetrates the steel body of the Automaton, only to reveal that it was motivated, all along, by one of the very human villains concealed inside it. The source of its superhuman strength was never divulged.

As serials went, it was not very much worse than most. Houdini was fairly stiff and unconvincing before the camera, but not nearly as stiff as heavyweight champion Gene Tunney in *The Fighting Marine* a few years later. And in the various episodes Houdini really did many of the things which he had performed "live" in vaudeville and for publicity stunts.

The Master Mystery was probably the first film to use the robot theme, which has since had a good workout in science fiction. The Automaton, as presented in the film, may well have stemmed from the *golem* of Jewish folklore, a monster made of clay and brought to life by cabalistic magic.

In Houdini's serial, the monster was so ludicrous that it had a truly terrifying impact—at least for the small fry. Its effect on adults was not quite so frightening; it seemed to the kids that the grownups had been afflicted by the Madagascan Madness in truth, for they certainly gave way to uncontrollable laughter. As a horror film it was a success, though not quite in the way Houdini intended.

The picture had two profound influences on the boys of the nation—imitations of the Automaton took precedence in schoolyards over imitations of Charlie Chaplin, and for a while it became impossible to keep clotheslines, on roof or in back yard—the ropes were being utilized by boys in tying each other up, playing Houdini. There was one corollary effect on schoolwork—every boy was able to tell you the exact location of Madagascar and some of them even learned how to spell it. But no rose without its thorn: *The Master Mystery* implanted the notion that an "emissary" was, by definition, a thug, usually unshaven.

The serial was issued under the aegis of B. A. Rolfe Productions. Then Jesse L. Lasky, under the Paramount-Artcraft banner, signed Houdini for two features which were released as *The Grim Game* and *Terror Island*. In both of these Houdini had a hand in the script—he would hardly have signed without this proviso, but the main script chore was performed by Arthur B. Reeve and John W. Grey, who had done their best to keep Houdini within logical grounds in his struggles with the deadly Automaton.

The writers were called on to revise the script of *The Grim Game* in the middle of the shooting because of an airplane accident. The story called for the hero to scale sheer prison walls and precipices and, among other feats, to leap from one airplane to another in mid-air. All of these deeds Houdini actually did without benefit of doubles or stunt men. His attitude was, "Who you going to get for a stunt man that's better than I, Houdini?"

The airplane jump was the big scene of the picture and, to serve as consultant for the airborne sequences, Houdini sent for Brassac, the mechanic from his aeronaut days. It was the great age of the barnstorming pilots and the beginning of acrobatics with flying machines, including wing-walking. This hair-raising feat is risky enough under any circumstances but it was made possible at all by a device unknown to the public. This was a "piano wire safety"—a strand of wire so thin as to be invisible at a few yards' distance yet strong enough to hold the weight of the daredevil if he should slip or be blown from the wing. It was anything but a foolproof gimmick but it gave the performer a big psychological assist.

Houdini rehearsed his plane jump carefully, then both planes took to the air, with a third plane carrying the cameras. The cameras started rolling. Houdini got the signal and stood ready to make his jump when, by some miscalculation, the planes locked wings and went spiraling toward the earth—the cameras grinding faithfully, recording the disaster. Luckily, the pilots were able to untangle their craft before reaching the ground and both managed to land safely, though the plane carrying Houdini came down in a swamp and nearly buried the escapist in mud. The script was rewritten to allow for the incident and it was featured in the ballyhoo of the picture.

Terror Island was shot on Catalina and in surrounding waters, where a bevy of husky Negro lads played the part of

South Seas cannibals, tying up Houdini approximately twice to the reel.

While Houdini was working in pictures, he rented a bungalow in Hollywood for himself and Bess. It was the first time in their twenty-five years together that they had ever stayed put in one place for more than a few weeks at a time. The bungalow was soon overflowing with Harry's books, files of clippings, playbills, programs, and general miscellany.

Houdini began to write a book on the wonder workers of the side shows, inspired by his acquaintance with these purveyors of "wild talents" in the dime museum days. It took shape gradually; the first seven chapters were devoted to fire eaters, going back to the first defiers of fire he could uncover. In this section Houdini quotes from *Hocus Pocus,* one of the earliest books on "natural magick" giving a supposed formula for making the skin heat-resistant. This magic formula begins, "Take half an ounce of samphire, dissolve it in two ounces of aquavitae, add to it one ounce of quicksilver, one ounce of liquid storax, which is the droppings of Myrrh and hinders the camphire from firing; take also two ounces of hematitus, a red stone to be had at the druggists' . . ."

This formula, according to Houdini, was the secret which enabled Richardson, the first famous fire-resister, popular in England, to walk unscathed on red-hot iron. The formula, as given in *Hocus Pocus,* was also to be found in Houdini's old guidebook to escapery, *Revelations of a Spirit Medium* but without credit to *Hocus Pocus.*

Houdini was of the opinion that this compound would actually fireproof the human skin. Recently a physician-chemist, Dr. John Henry Grossman, compounded this mixture and found that for heat-resistant purposes it is absolutely useless. Like many laymen, Houdini was sometimes overly credulous of what he read in books.

The next chapter concerned sword-swallowers and regurgitant acts; next he dealt with people who defy poisonous reptiles, a field about which he was lamentably ignorant. Other chapters concerned strength phenomena and "gravity resisters," such as Lulu Hurst, the Georgia Magnet.

The book was published the following year under the title: *Miracle Mongers and Their Methods: A Complete Expose.* It was hardly this. It does contain some interesting historical material about the early practitioners of the off-trail skills, but it actually exposes very little.

As a motion-picture star Houdini lacked one important talent—acting ability. Audiences then, as now, insisted on their adventure stories well spiced with romance and Houdini was much too bashful to kiss his various leading ladies without wincing, even with Bess standing off camera and cheering him on. His embarrassment was so evident that directors gave up on him. Romance before the camera was for Houdini a Grim Game indeed.

29. *The Knight's Tale*

Hou′di-ni, 1 hū′dĭ-nī; 2 hu̇′dĭ-nĭ, Harry (4/6 1874—   )
American mystericist, wizard, and expert in extrication and
self-release,—hou′di-nize, *vb*. To release or extricate one-
self from (confinement, bonds, or the like), as by wriggling
out.
    —*Funk & Wagnalls New Standard Dictionary* (1920)

Harry HAD at last hired a press agent, Arthur B. Chase,
in connection with his motion picture activities; Chase coined
the new verb *houdinize,* and insinuated it into the dictionary.
Houdini was immensely proud of this fact and used a facsimile
of the dictionary entry in his pitch book, *The Adventurous Life*
of a Versatile Artist.

For six years he had not crossed the Atlantic and he began
to suffer a gnawing fear—that the English public, which had
given him his first recognition, had forgotten him.

It was a different England to which he returned in February
of 1920. Peering through the peephole of the curtain before
a show, one saw an audience full of girls, row upon row of
girls, with a scattering of old folk. The young men of England
were dead. Scarcely a family had not lost someone—father,
brother, or son—during the War.

Without the plaudits of the young men, how would Houdini
go over?

He soon found out. His films, which had not catapulted him
into the ranks of the stars, had been well received in Britain,
and a whole new generation had arisen; too young to serve in
the war, they had seen the American Escape King on celluloid
and here he was in person, upside down in the torture cell and

215

safe outside a moment later. England once again took Houdini into a warm embrace.

He had left at home a number of literary projects interrupted by the tour. In charge of his mountains of notes, his trunks of scrapbooks, his files of data, letters, autographs, and curiosa, he left an elderly bookworm named Alfred Becks. This gentleman had been retired from the drama library of Harvard. A former actor and manager of stars, his declining years were spent in the company of books and memorabilia of the theater. In Houdini's brownstone castle of mystery on 113th Street he found a happy refuge.

The "working library" Houdini took with him, carrying it in the special Collins-constructed crate which became a bookcase when opened. But no bookcase could expand to keep up with Houdini's book-buying; particularly now that he was collecting everything he could lay hands on dealing with a subject which had fascinated him since the earliest days of his friendship with Joe Rinn in New York—the tricks of the fraudulent mediums.

It has been claimed that after his mother's death Houdini spent many hours with various psychics, attempting to receive some word which would be truly "evidential" of his mother's survival. This was true, in a sense, for after the death of Mrs. Weiss her flamboyant son did alter his attitude toward the spiritualists. Before, he had thought of them as more or less gentle grifters, and their patrons as marks. He was sorry for the deluded customers but had not felt that it was any of his business; they had a right to throw their money away on mediums if they wanted to.

Now, in his own séances—in which the ghostly whispers from the other side of the veil, purporting to be his mother, never spoke to him in Yiddish, never mentioned a single one of the myriad little personal things which would at once establish her identity; in short, when the "spirits" uttered nothing but platitudes and assurances that they were "happy"— Houdini raised a storm of bitterness. However, as he was interested in exposing the charlatans who had sunk so low as to impersonate his Sainted Mother, he did not yet affirm in public that there was no such thing as communication with the dead. That would have closed all doors to him in psychic circles, and it was not Houdini's wish to alienate his sources of research.

Although he railed at superstition in the séance room, Harry had quite a few superstitions himself. He would not, for example, start anything dangerous on Friday the 13th. Also, he often felt that unseen presences were trying to "get through" to him by means of subtle signs.

The Great Lafayette, an eccentric magician who was one of Harry's friends, had died several years before in a theater fire. When Houdini opened in Edinburgh, Scotland, in February, one of his first actions was to visit the grave of Lafayette, taking some flowers and a jar in which to arrange them. While cutting the stems of the flowers, he had placed the jar on the footstone. It fell off even though no wind was blowing. Houdini frowned and Bess could see that he was deeply stirred. "Bess—d'you think it's Laf, trying to get through to me?"

Bessie said that her skirt might have joggled the pot. He replaced it and went back to his work on the stems. The jar fell a second time and shattered. Harry made no comment but she could sense that he felt the unseen presence of the eccentric magician.

A great deal of Houdini's later violent denunciations of mediums undoubtedly stemmed from his desperate wish for communication to prove true.

He was constantly making "pacts" with his friends, giving them secret code words and signs by which the first one to die would try to identify himself to the survivor.

Houdini had started his British tour with a broken ankle and, true to his own code of "ignore it and it'll go away," he paid no attention to it until it got so painful that he could hardly walk. Doctors advised that unless he gave the bone a chance to knit firmly he might be a cripple for life. He reluctantly spent a week lying on a couch, getting caught up in his correspondence, which by this time was staggering.

It was a cold winter and when he hit Edinburgh, he was shocked at the number of children, in the poorer sections of the city, who were barefooted. Once an idea had taken possession of Houdini, it rode him like an Old Man of the Sea. Now it was the barefooted children. He put an announcement in the paper that children without shoes should come to the theater. He hurried to a bootery and bought three hundred pairs of shoes and then drafted all the other acts on the bill to help him as shoe fitters.

When the three hundred pairs were gone, there was still a crowd of disappointed kids. Houdini herded them all together and led the way to the nearest shoe store. At last every child in the crowd had a new pair. Houdini had the merchant send the bill to him at the theater. When he got back, he and Bess held a conference about finances for the rest of the week.

While trying to "favor" his ankle, Houdini used up some of the time allowed for his act by showing movies taken of himself doing bridge jumps and underwater escapes. Theater managers did not mind this intrusion of the "flicks," but drew the line at the Escape King showing films of his visits to the graves of dead magicians. To Houdini, anything which interested Houdini ought to interest everybody else.

By the 20th of March the weather was warm enough for him to set up an underwater stunt, which he did at Hull, England. His self-liberating diving suit had not brought any admirals of the U.S. Navy beating a path to his door but he had used it as a prop in *The Master Mystery;* and now, its special releasing properties quietly ignored, it made a beautiful stunt-escape which he could tie in with local diving-and-salvage companies.

Houdini gleefully sent a clipping of his Hull diving suit stunt to a British friend with whom he had been corresponding for some time but whom he had not met. This was none other than the King's most famous civilian subject—Sir Arthur Conan Doyle.

The relationship of these two oddly matched men has been recorded in a book of their correspondence, *Houdini and Conan Doyle; the Story of a Strange Friendship,* edited by Bernard Morris Lee Ernst, Houdini's lifelong friend and attorney, and Hereward Carrington, the noted author of a score of books on psychic matters.

The friendship was in many ways not strange at all: both were men of action, athletes who kept their prowess well into middle age. Both were crusaders, fearless as charging lions when sure they were right. Both were sentimentalists and romantics, devoted to their mothers and almost absurdly chivalrous toward women. Both loved animals and children. Both had been poor boys, the sons of gifted, poorly-paid fathers, who fought their way up in the world by their own talents and courage.

Conan Doyle was famous as an historical novelist and the creator of Sherlock Holmes when Houdini was still a lining cutter. In the Boer War of 1900 he had forsaken literature for his first profession, medicine, and served with heroism during the epidemic of enteric fever at Bloemenfontein. Later he wrote a pamphlet, *The War in South Africa—Its Causes and Conduct,* in which he demolished the smear campaign directed against Britain by Boer sympathizers slyly abetted by the Kaiser's emissaries. For this he had been knighted by King Edward VII.

He was in truth a "verray, parfit gentil knyght," descended from the Catholic gentry of Ireland who had been impoverished by their refusal to give up the faith of their fathers. This faith Conan Doyle had lost in his medical-school days and for thirty years he had been searching for a religion or philosophy to live by, meanwhile taking as his standard of behavior the ancient code of knighthood, fearless before the strong, humble before the weak, a righter of wrongs, and a redresser of grievances. His well-known powers of detection and deduction were ever at the service of the wrongfully accused and the imprisoned innocent.

Since 1887, Conan Doyle had been interested in spiritualism; he kept an open mind on the subject for nearly thirty years. Then, in the last days of 1915, a close friend of his wife's, a lady who had been experimenting with automatic writing, produced a "message" from Conan Doyle's brother-in-law, who had been killed in the war. This message contained a bit of intimate detail which the author was sure none knew but himself. It was the "evidential" test for which he had been searching all these years. It satisfied him completely as to the truth of survival and communication. Ever after, his life was devoted to preaching the new religion. He had a burning message, a message bringing joy to the hearts of a world which had lost its sons, even as he, shortly after, lost his own son, Kingsley.

Conan Doyle would never have made an amateur magician—even the innocent deceptions of magic, which are all in fun, would have subtly violated his conscience. The very idea of deception was so foreign to his nature that his brain rejected it, in himself constantly, and finally in others. And here he showed the paradox that honor itself, carried to fanatical extremes, can work evil, for it led him to ascribe to others the nobility which was his own, to refuse to suspect trickery and heartless fraud where they certainly existed, and to become pathetically credulous before the cunning sharpery of the lowest form of life—the fake spirit medium.

The will to believe is strong, as illustrated in this pathetically sincere account by J. Hewat McKenzie in his book *Spirit Intercourse*:*

> The last occasion on which the author, under strict test conditions, saw Houdini demonstrate his powers of dematerialization, was before thousands, upon the public stage of the Grand Theatre, Islington, London. Here a small iron tank, filled with water, was deposited upon the stage, and into it

* Simpkin, Marshall, Hamilton Kent & Co. London, 1916. Pp. 86-87.

Houdini was placed, the water completely covering his body. Over this was placed an iron lid, with three hasps and staples, and this was securely locked. The body was then completely dematerialized within this tank within one and a half minutes while the author stood immediately over it. Without disturbing any of the locks, Houdini was transferred from the tank directly to the back of the stage in a dematerialized state.

While the author stood adjacent to the tank, during the dematerialization process, a great loss of physical energy was felt by him, such as is usually experienced by sitters in materializing séances, who have a good stock of vital energy, as in such a phenomenon a large amount of energy is required.

Dematerialization is performed by methods similar in operation to those in which psychoplastic essence is drawn from the medium. The body of the medium may be reduced to half its ordinary weight in the materializing séance room. While in this state, Houdini was transferred from the stage to the retiring room behind, and there almost instantaneously materialized. The speed with which this dematerialization is performed is much more rapid than is possible in the materializing séance room.

Not only was Houdini's body dematerialized, but it was carried through the locked iron tank, thus demonstrating the passage of matter through matter. This startling manifestation of one of nature's profoundest miracles was probably regarded by most of the audience as a very clever trick.

Four years later, in what is generally agreed to be his best book, *A Magician Among the Spirits,* Houdini spent many paragraphs denying his supposed mediumistic powers, so dramatically inferred by the bemused Mr. McKenzie, who was President of the British College of Psychic Science. Houdini winds up by saying:

> Regarding the personally conducted tests of my work, by Mr. McKenzie, he did no more or less than all my committees are privileged to do while on the stage during my acts. Just as all Spiritualist believers do, so Mr. McKenzie relied on what he *thought* he saw, and therefore failed to affirm or negative

his misguided and misdirected vision by rational application of his conscious intelligence. Had he brought his reasoning faculties to bear, as all sincere, unbiased investigators should, he would have discovered the utter inconsistency of his deductions and never have gone on record as the author of such folly, without a particle of real evidence with which to substantiate his claim.

In private, the Mysteriarch would not have been quite so pompous about it: "The old Upside Down really had him beatin' his brains out!" Nothing pleased Houdini more than when some double-dome with a string of letters after his name found his reason staggering before the marvels of the Escape King, and finally gave in to an hypothesis of supernatural powers.

But at the same time it was with disgust that he saw men of the caliber of Conan Doyle taken in by tricks which would not fool a bright child of seven. And in this he was well within his rights; no one knew better than Houdini the years of labor, trial and error, and painstaking attention to detail that went into even a routine prison-cell escape, one which did not offer any special difficulties. Yet the determined believers in spiritualism could be taken in by the most arrant frauds, including mediums who had been caught and convicted of cheating time and time again.

Conan Doyle, early that spring of 1920, wrote to Houdini: "Yes, you have driven me to the occult! My reason tells me that you have this wonderful power, for there is no alternative, tho' I have no doubt that, up to a point, your strength and skill avail you."

Such was the knight's tale of how Houdini worked his wonders. Nothing the Self-Liberator could say or do—short of actually revealing his secrets—would have convinced the distinguished physician and man of letters that Houdini could not "dematerialize."

Finally, on the 14th of April, Harry visited Sir Arthur and Lady Conan Doyle at their home, Windlesham, in Crowborough, had lunch with them, met their children, and listened to the fervent accounts of their contacts with the departed son in the "Summerland." They were what spirit mediums call "shut eyes"—people who cannot be disillusioned or deprived of their belief under any circumstances.

Behind such powerful conviction lurks a good deal of unconscious vanity; the inference is, "I saw these things with my own eyes. If I cannot explain them they must be supernatural." Yet, as Houdini's pal Joe Rinn pointed out years later, such an intellectual "investigator" of psychic phenomena, on seeing a "nut worker" with his three shells and rubber pea at a carnival, would hardly ascribe the appearances and disappearances of the pea to dematerialization, though he could never explain its actions.

What had earlier begun in Houdini as a normal curiosity about the psychic miracle-mongers and their methods, became, for a time, an open-minded search for some word from his mother. But when his experiences with the psychics revealed only shrewd guessing on their part, the floating trumpets and cheesecloth ghosts set him in a rage. He determined to pile up plenty of séances and observations before he cut loose with his blast at the mediums in a projected book.

Thus, while on his tour of Britain from February to July, 1920, he had over a hundred "sittings" with mediums, including the hottest thing in the spook business of the year, an apple-cheeked French girl named Eva Carrière, who produced a frothy substance from her mouth which the psychists called "ectoplasm." Houdini was not impressed, though in his letters to Conan Doyle he takes the opposite tone without actually saying that what he saw impressed or convinced him. After all, he was getting to the cream of the mediumistic crop by introductions from Sir Arthur and he didn't want to antagonize the knight until he had more data.

In his private journals, Houdini recorded his true impressions—that the mediums were a bunch of chiselers.

On his visits to the séance rooms, Harry often took Bess with him and also her young niece, Julia Sawyer, who acted as his secretary. Julia became an expert at detecting trickery, and her appearance—she looked like a teen-ager long after she was out of her teens—made her a valuable undercover agent when Houdini opened up on the American mediums.

But before he set out as a professional "ghost breaker," he was determined to have another go at moving pictures. The sad wound in his self-esteem caused by the public's lack of enthusiasm for his films had now healed over and he ascribed the fiasco to bad writing and direction.

This time he would start his own production company and do the writing and directing himself, in addition to playing the star roles. When he sailed for home on July 3rd, it was with perfect confidence that he could achieve as great a place in pictures as he had in vaudeville.

30. *Movie Star or Bust*

The Grim Game, Houdini's first feature-length picture, had grossed less than $150,000 domestic, with foreign markets bringing in only another $50,000. *Terror Island* did $111,000 at home and about $54,000 abroad. Even in 1920 this was strictly from hunger. The first-run gross of the average film with a popular star was $375,000.

With a vengeance, Houdini prepared to conquer the new medium. By the beginning of 1921 he had formed The Houdini Picture Corporation and had prevailed upon Dash to put hand-cuffs, strait jackets, and the king-sized substitution trunk away in the cellar of his Brooklyn home and join in the picture enter-prise. (Hardeen never really got back into show business until after his brother was dead.) Harry proposed to write the script, choose the locations, supervise the photography, play the stellar role, edit the rushes, write the titles, and direct the exploita-tion campaign. Dash was put in charge of a film-processing plant.

With a great whoop and holler, Harry tore into his first inde-pendent production: *The Man from Beyond.* Its basic gimmick was good—a man is frozen in a block of ice and passes into suspended animation; a century later the members of an Arctic expedition chop him loose, whereupon he sets out looking for his lost love and discovers her replica in one of her great-granddaughters. This idea was probably suggested to Houdini by a story which appeared in *The American Weekly* about the body of a viking, complete with winged helmet and flaxen beard, which had been discovered in the Arctic, perfectly pre-served after a thousand years.

Closing himself into his office at "278" (West 113th Street),

225

a crowded den overflowing with books, old playbills, and letters, Houdini worked day and night for ten days and emerged
with the complete script. Then he assembled his company and
set off for Lake Placid to shoot his Arctic location sequences.

He began running into all the difficulties which beset amateur movie-makers trying to shoot on location: shadows don't
stay the same length for more than twenty minutes, the sun
clouds over, rain falls. Meanwhile your payroll is ticking away
like a taxi standing at the curb.

The tougher the difficulties grew, the more discouraged Houdini got. Finally, after his feet were badly frozen, he decided
that what was already in the can would have to do and betook
himself to Niagara Falls to shoot the big scene—his rescue of
the heroine on the brink of the cataract.

In the 1920's the special effect techniques of the films had
not yet been perfected; when airplane crashes were called for,
real planes were used. Houdini, in his big Niagara rescue, decided to do it "for real." This involved an elaborate apparatus
—a leather harness worn under his clothes, to which a steel-wire
rope was attached, operated by a drum on the shore. The same
safety device was required for the heroine's double. But the
rescue from the brink of the falls, after the heroine's canoe has
made the plunge, was one of the most hair-raising scenes ever
photographed, before or since.

Reviewers agreed on the excellence of the Falls scene, but
some remarked caustically that while the hero was supposed to
have been in suspended animation for a century, he expressed
no surprise at the many modern inventions which confronted
him on his release! This was a detail Houdini had lost sight of
in setting up his scenes of derring-do.

For his second venture, *Haldane of the Secret Service*, he
eschewed the more ambitious location stunts and kept the
action indoors. While the critics were good to him in *Beyond*,
what happened to *Haldane* shouldn't happen to a dog show.

Audiences were not overwhelmed by Houdini's films. In an
attempt to put his pictures across, he plunged into a series of

personal appearances. At the Times Square Theater he accompanied *The Man from Beyond* with a stage show in which he did two of his illusions—*Good-bye Winter* and *Arrival of Summer,* as well as the needle trick, the strait jacket, and a curtain speech that roasted the spirit mediums. When business was disappointing, Harry hired an elephant and did his vanishing-elephant illusion on the stage. This was an expensive way to sell a picture—the elephant ate up the profits in hay.

Houdini found a serious condition prevailing in his bank balance, a condition to which his attention was called several times a day by Bess in more and more urgent tones. Something had to be done, and done quick.

Vaudeville tempo had changed mightily during the time Houdini was away, selling Liberty Bonds and making motion pictures. The country seemed still to be marching to Georgie Cohan's "Over There." Autos were faster and roads were better for them to be faster on. Pioneer Station KDKA in Pittsburgh had begun daily broadcasts and America was in the grip of a new mania soon to replace the Ouija board—sitting crouched over crystal sets with earphones clamped to its ears. The big build-it-yourself radio boom was just around the next corner. And to a generation that had gone through the First World War, the sight of a man jumping off a bridge and getting out of handcuffs under water created no hysteria.

Now Houdini realized that he couldn't do it alone—"alone" for him meant him-and-Collins. So he let the word get out that he was open to suggestions re: publicity stunts, and that he would pay for them. And he started out on a long swing of The Keith time in the east and the Orpheum Circuit out west, working with his old friend, Martin Beck.

At Keith's in Washington, D.C., during the week ending January 9, 1922, his picture appeared on the front page of *B. F. Keith's Theatre News* along with the story of how he beat the Fiji Islanders at coin-catching. This little promotion piece, distributed to the theater patrons and sent out on the

mailing list, gave the Elusive American the lion's share of its
space, and included in the Houdini material a "poem":

TO HOUDINI

Oh, wizard of handcuffs, of bolts, bar and cell,
How he glides from thy clutches nobody can tell;
But he flits from thy bonds like a bird through the air,
Leaving naught but his fetters and wonderment there.

With steel chains you may bind him and shackle him fast
But he's vanished and gone e'er a moment has passed;
There is nothing can hold him—the marvelous elf—
Houdini, the mystery, to all but himself.

Straight jackets in which desperate maniacs pined,
The murderer's cell that held death-doomed confined,
The handcuffs and shackles, locking fast arm and limb,
Are but mockeries as fetters and useless to him.

From strong box or steel boiler where rivet and nail
Have been driven in vain to make for him a jail,
From every contrivance of bondage and pain
He escapes without effort and smiles in disdain.

—J. E. H.

Houdini knew that the specter of oblivion was haunting him
more closely than ever before in his life. The bill at Keith's
that week included an animated cartoon, the Pathe News, and
a short. There were also eight acts of vaudeville, with Houdini
in the "next to closing." They were tough acts to follow. With
the jacket, the needles, and Upside Down, Houdini just barely
made it.

The week beginning Monday, January 30, saw Harry in
Cleveland. He was still next to closing but he had to follow a
tab musical, *Varieties of 1922,* and a rising comedy star, Will
Mahoney. The postwar trend was all for sentiment, comedy,
and song—a trend which has kept on until the present day.

In Pittsburgh a musical-comedy star with jazz orchestra got more program space and bigger type than Houdini and his Water Torture. And at Keith's Orpheum in Brooklyn, in March, Houdini was spotted fifth in a nine-act bill which also starred John Steel, a romantic tenor whose recording of "The Love Nest" had taken his voice into nearly every home that boasted a wind-up phonograph.

The Superman would have to think fast.

That spring Sir Arthur Conan Doyle came over for a lecture tour, preaching his gospel of spiritualism. The tour opened at Carnegie Hall before a blue-ribbon audience. A few weeks later, Sir Arthur and Lady Jean Conan Doyle were guests of the Houdinis at "278" and the men went over Houdini's spiritualism library together, Sir Arthur remarking on the scarcity of what he termed "positive" books.

On June 18, when both families were vacationing in Atlantic City, Lady Conan Doyle suddenly asked Houdini if she could try to provide evidence of his mother's survival for him through her recently "developed" powers of automatic writing. Houdini agreed and the good lady did her best, in complete sincerity. The message, scribbed at top speed on sheets of note paper, was the usual kind of inspirational vaporings encountered in the work of most sincere "sensitives": "Oh, my darling, thank God, thank God, at last I'm through—I've tried, oh, so often—now I am happy. Why, of course I want to talk to my boy—my own beloved boy. . . ." This went on, page after page, precisely what the subconscious mind of a well-brought-up Englishwoman of the upper middle class would write if she subconsciously wanted to console a bereaved son. There was not one "evidential" word.

Houdini was, according to the Conan Doyles, "greatly moved" by the message, and his emotion was the only convincer the good knight needed that the message was highly "evidential."

Houdini was moved all right, but not by awe or overwhelming belief and conversion. He was, in all probability, boiling mad.

Before he had gone upstairs to the Conan Doyle suite for the séance, Bess had secretly cued him, by their old vaudeville mind-reading code, that during the previous evening she had told Lady Conan Doyle about Harry's devotion to Darling Mother. During the conversation, which must have been a lengthy one, Bess had mentioned how Harry had loved to lay his head on his mother's breast to hear her heart beat. She had told the knight's lady everything except two important facts— Mother Weiss didn't speak English, and June 18th was her birthday, a day Houdini always kept holy.

The lengthy inspirational ramble of Jean Conan Doyle must have infuriated him, but since the great author and his wife were embarrassingly sincere and were his friends, Houdini could not let go with the explosion which was obviously building up inside. Finally he took his leave, "obviously in the grip of strong emotion."

June 22nd was the day Harry and Bess always celebrated as their wedding anniversary and that evening they took Sir Arthur and his wife to the theater as a send-off, for the Conan Doyles were sailing for home the following day. The show was Raymond Hitchcock's *Pinwheel Revue,* and "Hitchy" was in rare form. He introduced the Conan Doyles to the audience and asked Houdini to favor them with a little something. Harry made a fine show of modesty but encouraged by Hitchy, Sir Arthur, and the clamorous audience, he stepped upon the stage and found, by an odd coincidence, that he had in his pocket five packages of darning needles and a spool of thread. . . .

He stopped the show, which skipped all its following scenes and went into its finale—the first time in the history of show business, it was claimed, that a guest artist, with an impromptu bit, ever changed the routine of a Broadway production.

Houdini's association with Conan Doyle only gave the creator of Sherlock Holmes another mystery. Holmes' method, as stated in one of the early tales, consisted of "observation and deduction" and Conan Doyle's observational powers, remarkable in criminal investigation, were not trained in the field of conjuring.

This Houdini tried to make him realize in many conversations and letters but to no avail—Sir Arthur grew more and more credulous and finally the inevitable break occurred.

Back to the three-a-day for the rest of the season, Houdini found himself devoting more and more time before audiences to denouncing spirit fakers. Occasionally, to give variety to his act, he included an exposé of mediumistic trickery, and it always went over big.

By the time he reached Los Angeles he was fighting furiously by means of publicity stunts—sometimes several in one week—to keep his place at the top of the vaudeville heap.

In L.A. he raised a furor with the theater manager when two other acts on the bill got their pictures in the paper and he didn't. He then set up an "escape from flames." Boy Scouts tied him to a stake and piled faggots around him, then applied a match. Houdini had to slip from the ropes before the fire got him. But the scouts, following their famous motto of "Be Prepared," had come prepared to make a good fire—not with bow drills but with a can of kerosene! By the time Houdini was out of his bonds his pants were on fire. More "miraculous" than the escape was the fact that he was not injured.

Houdini next settled on a completely safe-and-sane act: exposing the tricks of the mediums in such a way that a committee from the audience would be completely mystified while the majority of the crowd could see how it was done. He accomplished this by blindfolding the committee on stage, the blindfolds taking the place of the traditional darkness of the séance room.

The idea was not original with Houdini—his old friend Joe Rinn had been doing this sort of thing for years on a semi-pro or amateur basis. Rinn was no showman, but as he performed it, there was a certain degree of interest and it made good copy for newspapers. In Houdini's hands it became a sensation.

The time was ripe, spiritualism was rife; Conan Doyle's literary prestige had helped to sell his gospel of survival and communication, while the beloved author continued to be deceived by charlatans, both clever and clumsy. He now began ascribing psychic powers to legitimate vaudeville performers who did anything he could not see through immediately. One of these was Julius Zancig, a master mentalist, whose code act with his wife was uncanny; but Julius was a member in good standing of the Society of American Magicians and never claimed supernormal powers until he was old, ill, and in financial straits.

As a result of Sir Arthur's lecture tour, the *Scientific American* magazine, on November 18, 1922, offered $2,000 to anyone who could take a "spirit" photograph under test conditions and $2,500 to any medium who could produce physical phenomena—raps, lights, levitations, apports, or anything else —while strictly "controlled."

Conan Doyle, contacted by the press for a comment on this prize offer, replied, "I don't understand the necessity or wisdom of publicly offering prizes for conclusive manifestations or psychic photographs. This is a direct invitation to the rogues of two continents. Why offer prizes at all when there is already in existence a quantity of indubitable evidence?"

It was a very safe offer—a sure-fire publicity-getter for the magazine, a circulation builder of the first order. And few mediums were expected to submit to the test conditions, which were not announced. Nor could they be, for they would vary for every contestant—if there were any.

The committee which would set the conditions and test the mediums included Dr. William McDougall, formerly of Oxford and the British Society for Psychical Research and now of Harvard; the American Society's research officer, Dr. Walter Franklin Prince; Hereward Carrington, lifelong psychic investigator who had brought the Italian table-lifter, Eusapia Palladino, to America in 1910; and Houdini. McDougall and Prince were learned in psychic matters, Carrington a shrewd man with an open mind. But the hot spot in the committee, to the mediums, was Houdini.

This famous committee would be the center of one of the most violent storms ever to sweep over the world of psychic research. Its investigations led it down some bizarre trails before it was disbanded. The committee's secretary was a young, intellectual chap who was associate editor of the *Scientific American*—J. Malcolm Bird. He and Houdini were to lock horns more than once and, in the end, the Mysteriarch was to denounce Bird in a radio interview as a confederate of a medium. If this were true, then it was agreed that the medium must have brought unusual pressure to bear. She was a disturbingly beautiful woman.

31. *"Spooks–a No Come!"*

HOUDINI'S first invitation to address the undergraduates of a university came on his Midwest tour, in the fall of 1922, when a more than usually intrepid professor asked him to say a few words to his class on the subject of psychic investigation and psychic frauds. Or so the story was given out. Actually, Houdini most likely talked the professor into inviting him. In any case they made an agreement that Houdini was to speak for only ten minutes—when he heard the professor snap his fingers, that was the signal for him to wind up the speech and sit down.

The professor's signal was never given. Houdini spoke for the full hour. He was so full of his subject, and so voluble with his stories of the spook racket, that fascinating incidents and anecdotes kept tumbling out—not always in any particular order. Houdini sometimes left stories unfinished, for he was not a good extemporaneous speaker, but he got over his main thesis: that professional mediums who take money for their efforts are chiselers pure and simple.

In January of the new year, 1923, Houdini was polishing up his lecture technique by trying it out on students at the University of Wisconsin and later at Notre Dame. If the escape business, as such, was going into a decline, Harry was reconverting to postwar conditions in his own way.

Following the news of the *Scientific American's* award for psychic phenomena which its experts could endorse as genuine, Houdini made headlines by posting $5,000 of his own money in addition, the purse to go to any psychic who could produce physical phenomena which Houdini could not "duplicate by natural means." Now there is a logical hole in this argument, if argument it is: Houdini might have been able to reproduce by trickery anything observed in the séance room but that does not actually invalidate all such happenings. If a medium were genuine and able to cause a dollar bill to crawl around the surface of a table by true telekinetic power, this would have absolutely nothing to do with the fact that Houdini could have "reproduced the phenomena" by sticking a lively cockroach to the underside of the bill with conjuror's wax!

The offer to "reproduce the phenomena" is a good publicity gimmick for any magician—and very little else. The supposed telekinetic effect, produced by the adroit use of the roach, would be valuable only if some psychic researcher insisted that the magus had done it by psychic power.

In 1923 Conan Doyle was again in the States, lecturing to packed houses everywhere, accepting nothing but his expenses from the proceeds—all the rest of the intake went to further the cause of spiritualism as a religion.

In Denver, Colorado, he was "day and dating" with Houdini; Sir Arthur visited Harry's matinee at the vaudeville theater and Bess returned the compliment by going to Sir Arthur's lecture that night.

The press, which could not resist playing both of these two ardent campaigners against each other, misquoted them, ran hoked-up stories about them, and in the end had them apologizing to each other frequently during the American tour of the zealous knight.

By December, while he was playing in Little Rock, Houdini had gotten word from O. D. Munn, publisher of the *Scientific American,* that a medium had at last thoroughly puzzled the committee, which had been functioning minus Houdini, who was away on his vaudeville tour.

This medium was a young Neapolitan lad named Nino Pecoraro. In April of 1922, Nino had given a sitting in New York to Sir Arthur and Lady Jean Conan Doyle at which articles flew about and the voice of the famous deceased table-tipper Palladino came from the cabinet bearing greetings for the

Conan Doyles. Sir Arthur commented in one of his books on the startling and irrefutable quality of Nino's phenomena, stating that there could be no suspicion of fraud since Nino's hands and feet had been firmly fastened to his chair with picture wire, Dr. Hereward Carrington doing the tying.

Houdini canceled his bookings and hurried to New York to defend the honor of the *Scientific American* and trap the new fraud and fourflusher. When he questioned the committee they told a wondrous tale of having wound Nino up like a mummy with seventy-five feet of clothesline. Houdini exploded. "Seventy-five feet! Don't you know that nobody can be secured with a long piece of rope like that? That's the easiest of all rope ties to beat! I used to do it in the dime museums for twelve bucks a week when I was a kid! Let me tie this fellow Nino. I'll show you something."

Nino Pecoraro was again commissioned to sit with the full committee and this time Houdini supervised the tying, which was done with short lengths of fish line. The darkness was punctuated only by the singing of hymns by the committee in accord with the instructions of the medium. There were no phenomena, except the voice of "Palladino" complaining that the fish lines cut the medium's wrists. After an hour and a half, Nino came out of his trance and called for lights.

To the disappointed committee, he shrugged and offered his usual comment in such cases: "Spooks-a no come."

He would, on occasion, offer the same excuse for an unproductive séance when he was not closely confined but when his manager had failed to advance him sufficient spending money.*

* In 1928, two years after Houdini's death, there was a total of $21,000 offered in prize money for genuine phenomena—$10,000 by Joe Rinn, $10,000 by Beatrice Houdini, and $1,000 by the *Scientific American's* rival, *Science and Invention Magazine*. This wad of cash drew Nino Pecoraro again into the orbit of the investigators. With Houdini dead, Nino felt safe.

But at the 1928 séances he had another wily antagonist in Joseph Dunninger, who had taken over Houdini's post as unofficial ghost-breaker in chief. Dunninger tied Nino with ropes, sealed the knots, sewed mittens to Nino's shirt sleeves, and fastened the mittens to Nino's trousers. The only "phenomena" was the voice of Nino from the darkened cabinet: "Hey,

As Houdini's attacks on the slate messages, the trumpet voices, and the apparitions in luminous nightshirts increased in number and in volume of decibels, it was inevitable that Sir Arthur's patience would soon be exhausted.

The Kellock biography, commenting on the association of Conan Doyle and Houdini, says, ". . . The men had too much affection for each other to break, and their friendship survived to the end."

But this, alas, is an error, unless the author meant "to the end of the *year*." For in February Houdini wrote Conan Doyle for some information and received a reply which was as bitter as Sir Arthur could be: ". . . You probably want these extracts in order to twist them in some way against me or my cause. . . ." Another letter from Houdini was unanswered and the friendship came to an end.

But they cherished little ill feeling toward each other; this is easy to believe, for Houdini considered Conan Doyle as deceived but utterly honest. And Sir Arthur, in a book called *Edge of the Unknown*, gives a long description of Houdini and pays tribute to his courage, his cheery manner, his devotion to his mother and his wife. With a twinkle in his eye, figuratively speaking, Sir Arthur writes concerning Houdini's vanity: "I can remember, for example, that when he introduced his brother to me, he did it by saying, 'This is the brother of the great Houdini.' This without any twinkle of humor and in a perfectly natural manner."

Dunninge', thees-a Houdeen!" It was not considered "evidential." Later, Pecoraro made a full confession of his trickery.

In all his investigations, Houdini admitted that there were two fraudulent psychics who roused his admiration—Nino Pecoraro, the rope-tie expert, and "Doctor" Bert Reese, the message-reader, whose sleight-of-hand in switching paper billets was undetected by Houdini even though he knew, in principle, what was going on. Reese, unlike Pecoraro, made no "hard sell" of his psychic abilities, preferring to let his sitters do the ballyhoo for him. He convinced Thomas A. Edison, among other celebrities, that his powers were genuine, but a large part of his act consisted of clever misdirection and such humor, charm, and subtle knowledge of human nature that he was an entertainer of a high order, whether one believed him a genuine psychic or not. He was the exact opposite of Nino.

Here it is probable that Sir Arthur's memory misled him. Houdini would hardly have said, "This is the brother of the great Houdini." He never used the adjective *great* in reference to himself. To him, *Houdini* was synonymous with *great*. What he probably said was, "This is the brother of HOUDINI!" He was one of those who speak in capital letters.

Houdini might never have caught the crusading fire in his exposures of the mediums had it not been for the equal fervor of Conan Doyle on the opposite side—challenge and response. But once he got started, he gave everything he had. Most mediums were deathly afraid of him—and for good reason.

But, as we shall see, there was one who was not in the least afraid—or didn't admit it. In addition to being lovely to look upon, she was well supplied with brains. When the lights had been turned out, she sometimes removed all her clothes, let the ectoplasm fly where it may. She was known under the *nom du séance* of "Margery."

32. *The Blond Witch of Boston*

AT THE CLOSE of a swing around the vaude houses in February of 1924, Houdini decided to take the plunge into a brand-new field. The lecture circuit booked by the Coit-Albee Lyceum office had offered him a trial season of twenty-four lectures through the Middle West. This meant, to Houdini, playing one-night stands. Well, he and Bess had done it in the ten-twent-thirt melodrama, so why not now, when he could hitch his entertainment wagon to the crusader's star?

But old habits are hard to break. To "feed" his lecture audiences he did packing-box escapes as challenges, just like the old days.

He celebrated his fiftieth birthday back home on 113th Street with a grand family party. On that day he discovered something which surprised him as it surprises most people who reach the half-century mark—he didn't feel any different! Physically he was stronger than he had been at twenty and when it came to playing handball he was not only just as fast but a lot craftier.

He felt sure he could live to be a hundred. The problem was economic—how to make enough money to provide for old age (when he finally was old) and how to keep up the support of a score of relatives and decrepit performers on his pension list, not to mention his payroll of John Sargent, his secretary and copy-editor; Alfred Becks, his librarian; little Julia Sawyer, who was secretary and companion to Bess on their travels; and Jim Vickery and Jim Collins. He was the patriarch of a clan—a clan which, alas, contained no children of his own.

Harry's venture into the lecture business was profitable, and —with the tricks of the spirit fakers as its topic—had a good precedent. In March, 1879, the great magician Harry Kellar

had booked into Ford's Opera House in Washington, D.C.,
only to find that an equally great and witty magus, Robert
Heller, had "burned up the spot" with his magnificent show a
few weeks before. After starving to death for a fortnight, Kellar
was forced to think hard and fast to raise money to move the
show. He decided to give a Sunday evening lecture and chose,
as his topic, spiritualism. After all, he had traveled with the
Davenport Brothers as press agent. The lecture was a howling
success and he "kept it in." Lectures were permitted on Sunday
in states where blue laws prohibited all forms of Sunday entertainment or sports.

When Houdini got back from his lecture tour, in the spring
of 1924, he began building himself as an expert in the field of
psychic investigation. At the Church of St. Mark's on the
Bowery, he debated the existence of genuine physical phenomena with his co-committeeman, Dr. Walter Franklin Prince
of the American Society for Psychical Research. The write-up
was good but without any spread of pictures, naturally.

Then, on a visit to New England, Harry met the famous old
vaudeville medium and message reader Anna Eva Fay and
had his picture taken with her in the garden of her home. She
told Houdini the story of her "tests" with the famous British
researcher Sir William Crookes, who had publicly announced
his conversion to spiritualism after séances with Fay. It proved
to be trickery of a very high order, and the secret methods she
revealed to Houdini were useful anecdotes for his lectures.

Whenever a skeptic debates the existence of true phenomena
with a spiritualist, he sooner or later is confronted with the
"evidence" of Sir William Crookes, one of England's most distinguished chemists of the nineteenth century. Houdini would
point out that toward the end of his life Sir William refused to
make any statement of his beliefs and seemed bitter about the
whole thing. He had, in truth, made a fool of himself in print
by asserting his belief in the genuineness of a medium named
Florrie Cook.

This young woman was a materializing medium who produced repeatedly a lively shade named Katie King, a pretty, mischievous girl who deserved the title "mysterious elf." Katie floated from the medium's cabinet in very corporeal form, clad in daringly diaphanous draperies. She flirted with Sir William and once he asked her if he could hold her in his arms to assure himself of her complete materialization. This she not only permitted but encouraged and he found her very corporeal indeed!

Crookes, a man of honor in the best Victorian sense, was one of those gentlemen who found it hard to believe that human nature could sink so low as to imitate by fraud or mummery the sacred subject of spirit return. Houdini, a veteran of the circus side show and the dime *musée,* found no such difficulty.

One of the favorite arguments advanced by believers, in upholding the veracity of Florence Cook and the reality of the materialization of Katie, was, "But how do you explain it by fraud if the phenomena occurred in Sir William Crookes' own laboratory, with the door safely locked?" Houdini had the answer to that one, for he could point to his own exploits in being outside on the street beside a prison, passing out handbills, while the warden considered him safely locked within a cell, naked, searched, and manacled to the bars.

In Crookes' study of the mediumship of Florrie Cook—and before that, of the charming Daniel Dunglas Home—we are not told much about the conditions which prevailed in the séance room. If Sir William had taken the precaution of pasting a postage stamp bearing his initials over the edge of the door it might have provided a clue as to how Katie King managed to manifest so corporeally. In other words, if Houdini could get an impression of a key and make a duplicate for the lock of a prison cell, what could not a clever medium do with the darkness of the séance room to aid her?

One simple thing psychic investigators seemed to overlook was the possibility of someone dressed in black, wearing a black hood, softly entering the room during the séance and producing all the wonders, making his or her exit before the medium called for lights.

In the Victorian age there was a potentially "invisible man" in every wealthy household—the butler. If Dan Home had "gotten to" the butler and—either by bribes, blackmail, or a touch of both—made the butler "his man," the medium could have been searched to the skin and still have produced the ghostly high jinks.

This use of an "invisible man" Houdini knew only too well by long practice—with Jim Collins in such a capacity. Houdini was convinced that the marvels of mediums who had "never been exposed" often depended on secret assistants, coupled with constant vigilance on the medium's part, able misdirection, and the pre-sell of the investigator's belief in the possibility of genuine physical phenomena.

In 1910 the famous Italian medium Eusapia Palladino had been caught by Houdini's pal Joe Rinn while levitating her table in New York. Rinn had worked the medium's trick in reverse—himself crawling into the séance room privately and lying on the floor, watching Eusapia's feet.

As Houdini insisted in his lectures, it does no good to "control" a medium—by holding her hands and resting your feet on hers in the darkness—if her husband, manager, companion, or even a member of the committee known to be sympathetic with her, is left out of control. One committeeman with one hand free can produce a hatful of wonders while the medium takes it easy in her chair, closely "controlled."

This was such an elementary and self-evident fact that Houdini's wrath boiled over when serious investigators, with a parade of academic letters after their names, refused to include it in making their evaluations of "genuine" phenomena. Again and again, in public and in private, Houdini insisted that a distinguished career in one field, such as chemistry, physics, or astronomy, is of no value whatever in detecting fraud by a medium. The laboratory researcher, while familiar with the scientific method as applied to experiments with chemical compounds, electricity, or the physiology of white mice, is completely out of his depth when faced with a tricky, professional wonder-worker.

In Houdini's day the *grande dame* of psychic fakery was Anna Eva Fay, who had thoroughly mystified Crookes when he confronted her with a galvanometer. This was a simple "control" device consisting of a battery, two metal hand grips, and a dial which measured the amount of current flowing through the terminals. The medium grasped the handles firmly; outside the séance laboratory, in a well-lighted room, an assistant kept his eye on the needle of the dial which showed the passage of the current. At no time during the séance did this current stop or diminish, yet the phenomena continued as before in the darkness.

La Fay produced them all with her left hand, which was quite free. The galvanometer had been taken care of easily. When the lights were out Annie Fay pulled up her skirt—a maneuver no Victorian gentleman would be likely to anticipate in a lady—drew down her stocking and slipped one handle under her knee, holding it in place by bending her leg. The bare skin allowed perfect passage for the electric current as recorded on the dial in the other room.

A scientist who has spent his time observing the behavior of white mice is hardly equipped to out-guess this sort of ingenuity; Crookes' experiments with Fay proved only one thing—that people are smarter than mice.

Early in 1924 a young Spaniard caused a mild flurry in psychic circles by being able to see through the covers of metal boxes. Houdini showed that the lad's own boxes had loose covers through which he could get a glimpse of the contents. But this boy was small fry compared to Houdini's next psychic opponent.

Called by Walter Franklin Prince "the most brilliant star in the firmament of alleged physical mediumship that America has seen in fifty years," she was the "white hope" of the believers in their battle with the skeptics. Like the great Home,

she did not perform for money; unlike him, she did not perform
for jewelry either. She was a young Boston matron whose phenomena included just about everything that had ever been
heard of in accounts of physical phenomena—she produced
automatic writing in many languages, including Chinese; her
"apports" were frequent and sometimes living, such as a pigeon
which burst upon the séance room in a whirr of wings; her
powers of telekinesis were great—tables rose and danced, bells
rang, chairs skittered over the floor; she got clairvoyant visions
of distant happenings, came through with spirit messages full
of supposed evidential proof; she materialized full forms, and
when a bucket of melted paraffin was placed near her the spirits
would dip their hands in the mass, then into cold water and
dematerialize, leaving paraffin "gloves," smaller at the wrist
than across the knuckles—a sure proof to the believers that
dematerialization had taken place; thumb prints in soft wax
proved to be different from the thumbs of any of the sitters or
of the medium herself; and most impressive of all, she extruded
ectoplasmic pseudopods which rapped on tables, formed themselves into the semblance of human hands, and could be photographed by flash powder. Being an amateur of "unassailable
social position," accounts of her sittings found their way into
publication at first under the modest pseudonym of "Margery."
And in the summer of 1924 Margery decided to try for the
Scientific American award.

This magazine began to carry articles describing the marvels
obtained through the mediumship of the Boston lady. Beginning in the July issue of *Scientific American*, they were written
by the associate editor, J. Malcolm Bird, and he dwelt at length
on the medium's beauty and charm. It was stated that while
the cash award held no interest for Margery, she would nevertheless compete for it simply in the interests of the cause of
spiritualism. Bird took care to point out that since the medium
desired neither money nor "notoriety," she must be given more
consideration than the average psychic claimant. It sounded
good, and even the New York *Times* was moved to report that

MARGERY, THE BOSTON MEDIUM,
PASSES ALL PSYCHIC TESTS

Scientists Find No Trickery in a
Score of Séances

Versatile Spook Puzzles Investigators
By Variety of His Demonstrations

Houdini let out a roar which might have been heard all the way to Boston. Margery had by this time held over fifty séances with the committee. And J. Malcolm Bird, as secretary, had failed to invite Houdini to a single one. Some word of his rising wrath must have percolated to the magazine, for Bird finally wrote Houdini a letter, asking him to confer with Mr. O. D. Munn, the publisher.

When Houdini stormed into the office at last, Bird informed him that they were on the verge of giving Margery the prize. Houdini kept his temper, and offered to forfeit $1,000 if he, Houdini, could not detect Margery in trickery. Accordingly, Houdini and Munn set off for Boston on the 22nd of July.

The mysterious Margery was really no mystery as far as identity went—the Boston papers had often published her real name. She was Mrs. Mina Crandon, a Canadian girl who was the wife of one of Boston's most distinguished, if eccentric, surgeons—Dr. Le Roi Goddard Crandon. Her first husband had kept a grocery store.

Crandon was a year older than Houdini. He claimed descent from a score of signers of the Mayflower Pact. He had graduated from Harvard in 1894 and received his medical degree four years later. From 1903 to 1918 he was instructor in surgery at Harvard Medical School, leaving this post to serve in the First World War as a commander in the Medical Corps of the U.S. Navy. And he was a joiner, a member of both the British and American Societies for Psychical Research, the Harvard Club, the University Club, and the Boston Yacht Club. He was also the author of a well-known textbook on postoperative care and frequently contributed papers to scientific journals and symposia on psychic research. He was no "cheap fourflusher" to be kissed off lightly or frightened easily. When Houdini came up against Crandon, psychic believers asserted that the irresistible cannon ball had met the immovable post.

Mrs. Crandon, the former Mina Stinson, was—as the impressionable Bird had indicated in his articles—fully equipped with both brains and charm. Her photographs show a pretty woman but they do not convey the essence of her personality— a vivacious warmth which was contagious and, to a committee of staid professors, delightful. She had been a secretary before her marriage, was an accomplished musician, and she had that bold, self-confident poise which would have marked her as an American or Canadian woman anywhere in the world. She had a beautiful body and no false modesty about being searched. Her favorite garment for the séance room was a kimono—period.

This was the background, or as much as is generally known about it, of the greatest American medium since Dan Home.

The whole case is tantalizing, chiefly from the standpoint of motivation. Why did the lovely Mina Crandon ever become a spook worker? Why did her husband, who was unavoidably suspected of being a confederate—though there is reason to believe that he was not—why did he get into the act? What did they have to gain? Most of these questions must remain unanswered. Gossip about the Crandons hinted at bizarre tastes and grotesque goings-on, both in and out of the séance room. But there is no way of confirming or denying such rumors now.

When Houdini appeared on the committee and demanded to be allowed to witness a séance, the Crandons could not very well keep him out—he had seen to that, for he had the *Scientific American's* publisher, Mr. Munn, in his corner. Munn's position was complex; he stood to lose $2,500 if Margery were proved genuine; if she were a fraud, as Houdini had taken pains to point out to him privately before they started for Boston, the magazine stood to lose in prestige and "become the laughingstock of the country."

With this engaging skein of tensions tightly woven, the Margery sittings began. One of the control conditions had always been that Dr. Crandon held his wife's right hand while J. Malcolm Bird held both their hands with one of his, leaving his left hand free for "exploring purposes," as he once described it and as Houdini gleefully quoted him.

When Houdini and Orson Munn got to Boston, they were invited to stay at the Crandons' home, a stylish brick house on Lime Street near Beacon Hill. This Houdini flatly refused to do, and he and Munn, after having dinner with the Crandons, checked into a hotel. Houdini told Munn that, in his opinion, it was impossible for an investigator to retain his objectivity if he became too closely associated with the medium socially. Malcolm Bird and Hereward Carrington apparently did not agree with this theory for both of them had been house guests of the unusually hospitable Crandons for weeks at a time.

One of the most cogent criticisms made of Sir William Crookes in his famous laboratory testings of Dan Home was that he and the medium were on terms of close personal friendship; this made Crookes' observations suspect, to say the least.

Houdini was not taking any chances that the bewitching Mina Crandon would lull him into lax observation by her fascinations.

On the 23rd of July, 1924, Houdini had his first sitting with Margery. One of the conditions imposed on her investigators was total darkness. Some psychics, notably Home, had been content with dim light—but Margery's control spirit, her dead brother Walter Stinson, demanded Stygian night.

Before the lights were turned off, Dr. Crandon took his customary position, "controlling" his wife's right hand, with Malcolm Bird clasping both their hands—his left, or exploring hand, ready to do its exploring.

As a concession to their well-publicized guest, the famous bell box was placed between Houdini's feet. This was a small, rectangular box made of thin wood containing an electric bell, a couple of dry-cell batteries, and a pair of contacts. The top of the box had a wooden flap held open by a light spring. When this flap was depressed slightly, the metal contacts joined and the bell rang. It was explained that the box had to be placed within a certain distance of the medium's body since the psychic force which rang the bell was making use of pseudopods of ectoplasm extruded from the body orifices of the medium.

Houdini was given Margery's left hand to hold and, as a control for her foot, she pressed her left ankle against his right ankle. This sort of "control" would be deemed completely adequate by all believers in spiritualism and a great many psychic researchers distinguished in academic fields. It was not enough for Houdini.

He knew, and had known for many years, the old trick of holding a person's forearm in both your hands and then, when his eyes were closed and he declares he still feels both hands gripping his arm, touching him briskly on the head (or any other place) much to his surprise and chagrin. The nerves of the arm are sensitive to heat, pain, and other sensations but they do not register tactile impressions delicately enough to tell when one of the hands has been removed.

Houdini, as in the impromptu act at Hitchcock's show, had come prepared. All day he had worn a tight elastic bandage around his right leg below the knee; by now the leg was swollen and so sore and tender that the slightest movement or touch would be clearly felt.

Slowly and gently, Margery was moving her leg around to where she could tap the bell-box lid with her toe. Every time she gained a half inch by sliding her leg against Houdini's, she accompanied the action with conversation. But Houdini's attention was focused on the touch of her leg and he realized that soon she would be able to reach the box. And then the box rang. At each ring he felt the tendons of her leg in motion, due to the hypersensitivity of his own leg from the tight bandage.

When the spirit bell had performed sufficiently, he felt the medium slipping her leg back to its first position.

Nor was he in the least impressed by the spirit voice of Walter, which sounded exactly like the voice of Mrs. Crandon.

The only difference was that Walter was brash, slangy, impudent, and given to profanity, whereas—to all intents and purposes—Mrs. Crandon was a perfect lady.

At one point in the proceedings, Walter asked for a luminous plaque which was sometimes used to show a materialized hand in silhouette against its surface. Malcolm Bird got up to get it and Walter shouted for Houdini to control the medium. She gave him both her hands and then Walter announced that the trumpet was floating in the air and asked Houdini where he should throw it. There could be but one answer by the Mysteriarch: "Toward me!" Whereupon it fell at his feet.

Houdini suspected that Margery had simply picked up the megaphone, which served as a spirit trumpet, and put it on her head "dunce cap fashion" before giving him both her hands. When he told them where to throw it, she simply tipped it off her head so it would land near him.

The following evening Margery agreed to "sit" in a hotel suite. This time, with Margery again controlled by Houdini grasping her left hand, they sat around a table. By leaning forward in her chair in the darkness, she got her head under the table and lifted it up and over so that it crashed on its opposite end.

But Houdini suspected what she was going to do. As Orson Munn was holding his left hand, Houdini let go and placed his hand under the table where it came in contact with the top of Margery's head.

After this manifestation the bell was again put between Houdini's feet. And this time his garter clasp got hooked in Margery's stocking. When she claimed that it hurt her, Houdini obligingly took off the garter. Then the ankle-sliding proceeded as before until Margery could reach the bell with her toe.

Houdini whispered to Munn, "Shall I expose her now?" and the publisher answered, "No, better wait until the committee is all together afterward."

This the magician did. But when the committee met without the Crandons shortly after the séance, Malcolm Bird argued against immediate exposure and denunciation, suggesting that the committee wait until it had returned to New York before issuing a statement to the press.

Munn and Houdini went back to New York that night, but Bird stayed on as a guest of the Crandons. As was learned later, he told them all about Houdini's "discoveries" and what the exposer intended to do about them. This, in spite of the fact that Bird had been cautioned by his boss, Munn, not to reveal the Committee's plans to anyone.

Houdini insisted to Munn that Bird's forthcoming article in the magazine be carefully read by him (Houdini) lest Bird's claim that Margery was "fifty percent genuine" be assumed to be issued with Houdini's consent.

When Munn got to New York he stopped the press which was printing the September issue of *Scientific American* and killed the Bird article in that issue.

Bird was already in the doghouse with his boss and he soon broke out with a rash of statements to the newspapers which appeared under such headings as: "BOSTON MEDIUM BAFFLES EXPERTS," "BAFFLES SCIENTISTS WITH REVELATIONS, PSYCHIC POWER OF MARGERY ESTABLISHED," and then the red flag to the bull: "EXPERTS VAINLY SEEK TRICKERY IN SPIRITUALIST DEMONSTRATION. HOUDINI THE MAGICIAN STUMPED."

It was all Harry needed to be sure that his reputation would be ruined, his life's work demolished, and his career made a shambles.

Houdini's firm ally in all this fire and counter-fire of charges, claims, and insinuations was the clergyman member of the committee, Dr. Walter Franklin Prince. Had Houdini resigned from the committee, it might easily have been interpreted that the phenomena of Margery had mystified him. But Dr. Prince agreed that he, too, would resign, unless some way were found to curb the public pronouncements of J. Malcolm Bird. Hou-

dini was for barring Bird from the séances until the committee's
investigation was complete.

Meanwhile another committeeman, Dr. Daniel F. Comstock,
formerly of the Massachusetts Institute of Technology, agreed
with Prince that Houdini should design some form of cabinet
or box which would "humanely" control the medium's hands
and feet. Jim Collins got busy on this project and he and
Houdini built such a cabinet. It was shaped something like a
piano box but just wide enough and deep enough to admit a
person sitting on a chair. The lid sloped in front, where there
was a circular hole for the neck; at the sides were two openings,
through which the medium could thrust her hands for control
by sitters.

On August 25th, at the Charlesgate Hotel in Boston, the
Crandons met with the committee. Houdini and Collins were
on hand with the cabinet. The famous bell box was placed on
a table in front of the control cabinet within reach of any
ectoplasmic pseudopods which might materialize out of the
medium's body orifices; the glamorous Margery was properly
boxed and the lights extinguished.

The bell rang. When the lights were turned on again, it was
found that two thin strips of brass which had held the cabinet's
lid in place had been moved. Houdini pointed out that Margery
could easily have stood up in the cabinet, pushing up the lid,
and then have bent forward and knocked the bell box with her
forehead, causing it to ring. Margery claimed that if the cabinet
had been forced open, then Walter had done it. It is not an
unheard-of thing for girls to blame various types of mischief on
their brothers but in this case the brother was dead.

After the séance Houdini found the Crandons missing and
followed them into the séance room, where he caught them
measuring the neck hole in the cabinet. Or so he claimed.

The next night Collins fitted the cabinet's lid with staples,
hasps, and padlocks. Malcolm Bird had been excluded from
the room the night before, but he now came to the hotel and
asked why he was being kept out. Houdini informed him that

he wanted the proceedings of the committee kept secret. Bird finally admitted that he had intended to keep everything secret but that Margery had "worried" the facts out of him. In a huff, Bird resigned as secretary of the committee; his resignation was readily accepted.

This time the committee insisted that Houdini take one hand of the medium and Dr. Prince the other. Houdini, watching Margery as she settled herself in the cabinet, said that she seemed to be working hard on some project of her own; he could tell by the motion of her head and the muscles of her neck. He demanded that she put out her hands, which she did. He cautioned Dr. Prince not to let go under any circumstances. Margery retaliated by asking why, and Houdini bluntly told her that in case she had "smuggled anything into the box" she could no longer use it, since both of her hands were now firmly held.

Soon the personality of Walter took over and snarled, "Houdini, you are very clever indeed but it won't work. I suppose it was an accident those things were left in the cabinet?"

On being asked what he meant, Walter stated that a ruler had been dropped in the cabinet by Houdini's assistant in order to discredit the medium. Walter then cut loose, shouting, "Houdini, you god-damned son of a bitch, get to hell out of here and never come back. If you don't, I will."

Houdini insisted that this remark be allowed to stand in the record of the proceedings. Dr. Comstock interposed that the ruler in question might well have fallen accidentally from someone's pocket. Houdini urged Munn to step out and ask Jim Collins if it was his. Collins returned with Munn and denied knowing anything about any rule. His own folding carpenter's rule was safely in his hip pocket where he always carried it. Houdini made Collins swear a mighty oath that he knew nothing about the rule. This done, Houdini swore a mighty oath that he did not drop the ruler in the box—he swore it on his mother's grave.

The séance continued for a while after this fracas, but nothing happened. When the lights were turned on again and the cabinet opened, the rule was found on the floor of it, a cheap two-foot ruler which folded to six inches in length. Houdini had his own theory, which he strenuously voiced, as to how Margery could have smuggled the object into the box.

The next night Dr. Comstock, in all probability briefed by Houdini, asked for a special control—he brought a small box, sat facing Margery, and had her put her feet in the box. He did the same and a board was fastened over their knees. He held the medium's hands. The bell box, placed beside them, failed to ring.

Margery, while at dinner with the committee, said softly to Houdini (as he later told it) that she was afraid he would denounce her from the stage of Keith's Theater and that if he did a number of her friends would come up and give him a good beating. Houdini was not frightened. Similarly, Dr. Crandon, before the séance of August 27th said jovially that if Houdini were only converted to a belief in his wife's mediumship he, Crandon, would gladly give $10,000 to any charity Houdini would name. Houdini was not to be persuaded by $10,000, which he chose to consider a bribe.

Dr. Crandon then insisted that Dr. Comstock "control" Houdini's left hand and swear on his word of honor not to release it under any circumstances. This control of Houdini, while he was trying to control the medium, was the last straw.

Margery did not win the *Scientific American* award. Malcolm Bird shortly afterward left the employ of the magazine, when Houdini said in a radio interview, "I hereby publicly denounce Malcolm Bird as a confederate of Margery. Every time he's there something wonderful happens."

That fall Houdini published a pamphlet, *Houdini exposes the tricks used by the Boston Medium "Margery."* It was illustrated by cartoon sketches of the way Margery did her faking, according to Houdini, and also contained a number of photographs of Houdini and the famous cabinet. The cabinet he took with him on his lecture tour to the Pacific coast, where spectators watched delightedly as he maneuvered a two-foot rule up through the neck hole, held it in his teeth, and made a bell box ring.

Years later, when the Self-Liberator was dead, Jim Collins was asked about the mysterious rule. Collins smiled wryly. "I chucked it in the box meself. The Boss told me to do it. 'E wanted to fix her good."

"But he swore on his mother's grave. . . ."

"Sure—that was *after* 'e told me to do it. By that time 'e 'ad it all figgered out in 'is mind that 'e 'adn't done it. There's one thing you got to remember about Mister 'Oudini in his last years. For 'im the Truth was bloody well what 'e wanted it to be." Collins added, with a burst of old loyalty, "But 'e was a good one to work for. Never forgot birthdays an' such. And generous at Christmas."

Margery's fame increased among the devout believers as she was attacked by skeptics and scientific investigators. One of her most convincing tests was the production of ghostly thumb prints in slabs of dental wax; the prints did not match the whorls and islands of her own thumbs, nor were they the prints of Dr. Crandon or of anyone in the séance room.

Petted and worshiped by the spiritualists, glorified in the columns of their publications, she became the greatest medium of her age. Then one skeptical investigator, under a plausible pretext, began collecting thumb prints of *everyone* who had ever been to a Margery séance. He found the prints ascribed to the dead Walter—they were actually the prints of a Boston dentist, very much alive, who not only took care of Margery's teeth but had shown her how to prepare dental wax to receive impressions and had given her two slabs with his thumb prints deeply pressed into them. All she needed to produce the mysterious marks were two tiny plaster casts made from these impressions which she could easily have hidden about her before a séance.

Spiritualists, as well as investigators who remained neutral, have pointed out that Houdini never exposed Margery—it was merely his word against hers and it was hinted by those who knew them both that Houdini was not above threatening a blackmail type of operation to keep Margery and her champions from retaliating too fiercely. He possessed, apparently, information about her that she was not eager to have him circulate.

The controversy did not easily die, and for awhile was waged fiercely in the columns of newspapers, particularly in Boston. When Houdini played the city, demonstrating his "Margie Box" as he called it in private, he "packed 'em in."

That, after all, was the main thing. He had found his new gimmick—demonstrating spiritualist tricks, with several members of the audience on stage blindfolded and mystified at what he was able to do when they believed that they were "controlling" his hands and feet, while the audience howled its glee.*

* Not long ago I was walking down Fifth Avenue on a spring evening with a polished, cosmopolitan gentleman, at home in many lands and comfortable in many languages. I knew he was a lifelong student of mediumistic trickery, had done a great deal of psychic researching both here and abroad. I brought up the question of Margery.

"Ah, yes, Mina Crandon. Beautiful, beautiful girl. Utterly fascinating. You know that was a hellish hot summer, there in Boston that year. Mrs. Crandon was all for going on picnics at the seaside or sailing on her husband's boat. Anything except sitting in a stuffy room. But the doctor—crisp sort of chap he was, called his wife 'Psyche,' never Mina or Margery—he was red hot for séances. He spoke of that damned control spirit, Walter, as if he lived just around the corner. Crandon was a puzzling sort of fellow; brilliant surgeon—could knot sutures with one hand and all that—but puzzling. I never could figure him out, nor could anyone else.

"But Mina—ah, there was a heartbreaker for you. A natural blond with the most devilish blue eyes I ever saw in my life. And there was pure enchantment in her voice, no other way to describe it. I understand that she went to pieces rather badly before she died and all the loveliness and the laughter were no more.

"It was quite a tragedy. I had occasion to visit Boston a few years ago and I went out of my way just to walk past the Crandon house. I have no idea who's living in it now. It was a foggy evening when I came close to it and I stopped for a bit on the other side of the street, looking up at the lighted windows. I never put any faith in all her psychic wonders but the girl was an enchantress. Now it was just a house; quite a posh house of course, but empty. '. . . *All the grey night In chaos of vacancy shone; Nought but vast sorrow was there—The sweet cheat gone.*'"

33. *Dreams Come True*

HOUDINI'S farewell tour of vaudeville, though he did not know it as such, opened at the New York Hippodrome in the spring of 1925, where he demonstrated his reconstruction of what Margery would have done had she been able to use the folding foot rule by holding it in her teeth and tapping the bell box.

His act consisted almost entirely of spirit exposés. He used the old Davenport rope tie, but with comedy business. The inspecting committeemen blindfolded with special strips of black velvet, Houdini would ring the dinner bells and tambourines with his toes, his foot drawn from a shoe on which a committeeman held his own foot—Houdini's shoe had a firm shell built into it for the purpose. This act, often climaxed by the old favorite, the Water Torture Cell, was hailed as the greatest novelty ever to be presented to a vaudeville audience.

At times, when he felt the need of a rest, Houdini would change the act entirely, opening with the strait jacket, then doing the needles, and closing with Bess in the Substitution Trunk. For $1,200 a week—the old $12 a week act of thirty years before; the only difference was that Bess had at last a few curves, where in her girlhood she had been as slim as a match stick.

On this final vaudeville tour, Houdini was preceded by his own undercover squad of psychic investigators, among them Julia Sawyer. Having gotten a line on one of the boldest "direct voice" trumpet mediums or materializing psychics in a town, Houdini was all set to appear in his favorite disguise—a bent, doddering old man, with white wig and beard, who would beg piteously in a quavering voice for some word from his dead son. When the money had been paid and the medium produced a message or a shade purporting to be the mythical son, Houdini would pull out his powerful flashlight, focus it on the medium with the trumpet to his lips or the luminous gauze draped over his shoulders, and denounce him in ringing tones. He usually took a detective with him on these raids. When the lights were turned on and the medium remonstrated with the boorish skeptic, Houdini would dramatically whip off his wig and beard, and thunder, "It is I, HOUDINI. I hereby accuse you of fraud and deception. I've got you dead to rights."

Reporters had a fine time with these exposés and Houdini found that they were much better publicity stunts than even his underwater box or his upside-down jacket.

His fifty-first birthday that year fell on Easter Sunday. His birthday present for himself was a new Easter outfit for Bess.

The tour ended where it started, at the New York Hippodrome, where he did the needle trick with one hundred and twenty needles.

The more for Bessie's sake than his own, he rented a cottage at Glen Head, Long Island, for the summer, intending to take it easy. It was too late for Houdini to take it easy. After a few days of swimming and sunning himself, he began thinking up new ideas for the dream of a lifetime—a full-evening magic show, combining everything into one gala extravaganza of Houdiniana: magic with cards and silks, illusions with beautiful girls appearing and vanishing, escapes with the good old Upside Down to climax them, and a spook show of materialized ghosts from a cabinet, messages on slates; anything and everything that would cause talk, and pack 'em in.

While he bided his time for such a show to begin, Houdini gave a series of lectures on the tricks of mediums and fortune tellers before the New York Police Academy. He was still working out more gimmicks for a grand crusade against mediums. But the thought began to form in the back of his mind —"after the mediums, then what?" He was too canny a showman to think that his anti-spook crusade would last forever and he began casting about for something to replace it when it was worn out.

Houdini was an inveterate performer of card tricks and when demonstrating his dexterity to the police force he found that the boys in blue were most interested in the moves of the professional gamblers, since they were constantly being approached by suckers who had been taken for large sums in crooked games. When asked "How did they do it? They beat me with my own cards," the police were often at a loss to explain.

Houdini laid plans, which he confided to very few of his associates, for another campaign, after the mediums wore out. This was to be an anti-gambling foray, exposing the tricks of the "card mechanics" and "dice hustlers."

For this he would have to practice like mad. From his years of escape work and spook-chasing, he was out of practice, and the smooth execution of gambler's sleights are among the most difficult moves in magic.*

Like so many of his exploits, Houdini's thoughts on a possible gambling exposé were not original with him. There had been "reformed" gamblers for years playing the dime *musées*, among them "Kid Canfield," whose demonstration of the second deal and of card-stacking and false-shuffling was a wonder to behold.

Meanwhile, there was gold in the hills of spook fakery. In the words of Houdini's friend Al Jolson (with whom he founded a club of people in show business who were the children of rabbis), "Don't go 'way, folks—you ain't seen nothin' yet!"

In the fall the dream came true. Houdini put his full-evening

---

* Many years later the fabulously dexterous John Scarne rode to fame by just such demonstrations, as did Mickey Macdougal and Audley Walsh. The exposing of gamblers' tricks had been one of the specialties of Houdini's old idol, Robert-Houdin, and the latter's book, *Les Tricheries des Grecs,* is still one of the handbooks of the art. Houdini was again trying to surpass his deposed hero.

show on the road. Twice he had tried it before and it had
failed. This time he was going to make it go over or bust every
bone in his body.

Vaudeville was fighting for its life but the full-evening magic
show could penetrate the sticks where there were no big-time
vaude theaters, and where, Houdini was sure, the people were
starved for sensational live entertainment.

The show, when he took it out in the fall, played two hours
and a half with Houdini on stage nearly every minute. In the
first act he did his version of the Miser's Dream called Money
for Nothing. He also did a version of Harry Kellar's famous
"Yogi's Lamp," in which a lamp is wrapped in a foulard and
is seen glowing through the cloth until the pronouncement of
the magic words, when the silk is whisked away and the lamp
is gone. This he followed with a bright medley of silk effects; he
produced a live rabbit, turned a girl into a rosebush, burned
and restored a handful of cloth forming part of a turban worn
by one of his assistants. He did his needle trick. He brought
on Bess, announcing proudly, "Been traveling with this girl
for thirty-one years." They did Metamorphosis. A radio, playing loudly, was covered with a silk and vanished, the music
stopping on the instant the radio cabinet dematerialized. He
presented to the audience a trick so old that most of them had
never seen or heard of it—five cards, chosen by spectators, are
torn to bits and loaded into a magic blunderbus pistol, which is
fired at a gilded star; the cards appear, restored, one at the tip
of each arm. He produced glass fish bowls, complete with live
goldfish, from silk foulards; half a dozen alarm clocks were
vanished and made their reappearance, all ringing lustily.

For the second act, Houdini opened with the strait jacket,
did a couple of fast releases from pillories, coffins, trunks, or
whatever he felt like doing that evening, and closed with the
Torture Cell.

After an intermission during which he got dried off, he
opened up with his siege guns on the local mediums, who had
been investigated a few days before he came to town by Hou-

dini's private eyes. The mediums seemed fascinated by what Houdini was going to say about them; they would even come to the show. When he spotted them in the audience, Houdini would have a spotlight turned on them while he recounted the experience one of his lady investigators had had with them, getting messages from dead husbands (the lady in question was a spinster) or from a dead mother, when the girl's mother was safely home in Brooklyn in the best of health.

The mediums, so confronted with Houdini's invective and the spotlight, would retire from the auditorium in confusion. If, once in a while, the "medium" so attacked from the stage was really one of Houdini's spare relatives or in-laws pressed into service, it was all in good clean fun.

It has been suggested that some of Houdini's best publicized "ghost grabbings"—at séances where he appeared in the disguise of the senile old man—were put-up jobs; some mediums, knowing that nothing could shake the faith of their firm believers, were willing to be exposed by Houdini for a consideration. This seems likely enough, but we cannot know now how many of the famous exposures were on the level, without the medium's collaboration, and how many were fixed. Whatever the count, all of the exposures made good newspaper copy.

A typical quiet week with the Houdini show in town can be observed from the headlines in the Baltimore *News,* beginning Tuesday evening, November 3, 1925. The front page carried this banner headline:

HOUDINI TO EXPOSE BALTIMORE FRAUDS

The *News* Will Help in Baring Schemes

A sweeping challenge is hurled at Baltimore mediums, fraud spiritualists and fortune tellers by Houdini, psychic investigator, lieutenant in the New York City Police Reserves, and world famous "Man of Mystery" who comes to the Academy of Music the week of November 9.

The story went on to list the many cash awards of thousands of dollars offered for genuine phenomena or messages under test conditions.

The next day, a thing unheard-of in journalistic practice, the same paper carried the same identical head:

HOUDINI TO EXPOSE BALTIMORE FRAUDS

This time the story was under Houdini's by-line! The picture, two columns wide, showed Houdini tied and chained to the drive-wheel of a locomotive.

The next day, November 5, the banner (eight columns wide) proclaimed:

HOUDINI ON TRAIL OF BALTIMORE SEERS

The picture showed him in handcuffs and chains.

November 6:

HOUDINI TO ANSWER MEDIUM QUESTIONS

The story concerned Houdini's many pacts with friends who had died and his failure to get any evidential material in his years of psychic research. He answered the questions supposedly sent in by readers on the "how" of mediumistic wonders. The picture, three columns wide, was a still from *The Master Mystery*, showing a gang of emissaries tying Houdini up.

November 7:

HOUDINI ON WARPATH AGAINST SEERS

(with a two-column picture of Houdini being put into a strait jacket by a cop.)

Monday Evening, November 9 (when the show finally opened):

HOUDINI BEGINS HIS WAR ON MEDIUMS

Story: account of how Houdini's agents constantly had themselves "ordained" as spiritualistic reverends on payment of $25.

Illustration, two columns: a movie still of Houdini being tied to an old water wheel.

Next evening:

HOUDINI EXPOSES DARK SEANCE SECRETS

Wednesday, November 11:

HOUDINI CHALLENGES MYSTICS TO TEST

(first time the story carried no front page pix) Story: $50,000 offered for a real spook.

Thursday:

MEDIUMS SILENT ON HOUDINI'S OFFER

Friday, November 13:

HOUDINI'S OFFER STILL UNCHALLENGED

For ten days, Houdini monopolized the front page of a newspaper in one of the largest cities of the land. A careful reading of the stories fails to show that he ever actually exposed a single Baltimore medium. And this publicity record was duplicated again and again on his tour.

One feature of the show, which was not publicized in the foofaraw about mediums, was Houdini's invitation to the Baltimore magicians of the S.A.M. He gave twenty minutes of his show over to them and they did their best tricks before the citizens of their own home town.

Houdini was now serving his eighth term as president of the Society of American Magicians.

On the eve of one of the S.A.M.'s annual banquets in New York, Houdini got a frantic phone call from a teen-age magical devotee, a youth who had set his heart on going to the banquet show. At the last minute funds were not available. He called the Great Man: "Mr. Houdini, I hate to trouble you, but . . . well, I've *got* to get to the show tonight. I've just *got* to."

"Yeah, sure. I understand, son."

"Well, I thought, maybe I could get a ticket on credit, or something. . . ."

"Think nothing of it, my boy. You'll sit at my table with Mrs. Houdini and my own crowd. Just give your name to the fellow taking the tickets at the door. Let me make a note of it. What's your name?"

"Keating, sir. Fred Keating."

That teen-age boy was to grow into one of the greats of magic, a star in films and on Broadway.

It was little, generous acts such as this on the part of Houdini which made him devoted friends by the hundred.

At the end of the season with the ghost-breaking show, Houdini was in New York, meeting with his fellow magicians, when young Keating came in, looking subdued and downcast. Houdini asked him what the trouble was and Keating told him— he had lost his mother. Houdini's eyes filled to the brim with quick tears. He patted the youth's arm and said huskily, "I know how it is, my boy. It's tough. Tough. I know."

Young Fred admitted that he had thought of trying to establish contact with his mother through one of the more reputable mediums. At this Houdini smiled his faint, sweet faraway smile as from Olympus.

"Don't try it, my boy. There is no such thing as speaking with our loved ones who have gone. I know. There is no communication with them. We must suffer alone."

Keating persisted, saying that he still felt that he had to give it a try. Houdini frowned. "But my dear boy—how can you say such a thing? I, Houdini, have told you that it is impossible!"

34. *Spoiled Egyptian*

WASHINGTON, D.C., the nation's most beautiful city, heart of the democracy, hub of the forty-eight sovereign states was in 1926 also the city most infested with palm readers, astrologers, message mediums, slate writers, crystal workers, and "rag head rackets"* generally. In the shabbier residential neighborhoods their shingles, showing an upraised palm, were thick; sometimes almost every brownstone house to the block had its prognostication parlor.

Why Washington should have been such a Mecca for mediums and fortune tellers is a moot question. But on February 26, 1926, the House of Representatives' Subcommittee of the Committee on the District of Columbia opened its meeting with a consideration of a bill, H. R. 8989, that was co-sponsored by Senator Royal S. Copeland and Representative Sol Bloom of New York State. The bill, "Amending subchapter 5 of the Code of Law of the District of Columbia, as amended to June 7, 1924," related to offenses against public policy.

The amendment stated:

> "Any person pretending to tell fortunes for reward or compensation where lost or stolen goods may be found; any person who, by game or device, sleight of hand, pretending, fortune telling or, by any trick or other means, by the use of cards or other implements or instruments, fraudulently obtains from another person money or property or reward, property of any description; any person pretending to remove spells, or to sell charms for protection, or to unite the separated, shall be con-

* Rag head: one who wears a turban, hence, by inference, anyone engaged in professional occult fakery whether in the guise of a Hindu swami or not. The term originated on the midway.

sidered a disorderly person. Any person violating the provisions of this law shall be punished by a fine not to exceed $250 or by imprisonment not to exceed six months, or by both such fine and imprisonment."

Congressman Bloom brought with him to the hearing a witness; said witness, on being asked his full name, replied, "Harry Houdini." When asked his occupation: "I am an author; I am a psychic investigator for the scientific magazines of the world; and then I am a mysterious entertainer."

He brought it to the attention of the gentlemen of the committee that, in the District of Columbia, anyone could set up in business as a fortune teller on payment of a $25 license fee. He further stated that he had no wish to attack spiritualism as a religion but ". . . this thing they *call* 'spiritualism,' wherein a medium intercommunicates with the dead. . . . There are only two kinds of mediums," he said, "those who are mental degenerates and who ought to be under observation, and those who are deliberate cheats and frauds. I would not believe a fraudulent medium under oath; perjury means nothing to them."

Some mediums had shown up for the hearing, too, and these Houdini challenged to read the words of a crumpled telegram he snatched from his pocket. When the mediums remained silent, one member of the Subcommittee jocularly offered to act as a clairvoyant; he guessed that the telegram read, "Please send more money" since that, presumably, was the type of wire most often received.

The legislators eventually agreed that the bill as worded would make it a crime for children in their own homes to deal out a deck of cards and tell each other's fortunes, and would likewise prevent a country swain from putting a dime into a machine and getting in return a picture of his future bride. They pointed out that the laws already on the books of the District of Columbia gave the citizenry full legal remedy in case of loss suffered from a conspiracy with intent to defraud, whether said conspiracy took the form of fortune telling or not.

At one point Houdini was questioned about the claim of

psychics that he himself did his marvels by supernatural powers. He emphatically stated that he did NOT have supernatural powers—and then one of the learned gentlemen threw him a real poser: "Can you prove it?"

Houdini stated again that he did not possess such powers, and cited the claims of J. Hewat McKenzie that he dematerialized himself to get out of the Torture Cell. When pressed to tell the committee just how he did get out, he replied, "I do it like anybody else would do it." This seemed to stymie the query successfully.

When asked if he believed in astrology, Houdini shot back: "I do not believe in astrology. They cannot tell from a chunk of mud millions of miles away what is going to happen to me."

One of the witnesses called by Congressman Bloom was Houdini's chief investigator of mediums, Miss Rose Mackenberg, whose testimony of what a medium, Mrs. Jane B. Coates, had told her the day before regarding her supposed illicit love life spiced up the proceedings no end. Miss Mackenberg was a respectable spinster.

When questioned about further disclosures made to her by Mrs. Coates, she mentioned a list of U.S. Senators who, Mrs. Coates had claimed, were ardent believers in mediumistic phenomena, and followers of spirit advice.

This was getting the hearing into deep waters—and Houdini promptly created a diversion by demonstrating to the committee and the spectators how mediums produce voices from a trumpet.

The hearings were postponed and reopened in May. This time the spiritualists of Washington had their line of attack well thought out. The Rev. H. P. Strack, secretary of the National Spiritualists' Association of America, a portly, dignified, and eloquent individual, made a graceful defense of spiritualism as a religion and by inference accused Houdini of attacking the right of freedom of worship.

Houdini introduced a reformed medium's sworn statement, describing her life as a trumpet worker and the load which had been lifted from her conscience when she "packed in" the racket.

He finally got the committee to allow him to give them a demonstration of slate-writing; he picked out a lady in the room—the wife of a senator—whom he had never met, and produced an "evidential" message for her between two slates previously shown blank. On the request of the committee chairman he revealed that the day before, when she had come into the room, Houdini had been walking in front of her and had heard her say, "I would like to get a spirit message." He had, thereupon, done some research on her after learning her name. Then he demonstrated how he had apparently shown all four sides of the slates but had, by misdirection, only shown three; the other contained the bogus spirit message.

When Mrs. Jane B. Coates took the stand, being duly sworn, the committee and spectators were treated to the agile performance of a really expert medium when in a tight spot. She attacked Houdini's investigator, Rose Mackenberg, in a dozen subtle ways and some not so subtle.

The spiritualists finally nailed the committee down to the point that the bill, as presented by Sol Bloom with the advice of Houdini, would make it illegal for spiritualists, in the practice of their religion, to indulge in the divine gift of prophecy. Further, they implied that everything had been going along smoothly in the District of Columbia, with the police fully capable of taking care of frauds and swindlers, until Houdini burst upon them with advice on how to run their fair city.

In this kind of parliamentary rapier-play, Houdini, with his verbal mace-and-chain, was outmatched. This was particularly evident when the Rev. Alfred H. Terry, pastor of the First Spiritualist Church of Washington, stated that the existing law, *if enforced,* would prevent even one fraud from operating in the capital. This was tossing the hot potato right into the laps of the Congressmen.

When asked why a man's dead mother, to get in touch with her son, must needs come back by way of a medium, Terry explained that it was due to the greater spiritual development of mediums, who take time to bring out the psychic powers latent in all men. A medium was only an instrument; so is a telephone, by which we talk to our loved ones when we are separated by mundane miles.

Speaking against the bill, there appeared a gentleman named Palmer who had spent thirty-five years in the government employ as a clerk in the Pension Office. Mr. Palmer was a devout spiritualist and made a well-informed summary of the evidence for his belief, as gathered from the writings of Lodge, Crookes, Lombroso, Flammarion, and Hereward Carrington.

At the mention of Carrington, Houdini was on his feet. Pouncing on the name like a hawk on a pullet, he denounced the famous author in violent terms and wound up almost incoherent in his rage.

When he finally got off the subject of Hereward Carrington, Houdini went back to an earlier point of attack: the sale of supposed lucky charms as a menace to the citizenry. In the matter of the sale of charms and amulets for protection, a woman lawyer, Miss C. Larrimore Keeley, took the stand and expressed an opinion that the wording of the bill would make illegal the sale of miraculous medals by the Catholic Church.

The legislators of the committee seemed to be getting more and more confused by the minute. This was not helped any by a strident witness who opened a defense of his faith—spiritualism—by declaring that the whole business of this here bill is an attack by organized religion on the spiritualist churches! The witness, in high dudgeon, reminded the committee that 2,000 years ago Judas betrayed Christ, that Judas was a Jew and that this here bill was being put through by a couple of . . . (loud raps by the chairman's gavel).

Very little was done to clarify the issues by a lady who testified that, at a séance in St. Louis, she had met the materialized form of her mother; in order to see if there was some fake to it, the sitter had put out her hand and touched the robe of the spirit and discovered that it was a *creepy* substance.

THE CHAIRMAN: A creepy substance?

THE WITNESS: A creepy substance, you know, just like when it would be creepy—like crepe de Chine . . .

The bill was never reported. But the results of the hearing were nonetheless gratifying to all concerned. It got Houdini on the wire services for several days. The mediums, palmists, and astrologers of Washington got so much publicity they had to keep open far into the night to accommodate all the new business. And the published minutes of the hearing served as an excellent guide to spiritualists when facing a ghost-breaking campaign.

Hardly had he simmered down from the strenuous session in Washington, than Houdini went into eruption again.

Some time after midnight on the 31st of May, Jim Collins and his wife Maude were awakened by the insistent ringing of their telephone. The instant the receiver was raised there was no doubt as to who was on the other end:

"Collins, Collins! We got to do him something! It's Carrington, that trickster—he's got some kind of a fake yogi he's going to take into vaudeville, being buried alive on the stage—a cheap carny act, trying to book him into good houses! Psychic power, that's what he claims he's got; supernatural power. We got to stop him!"

Collins finally got the Boss cooled down, promised to give the matter his immediate attention, and went back to sleep.

The cause of all the rumpus was a dark-skinned performer billed as Rahman Bey. He was a supposed Egyptian dervish, purportedly able to control his body functions by occult practices. Hereward Carrington had seen him in Europe and become interested in some of the things the fakir could do.

The detonating charge which set off Houdini's wrath was a trial performance Carrington had secured for the dervish at the Selwyn Theater. As the fakir's manager, Carrington made a brief introductory speech, carefully worded, in which he mentioned some of the peculiar powers of the human body developed in the Orient by devotees of Oriental disciplines.

Rahman Bey himself, to build the act, began with a number of typical carny side-show stunts, "stopping his pulse" at will, pushing hatpins through his cheeks with only a little bleeding afterward, lying with shoulders on one scimitar and his feet on another while an assistant broke a large lump of sandstone with a sledge hammer, the stone resting on the fakir's middle. He did some simple "eyeless vision" tricks. He tried, without spectacular success, some muscle-reading effects on members of the audience. He lay on a bed of nails (spaced so close together that they did not pierce his skin, in the best side-show tradition). And then came the *pièce de résistance*—burial alive.

It was Rahman Bey's talent for this feat which interested Carrington. The other tricks were standard stunts, many of which had been described years before by Carrington in a book called *Side Show and Animal Tricks*—a book which, incidentally, is more informative than Houdini's *Miracle Mongers*.

For his "living burial," Rahman Bey made quite a show of putting himself into a cataleptic trance; he was then placed in a coffin, the lid was nailed down, and the coffin was placed on a sheet of linoleum in the center of the stage and covered up with shovelfuls of sand.

Houdini's old friend Joe Rinn had come forward as one of the committee and by edging around to the head end of the coffin, which was placed upstage and out of sight of the audience, he observed that there was a crack in the boards of the head panel through which the coffin's inhabitant could push out a straw or a putty-blower and so breathe easily.

Rahman Bey would not have needed even this device, however, for his interment lasted only a few minutes.

What concerned Houdini more, and caused his outburst over the telephone to Collins, was the Bey's stated plan of being lowered into the East River in a watertight metal coffin. This was stepping on the toes of the World-Famed Self-Liberator with a vengeance. For years—since 1911, in fact—Houdini had been experimenting with just such an effect. And he knew that no "cataleptic trance" was required; by keeping calm and breathing as little as possible, one could live for a surprisingly long time in a box or coffin!

In July the Egyptian finally got his stunt organized. He was placed in a zinc coffin, the lid soldered fast by tinsmiths. But before the coffin was fairly sunk, an alarm bell, with which it was equipped, began ringing insistently. When the coffin was hoisted up and ripped open, the dervish was found, still apparently in catalepsy, and by inference, able to ring a bell while unconscious.

Accounts of this performance in the papers gave the information that Rahman Bey was an Italo-Arab, who accomplished his feats by using the secret lore of the East which he had studied for twenty-six years.

The second water burial of the Italo-Arab took place in the pool of a well-known swimming school. This time Rahman Bey stayed in the coffin an hour—twenty-four minutes of it under water with relays of men standing on the box to keep it submerged.

Houdini did not attend the demonstration, but he was represented there by Joe Rinn, who took careful notes so that Houdini could "expose the faker." Then Houdini issued a blast in the press to the effect that he stood ready to duplicate, *by natural means,* the performance of the dervish. He set as the date, August 5; the place, the swimming pool of the Hotel Shelton in New York.

For Houdini's test, Joe Rinn was appointed timekeeper. Among the witnesses was Joseph Dunninger, a close student of the occult arts in the best ghost-breaker tradition, a friend of Houdini's and an admirer of the Master's methods, particularly as they applied to press relations and stunts.*

Except for a committee chosen to remain beside the pool, Houdini shooed all the observers up into the spectators' gallery.

* Dunninger is today the most famous figure in the world of professional mystification, the greatest mentalist of all time, and he has, through the years, beat Houdini's newspaper-space record in publicity. He would be the first to give credit to Houdini as a trail-blazer in creating sensational publicity stunts.

Then, in the gallery, he spied a familiar face and shouted, "What's *that* man doing here? He's got to get out of here."

"That man," Hereward Carrington, said quietly that he was there as a bona fide reporter for a magazine, which was perfectly true. Houdini decided to allow him to stay—in the gallery.

The casket designed for the pool test by Collins was built of galvanized iron with angle irons at the edges. It was equipped with an emergency bell, similar to that of Rahman Bey, and also a telephone. Collins remained in communication with Houdini throughout the test by this telephone, speaking to the Boss every five minutes to make sure he was safe.

The coffin, with its lid soldered tight by a tinsmith, was submerged in one corner of the pool and kept down by relays of men standing on it. After a half hour they accidentally slipped off and the coffin shot to the surface, but Houdini reported that he was not hurt and the casket was pressed down again and held fast.

When an hour had passed, Collins began calling Houdini every minute. Still he did not get the command to raise the coffin. Fifteen minutes after the hour mark, Houdini reported that water was beginning to seep in. Still he did not ask to be raised.

Time was now called every thirty seconds. When an hour and a half had elapsed, Houdini told Collins, "I guess I had better come up; I'm getting a little numb down here."

On his release, his pulse, which had been 84 before the experiment, was 142; diastolic blood pressure, which had been 84, was down to 42. Houdini looked shaken and haggard but he made a bold speech to the assembled newspapermen, asserting that he had proved that a man does not need supernatural powers to sustain himself in a coffin for quite a time without additional air.

Joe Rinn, writing about the famous water burial years afterward, hints that Houdini had a "gaff" in the coffin—some device for releasing oxygen and/or absorbing carbon dioxide.

Hereward Carrington, in his book *The Science of Psychic Research* (1931), makes much of the fact that Houdini's pulse and blood pressure were all askew after his test and that he was deathly white and dripping with perspiration—while Rahman Bey, or so he claims, under similar circumstances showed no physiological changes. Carrington also points with suspicion to the mysterious batteries of Houdini's alarm bell which were inside the coffin, hinting that oxygen-liberating chemicals and soda lime to absorb the CO_2 could easily have been hidden in these "batteries"; the bell was not used in the test and the excuse given for its presence was that it was a safety measure, in case the telephone failed.

All these points are well taken but the true secret of the coffin, which was apparently unknown to some of the medical men quoted at the time, was that there was enough air in it to last a man an hour and a half. The doctors had "estimated" that the air would only be sufficient for three or four minutes.

One of the things not generally recorded was the size of Houdini's famous coffin. According to Frank Sanchez of the hotel staff, the coffin measured twenty-two inches by twenty-two by six feet, six inches; much higher than necessary to hold the master mystifier. Information supplied by Sanchez has enabled The Amazing Randi to duplicate it.

Much research has been done in this field since Houdini's battle with Rahman Bey; and interested parties can find tables, by which they can work out the survival time exactly, in the U.S. Navy's *Handbook of Submarine Medicine*. This same source indicates that if, for twelve hours before such a test, the performer were to confine his diet to proteins and fats with no carbohydrates, his oxygen consumption would be almost half what it would be if he had taken in a large amount of sugar before the experiment.*

* On February 7, 1956, for Dave Garroway's TV show, "Today," the contemporary escapologist, The Amazing Randi, stayed under water in a coffin in the Shelton pool for one hour and forty-four minutes. In November, 1958, in London, Randi stayed down two hours and three minutes.

But the feat captured the imagination of the country; Houdini was in the headlines again, his name on everyone's lips.

For the fall season of his full-evening show, he got out special paper on his "buried alive" stunt—a lithographed "eight sheet" in four colors, proclaiming that The Master Mystifier HOUDINI—The Greatest Necromancer of the Age, Perhaps of All Times—would introduce his BURIED ALIVE!—Egyptian Fakirs Outdone! A copy of this poster, in the collection of Mr. George Pfisterer, pictures an elaborate bronze coffin with a cut-out section to show Houdini inside it, leaning against an Egyptian tomb, apparently about to be buried under the sand.

This setting may have suggested some stories ghosted for the Master Mystifier by the late, great H. P. Lovecraft which appeared in *Weird Tales Magazine* and concerned Houdini's supposed escape from an Egyptian tomb in which the sudden closing of a secret pivoted rock had imprisoned him while on a fictional visit to Egypt.

In the wake of the Houdini-Rahman Bey controversy, the Brooklyn *Daily Eagle* got hold of a real Egyptian and had him interview Rahman Bey. The Bey did not speak Arabic.

But the water-burial stunts did have one salutary and educational effect—they served to teach the American public that if you are accidentally locked in a closet, vault or whatever, you are not likely to smother in five minutes. If you keep calm and breathe gently, as Houdini did, you can live quite a time, while signaling and waiting for help.

This was illustrated some years later in Florida where a man, his wife, and their two children, were driving along a highway which bordered a canal. Their car blew a front tire and shot off into the canal where it settled until its roof was five feet under water. When the State Highway Patrol arrived and spotted the car, a volunteer swam down and tied a rope to the bumper. Hoisted out, the car was intact and the occupants all alive and uninjured.

As the car sank, the father had quickly cranked up the windows. He then quieted his family, pointing out that water was leaking in very slowly, that there was enough air in the car to last them if nobody cried or got panicky and all breathed evenly and slowly. The highway was crowded, other motorists had seen the plunge and help would soon arrive. He had remembered the story of Houdini in the Hotel Shelton pool!

35. *The Final Challenge*

THE REST of the summer Houdini spent getting ready for the coming season with his two-and-a-half-hour show. If he had worked hard back in the old handcuff days of bridge jumps, now he labored like one possessed. He *was* possessed—by a dread of obscurity, of becoming a has-been.

His brain swarmed with plans. The published minutes of the Washington hearings had shown that whatever else he was, Houdini was no courtroom orator. This stung him; he was always aware of his lack of formal education; now it became a threat to his greatness. He confided to Bess, Collins, and his closer friends that when the season was over, next summer, he was going up to Columbia University and cram in as many English courses as they would give him. For a fifty-two-year-old man, who was an international celebrity, this took a very special brand of courage.

Joseph Dunninger recalls several interesting anecdotes about Houdini in the final act of the melodrama which was his life.

"Like many geniuses," Dunninger says, "Houdini was almost completely self-centered. When his attention did turn to another person it was almost invariably concerned with that person's relation to Houdini. Because he never slept more than four or five hours a night it was hard for him to realize that other people needed eight. When my telephone rang at three or four in the morning I always knew who it was. One morning I received such a call; Houdini was wildly excited. 'Joe—Joe, come down here right away. I've got a pair of *live hands*!' I tried to get more details but he would say nothing more: 'I can't describe them. They're a pair of human hands. And they're

alive, Joe. They're *alive!'* To myself I said, 'This I have to see.'
I got dressed and drove to the house on 113th Street.

"Houdini let me in, obviously in the grip of some overwhelming emotion. 'Here, Joe—they're in here.' He led the way into
the library where, on a table, I saw plaster casts of Houdini's
hands. He was choked with emotion. 'There they are, Joe.
Don't they look as though they're really alive? Just to think of
it—my hands, *my poor hands* immortalized, preserved forever!
Isn't it wonderful?' I admired them properly and, as soon as I
could, headed back home to try to snatch a few hours' more
sleep. Houdini's vanity had such a strange, childlike quality
that many of its manifestations were touching rather than annoying.

"There is no doubt in my mind whatever but that Houdini
at first had a desperate hope that communication with the dead
was possible. When, one after another, every medium he investigated turned out to be a callous fraud, usually crude in technique and insulting to the sitter's intelligence, he began to
seethe. His prejudice against the spook-fakers, which my own
years of psychic research have proved well founded, unfor-
tunately also came to include everything which he could not
explain in the simplest terms. He convinced himself that hypnosis was a delusion of both operator and subject, in spite of
the vast medical literature on the science. I knew by long practice of hypnosis myself that it was a fact and a highly important
one to our study of the mysteries of the human mind. But to
Houdini it was a 'fraud' and that ended it. I could never convince him otherwise. Had I insisted in pressing the point, it
would have developed into an out-and-out quarrel between us.
Also he positively denied the possibility of the genuine tele-
pathic 'flash.' He had been at sea when his mother died and
Bess Houdini often told the story of his waking in the night and
rousing her, telling her of a dream that his mother was dead.
Later he ascribed this to 'coincidence.'

"Yet, in spite of his die-hard skepticism he seems to have
really had some presentiment of his own death. About two

o'clock one morning in October, 1926, I got a phone call from Houdini. He said, 'Joe—I just got in town today and have to hurry right out again. I want to move some stuff from the house. Can you come up with the car?' I told him I was on my way. When I got to 113th Street Houdini was waiting for me in the doorway. It was raining cats and dogs. A Holmes patrolman was with him to let him in the house so as not to set off the burglar alarms. Houdini had some bales of paper and magazines to take out and the Holmes man helped us stack them in the car. Houdini was wearing old clothes and a straw hat—this was in October, mind you—a hat with a 'bite' out of the brim in front. Bessie had been trying to get that hat away from him for years. After we had the stuff packed in the car he tipped the Holmes man fifty cents and then said to me, 'Hey— let's get something to eat.' We went around the corner to a delicatessen and had pastrami sandwiches. We came back, got in the car and Houdini said, 'Drive through the park, Joe.' When we got to the exit on Central Park West around 72nd Street he grabbed my arm; in a hollow, tragic voice he said, 'Go back, Joe!'

" 'Go back where?'

" 'Go back to the house, Joe.'

" 'Why—did you forget something?'

" 'Don't ask questions, Joe. Just turn around and go back.'

"I drove back to the house. By this time it was raining even harder, if that was possible, but Houdini ignored it; he got out of the car, took off the straw hat and stood looking up at the dark house with the rain streaming down his face. Then he got back in the car, saying nothing. When we again approached the western exit of the park his shoulders began to shake. He was crying. Finally he said, 'I've seen my house for the last time, Joe. I'll never see my house again.' As far as I know, he never did. We drove for a way in silence and then he said suddenly, 'Joe—you know that bronze coffin I made to expose that faker, Rahman Bey? Not only for that, Joe. I made it to be buried in.'

"Like so many of these incidents, we have no way of know-

ing how many other 'presentiments of death' Houdini had before, which did not come true. But this one I know about for I
was there." So Dunninger contributes to the Houdini legend.

Houdini's plans for the future, in more optimistic moments,
were ambitious and elaborate. One of them concerned a University of Magic, and it is interesting to trace this idea from
its source. It seems to stem from his offer to teach magicians
(and would-be spirit mediums) back in the Nineties when in
desperation he started the mail-order magic business, operating
from the flat on 69th Street. Now the plan burst into full bloom,
sparked with ideas from his old enemy, now a close friend, Dr.
A. M. Wilson, editor of *The Sphinx.*

Between them, Houdini and Wilson worked out a whole
curriculum for their proposed University, nine courses in all,
consisting of an orientation course for beginners on Magic as
an Art and a Science, proceeding to the History of Magic (always one of Houdini's enthusiasms), the Philosophy of Magic
(Prof. Brander Matthews, a highly skilled amateur, would be
perfect for this course), the Psychology of Magic (which would
reveal to the student Houdini's own vast fund of experience
in misdirection, the true secret of the jail break, and other
spectacular stunts), the Ethics of Magic (on which Houdini
had passionate convictions regarding the use of magical principles while claiming supernormal powers, as well as that field
of ethics involving swiping other people's ideas), Preparation
for a Career in Magic, Presentation of a Magical Entertainment, Advertising for Magicians (at which Houdini was a past-
master), and last and all-embracing, Showmanship for Magicians. This was, in the sense that it broke down the field of
magic into many important component parts, a novel approach and has since been covered in many fine textbooks, such
as the famous Tarbell Course in magic, and the works of John
Booth and Dariel Fitzkee.

But all these plans were shelved when Harry took the big
show out that fall. With him on the tour he carried a bronze

coffin, and in Worcester, Massachusetts, he used it in a publicity stunt.

The strain of managing a show of that size, even with Collins as stage manager and Bess as chancellor of the exchequer, was exhausting. The format was the same as the previous season, with a few added marvels. The three acts consisted of magic, escapery, and the spirit exposé. This was, for Houdini, two hours and a half before the audience, selling it hard every minute. If he felt the strain unduly he was much too proud to reveal it. To him the sweetest sight in the world was a packed house, the sweetest sound, the crash of its applause. "Let's get out there and give 'em a show!"

They opened in Providence, R. I., on October 3rd. Then, on Thursday of that week, Bess came down with an attack diagnosed as food poisoning. She was so ill that Houdini got relays of nurses to look after her. The following day, Friday, he sat up with her all night, too worried about her to sleep. Nor did he sleep all the next day. Bess had started to improve but was still very weak when he went to the theater for the closing show. After the show he supervised packing and loading for the next jump, which was Albany, N. Y. He sent Bess on to Albany with a nurse and shortly after midnight he and Collins took a day coach for New York City. Houdini had a list of chores for them both and on the train he worked away on publicity ideas with Collins. All day Sunday he was busy in the city, tying up a number of loose ends preparatory to heading west.

When pressed for time Houdini would stir a dozen eggs into a quart of milk in place of a meal, but that evening he had a dinner date at the home of his attorney, Bernard M. L. Ernst. When he got to Ernst's apartment, the family had not yet returned from a weekend in the country. The maid let him in and Houdini lay down on a sofa in the living room and slept for twenty minutes, his first sleep in nearly three days. When the family arrived he snapped awake and visited with them. He had legal business to go over with Ernst after dinner. He had planned to make the eight o'clock train for Albany but decided to stay a few hours longer. He phoned Frank Ducrot, a magic dealer and manufacturer who had taken over Martinka's Palace of Magic shop. Finally Houdini got a train for Albany which arrived there at seven in the morning. This, too, was a coach. When he reached Albany, Bess was much improved. He lay down and got an hour's rest before hurrying out to set up a publicity stunt and make special arrangements for Monday night's opening, which his old friend Al Smith, now governor of the State, was expected to attend.

The complex of circumstance which eventually led to disaster began that evening, Monday, October 10th.

As Collins was fitting the mahogany stocks of the Water Torture Cell to his ankles at the close of the second act, Houdini was obviously suffering from extreme fatigue if not exhaustion. As the assistants hauled on the hoist which raised him in the air for his descent into the water-filled tank, Houdini gasped. Collins hurriedly motioned for them to lower him to the stage and released his feet. Houdini sat on the stage, rubbing his ankle and then had Collins help him up. Turning to the audience with his warmest smile, he asked if there was a doctor in the house—he had felt something snap in his ankle. There happened to be a doctor present who was also a bone specialist, Dr. Hannock. The curtain was lowered while the doctor hurried backstage. By exploring gently with his fingers, he determined that a small bone in the ankle was broken and advised immediate X-rays. Houdini grinned. "But, doctor—I've a show to finish!" The doctor shook his head, and put on an emergency splint. He had done his best.

Houdini did his needle trick in place of Upside Down, hopping on one foot backward across the stage as the needles appeared from his mouth. He rested during the intermission, then gave his full repertoire of spirit-medium tricks for the third act. Only then would he consent to proper examination.

At Memorial Hospital the X-ray confirmed Dr. Hannock's

diagnosis—there was a fracture of the ankle. The bone was set and put in a cast.

Back at the hotel Houdini sat up all night again; his ankle was so painful he could not sleep anyway, so he used the time in devising a special support for the ankle so that he could continue working in the show.

Albany was a split week. On Wednesday he closed and loaded for Schenectady.

Even with the brace the ankle was painful, but he gave no sign of it when he was on stage.

The next jump was Montreal, Quebec, opening at the Princess Theater on Monday, October 17th. The ankle was knitting well; a doctor in Montreal confirmed this and advised Houdini to give it complete rest for a few weeks. To this advice he got a typical dose of good-natured scorn from the superman. Houdini was used to minor injuries—cuts, bruises, abrasions, torn muscles, breaks, and strains—they were all alike to him. His way was to ignore them—get out there and give the folks a show.

At Montreal's famous McGill University, Houdini had arranged to give a lecture on spiritualism and it went off with a bang to the delight of students and faculty. One of the undergraduates, an art major, made a sketch of Houdini and showed it to him after the talk. Houdini admired the drawing and invited the lad to visit him backstage and make some more sketches.

On Friday morning the young artist appeared at the theater bringing with him his sketch pad. He also brought along two friends, one of whom was a college boxing star.

By this time, Houdini's mail had risen to staggering proportions. His fraternal activities—he was now an Elk and a Mason in addition to being national president of the S.A.M.—accounted for some of it. Letters from skeptics congratulating him on his exposés of fakers made up a large part. An even larger part consisted of letters from believers denouncing him.

Houdini was lying on a couch in the dressing room, going

over his mail, when the three boys came in. He excused himself for reading and explained that he wanted to sort the mail,
looking for personal letters of importance.

The young boxer referred to a statement which Houdini had
made in his lecture that by clean living and regular exercise he
had kept the physique of youth and that he could let the strongest man aim a blow at any portion of his body above the belt
except the face.

"Mr. Houdini—could you let me throw a punch at your midriff with all my might?" the young boxer asked.

"No 'Mister'—just Houdini. Yes, certainly."

"Could I try it—right now?"

"Sure."

Houdini started to get up from the couch when the lad let
fly a punch to the midsection with everything he had.

Houdini gasped and clutched his middle. The boy fell back,
horrified. The master magician struggled to his feet, fighting
for breath, his face white. Then he got command of himself
and seeing the look on the boy's face he said, "Not that
way . . . got to get . . . set for it." He stood up straight, tight-
ening his belly muscles. "All right—now hit me. Go on—hit
me."

The boy hit him; this time Houdini's midsection felt like an
oak plank. The lad was duly impressed.

When the students had gone, Houdini rubbed his abdomen
for a time, feeling that the first blow, for which he had been
unprepared, had torn a muscle strand. Finally the pain subsided and he plunged into the day's work.

During the matinee he suffered intermittent pain in the right
side and faithfully ignored it.

By evening the pain was getting worse. It bothered him all
during the show and when he was finally back at the hotel with
Bess he mentioned it. He asked her to rub his side with alcohol;
thought he had a torn muscle. He couldn't sleep. The nurse,
still in attendance on Bess, suggested getting a doctor but to
no avail.

The next day, during the matinee, fatigue seemed to sweep over him in waves; the stage, the glittering props, the scurrying assistants quivered in a dancing haze. Then his head would clear and he would go on with the show.

During the interval between matinee and evening performance he lay on a cot in the dressing room. He was having spasmodic chills and sweats.

Still he forced his way through the evening performance but at the end of it, in the dressing room, he had to have Collins help him into his street clothes.

That was Saturday night—closing. Next jump, Detroit.

Urged by Bess, Collins sent a wire ahead of them from the train. When they pulled into Detroit, they were met by a doctor. Houdini's temperature was one hundred and two degrees.

He scorned going to a hospital. But when they got to the hotel he crawled into bed and had Bess pile blankets on him. His chill, which shook the bed, lasted a half hour.

In spite of his loud refusals, Bess sent for a committee of doctors. They were unanimous—Houdini had appendicitis and needed an operation at once.

Bess wept and argued all day when Houdini was not dozing uneasily. When curtain time approached he asked for news from the box office. The report came back, "Sold out. Not a vacant seat in the house." That settled it.

"Help me up. They've paid their money to see Houdini. By God, they're going to get a show." His temperature was now one hundred and four.

There is such a thing as too much courage and Houdini showed it now. From the front, the audience could hardly suspect what was going on across the footlights. They were watching a dying man.

The smile, by long habit, was as broad and captivating as ever. But the magician moved slowly with a detached, dreamy air. When off stage, he had to be held up. Once he was before the footlights, he straightened and went through the motions.

In one illusion, in which he produced a number of girls from a supposedly empty cabinet, Houdini's "business" called for him to walk around to the rear of the cabinet and jump through it to show that there were no mirrors.

This time he tried to lift one foot to the floor of the cabinet and froze, staring down as if something in the cabinet had caught his attention. The agony in his guts had paralyzed him. Collins hurried on stage and Houdini grabbed hold of him to steady himself.

When he came to a magic feat where he reached into a tiny glass bowl and from it drew yard after yard of bright silk, he began and then froze again. He whispered hoarsely, "Collins—take it."

Jim Collins finished the trick.

That was the end. Houdini had collapsed in the wings.

The operating room of Grace Hospital was alerted.

As Houdini was wheeled in, he said huskily to the two orderlies, "Go on, I can still lick the two of yez."

The exploring surgeons found a gangrenous appendix and peritonitis far advanced. In the days before antibiotic drugs, a virulent infection of the peritoneal cavity was a death sentence; survival was a miracle.

Houdini regained consciousness with drains in his abdomen. Bess had taken a turn for the worse and was put to bed in the same hospital. She was wheeled in once a day to Houdini's bedside.

The battler of handcuffs and strait jackets had a different adversary now, but he entered this final fight with his old bulldog tenacity. He held his own day after day, every twelve hours seeming like a miracle to the attending physicians.

The accident had occurred on the morning of October 21st. The operation was performed on the night of October 24th to 25th.

On the 29th he was still fighting and seemed a little stronger. When Bess was wheeled in for her daily visit he called her close to him and whispered, "Mother never reached me. If . . . anything happens . . . you must be prepared. Remember the message: *Rosabelle, believe*. When you hear those words . . . know it is Houdini speaking. . . ."

Nurse Sophie Rosenblatt bustled Bess away in the interests of both patients.

Still, the defier of restraints, the conqueror of prison cells fought on.

Hardeen had been sent for and sat with his brother through the hours. Finally, a little after one o'clock on October 31st, Houdini muttered, "Dash . . ." His brother gripped his hand. "Dash . . . I'm tired of fighting. Guess this thing is . . . going to get me." He closed his eyes. He never opened them again.

Dash took over the show and finished the tour.

Houdini returned to New York in the great bronze coffin of his underwater burial challenge. And in it he was buried, a packet of his mother's letters serving him for a pillow.

The funeral service was held in the Elk's Clubhouse on 43rd Street in Manhattan, beginning at 11 o'clock, the Elks' "hour of remembrance." A Masonic ceremony followed, with a white lambskin laid across the coffin and the assembled Masons filing by, each dropping a bit of evergreen, symbol of everlasting life. At the close, an officer of the Society of American Magicians broke the ceremonial wand over the casket. Rabbi Drachman gave the funeral oration.

Among the honorary pallbearers was Martin Beck, who had given the young magician his first break twenty-seven years before; there was William Morris, the happy warrior of the Morris-Keith feud of vaudeville's stormy days; there was Joe Rinn, Houdini's boyhood friend, and old Oscar Teale, who had done illustrations for Houdini's books; Bernard Ernst, his attorney, was there with Adolph S. Ochs of the *Times* and Orson Munn of the *Scientific American*. Show business was represented by Charles Dillingham, Adolph Zukor, and Lee Shubert.

Above the grave in Macpelah Cemetery where he was buried beside his father and mother rises a monument to Houdini, surmounted by a stone bust of the great escapist. It is an elaborate tribute. He designed it himself.

Epilogue—Telegram from Heaven

THE TORNADO was still, the maelstrom had ceased its spinning. Bess Houdini could sleep the whole night through, without being wakened to admire the fruits of genius or listen to the denunciation of some fourflusher, some faker.

She could sleep the whole night undisturbed—if she could sleep.

Thirty-two years she had lived on the slope of a volcano in more or less constant eruption and now there was no more white-hot enthusiasm, no more challenges, no more tender love letters left under her pillow.

Houdini's death found his affairs in their habitual state—mad confusion, to all but himself. And now he was not there to bring order out of the chaos.

Beatrice put up the house for sale and in a few months it was sold, with all its secret trap doors, its sliding panels.

The collection of books on magic—5,200, many of them rarities—was left, by Houdini's will, to the Library of Congress.

That will was a revealing document which had been redrawn time and again by Bernard Ernst as his stormy client patched up old feuds and started new ones. Houdini added codicils and struck out beneficiaries as passion moved him. The collection of playbills and letters, with many Lincoln items, was to be sold, too, and when the various bequests had been met, the moiety of the estate was to be invested in improved Manhattan real estate, the income from which went to Bess.

Hardeen got the magic equipment, the handcuffs, the Water Torture Cell (which he was too tall to operate).

The Lincoln holograph letters were said to be the largest private collection in the world. Houdini had, also, autographs of all but two of the signers of the Declaration of Independence.

As fast as these were sold, Bess received shipments, ordered by Houdini, from dealers all over the world. In the end she paid over $20,000 for posthumous deliveries.

On the other hand, the nonmagic playbills sold for $35,000. When the Gordian knot was finally untangled by Bernard Ernst, it is said that the liquid assets of the estate came to $500,000. After the bequests, Bess had a comfortable income for life. It was not as much as was rumored but she would never want.

Then a crucial question arose—what was she to do now? It is hard to break the pattern of thirty years. Ever since she was nineteen her main concern had been to keep Houdini well clothed and fed as often as he would take the time, to squirrel away enough money for them to move the show at the end of the week and meet their payroll; Houdini, in an auction room, could run wild when a treasure came up that he had to have. Now there was no more worry about money—she had money. There was no more waiting for Houdini to get out of a box underwater or untie himself from a skyscraper girder. There was nothing. . . .

One of the most destructive experiences a writer can have is to sell a novel to the movies after years of a grinding, hand-to-mouth existence. Like a deep-sea fish, accustomed to the pressures of the deep, when brought to the surface suddenly by a net, he often explodes when the pressure is removed.

Beatrice Houdini did not exactly explode but she drifted. She tried running a tea room in New York, which kept her busy enough, but she could never allow a magician to pick up a check and the venture did not prosper.

She thought of getting up an act of her own—after all, she had worked the trunk trick with Harry off and on all their married life. The act got as far as a tryout date and then fizzled.

A middle-aged widow, still attractive and with an income, is a target for assorted characters and Bess was always a trusting, generous soul.

Now at last, there was no one to boss her, no one to tell her she should drink no more than two glasses of champagne. There wasn't any champagne but there was bathtub gin and grapefruit juice at the parties, the constant parties which brought the Jazz Age to its skyrocket close.

Making one's own decisions is an art which requires practice. From the moment Harry had put his arms about her at Coney Island that night so long ago, he had made the decisions. So Bess drifted, worried over by a legion of old friends, most of them in magic or the newspaper business.

One of Bess's newspaper friends was a chap who lived in Greenwich Village and with him she frequently went to the famous Hubert's Cafeteria on Sheridan Square. And there she met many of the *Evening Graphic* staff, among them a tall, ash-blond, hard-faced woman who wrote under the by-line of Rea Jaure.

Bess still had a standing offer of $10,000 to any spirit medium who could produce the secret code message which Houdini had arranged with her and of which he had reminded her when he was dying. Messages had come thick and fast but not the real message, nothing Bess was inclined to take seriously. Finally, toward the end of 1928, she withdrew the offer. There had been no real claimants, no psychics had brought the two revealing words.

The stage was now set for the entrance of one of the most enigmatic figures of our time, the Rev. Arthur Ford.

Several years before, a good-looking young minister, ordained in the Christian Church of the Disciples of Christ, had taken the lecture platform on the Chautauqua circuit, speaking about psychic research, its difficulties and triumphs, the evidence so far accumulated of Survival. He was a Southern gentleman of exquisite manners, a native of Titusville, Florida. Arthur Ford seems to have taken as his touchstone the admonition of the Nazarene on sending disciples out to preach "as sheep in the midst of wolves": "*. . . be ye therefore wise as serpents and harmless as doves.*"

Wise as a serpent, gentle as a dove was the Rev. Arthur Ford. He had challenged magician Howard Thurston to a debate in Carnegie Hall and come off the winner. Thurston's press agent was blamed for claiming feats of medium-exposure which the magician could not back up with evidence in black and white.

Rumor had it that the engaging young "medium"—Ford was now pastor of the First Spiritualist Church of Manhattan—was planning a lecture tour with Bess. Presumably Beatrice Houdini would uphold the beliefs of her late husband and tell the stories of his exposures of frauds, while Ford would recount his belief in the genuineness of some phenomena, notably evidential messages which could only come from discarnate entities.

Rea Jaure represented the type of sob-sister which developed in the Roaring Twenties and has since, mercifully, become all but extinct in American journalism, along with that daily magazine-called-a-newspaper, the notorious *Graphic*.

This tabloid performed one valuable service for the other newspapers of New York—by contrast it made the other tabloids look respectable. It had been founded by Bernarr Macfadden, fiery advocate of the physical culture life, fasting, vegetable juices, and any passing fad which took his fancy. To build the paper he had secured as publisher one of the country's ablest editors, Emile Gauvreau, a crusading fugitive from an ultraconservative New England paper. The managing editor was another New Englander, a tall, gray-haired, craggy man, also a newspaper ace—Bill Plummer. To the staff, Gauvreau was known as "Little Napoleon," Plummer as "The Iron Duke." How newsmen of such caliber could get out a thing like the *Graphic* year after year is one of the mysteries of a mysterious profession. The *Graphic* cared little about news. It made its own news, much of it created fresh on the typewriters of its rewrite men, of whom the most adroit was Bob Campbell.

If F. Scott Fitzgerald was the conscience of the Jazz Age, Gauvreau and his boys were its raucous cheer-leaders. One of their contributions to the fine arts was called the "composograph," which grew to be a highly-skilled production under an artist proficient with an airbrush. The composograph was a faked photograph-layout, in which the heads of celebrities in the news were superimposed on the bodies of models, in order to show what may have happened, should happen, or was happening now in places barred to photographers. One of the most successful of such layouts showed the recently deceased Rudolph Valentino being escorted through Heaven in angel robes by the equally deceased Enrico Caruso. A message from Valentino, supposedly secured through a spirit medium, graced the story.

Rea Jaure covered things from the woman's angle. When the *Graphic* was "put to bed" at two in the morning, Rea frequently dropped into Hubert's Cafeteria for a snack. Also she kept her ear to the ground for the makings of good stories. When she met Bess Houdini she began boring in to find out if her long married life with the Self-Liberator had been as idyllic as Bess had portrayed it in *Houdini: His Life Story from the Recollections and Documents of Beatrice Houdini*. The author of the book, Harold Kellock, was an able writer on business and finance, assigned to Bess by the publishers. He knew nothing about magic but turned out a workmanlike job, telling everything just as Bess wanted it. The book was full of sentimental anecdotes which showed the Mysteriarch as an ideal lover and husband. Rea Jaure had her doubts.

These were probably encouraged by one of the most mischievous little minxes ever to be shot through a trap door into a magician's trick box—a natural redhead named Daisy White. She was a tiny thing, beautfully formed and with mocking green eyes. Knowing Houdini's prudishness and ultraconservatism in his attitude toward women, Daisy had written him several torrid love letters just to see what would happen. Houdini never threw away any scrap of paper unless it was a clipping which boosted an imitator. He kept the gag-love-letters hidden. After his death Bess found them and is said to have pitched quite a fit until Daisy explained the circumstances and managed to pacify her.*

During December of 1928, Rea Jaure got Bess in a mellow mood and extracted a promise that she would do a series for the *Graphic*—to be written by Rea and signed by Bess—called "The Life and Loves of Houdini."

Bess interrupted this project by being taken sick. She was in the hospital over Christmas and had a Christmas tree in her room.

Rea wanted a picture of Bess in her hospital bed to run with the first installment of the Life and Loves but at the desk the hospital officials sternly refused to have any newspaper photographers bothering the patients. Rea departed to map out her strategy. On the paper she was known as a woman who would stop at nothing—literally at nothing—to get a story.

What Rea did was to call the *Graphic* and ask them to send her Big Mac. Big Mac was a unique character, an elderly man, six foot four, with an enormous paunch. When washed, shaved, and dressed in cutaway coat and striped trousers, he could pass for a senator, a judge, a special agent of the medical examiner's office or anything impressive which would get him past barriers for the purpose of stealing photographs or smuggling in cameras. In this case, Big Mac appeared at the hospital as a specialist, sent for by Mrs. Houdini for a consultation. When he got to her room, carrying his black bag, he took from the bag a camera, a flash pan, and a can of magnesium powder. Big

* Daisy White, formerly with the Ducrot show, worked for a time behind the counter of Martinka's magic shop, where the author of this history was duly impressed by her. She was given to wearing low-necked dresses. When she demonstrated a trick her misdirection was perfect—she had but to lean over and she could switch decks of cards or do anything else without fear of detection. It was impossible to take one's eyes from the delightful cleavage.

Mac, in a pinch, served as a photographer. In this case, however, he bungled it badly for when he set off the magnesium powder it ignited the dry needles of the Christmas tree. In the ensuing commotion, Bess became hysterical and delivered her candid opinion of Rea Jaure and all her works and emissaries. Jaure was boiling, since Bess told her that the article series was all off and she wanted nothing further to do with Rea, Big Mac, flash powder, or the *Evening Graphic*.

Leaving the hospital under protest and some say with assistance, Rea Jaure swore she would get even with Bess for welshing on the story. She may have tried later to patch up the quarrel.

Bess left the hospital and took refuge at the house of her sister in the Inwood section of upper Manhattan.

Meanwhile the Rev. Arthur Ford, on going into trance, had produced, through his control spirit "David Fletcher," a message purporting to come from Houdini's mother mentioning the key word *Forgive*. Or so it was claimed. Ford, like most message mediums, always stated that what happened when he was "in trance" was not available to him and he had to take the word of the sitters as to what his control spirit said. The Forgive message, Ford's sitters claimed, had come through via Fletcher on February 8, 1928.

Then, on January 7, 1929, Daisy White ran into Joseph Dunninger on the street and told him that a big story was about to break involving Houdini and Bess. She refused to go into details.

On January 8th the *Graphic* burst out with the following:

> From the depths of the great unknown, the voice of Harry Houdini came back today to allay the feverish suffering of his widow Beatrice, as she tossed restlessly on a sick bed in her home. . . .
>
> Although near death herself, Mrs. Houdini has not the slightest doubt that the voice from the grave was that of her beloved husband, for it spoke in a code known only to the great magician and his faithful helpmeet on earth.

Slowly, the words, nine in all, fell from the lips of the medium, who, with a party of spectators, were grouped about the sick bed.

"Rosabelle—answer—tell—pray, answer—look—tell—answer, answer—tell—"

And, according to the code devised by Houdini some four years ago, the mystic utterances translated signified the single word:

"BELIEVE."

The Rev. Ford had, while possessed by his control spirit Fletcher, given out with a message from Houdini containing the code words. That this had actually taken place was attested by several friends of Ford; their integrity was never questioned. They got in touch with Bess and arranged a séance at her home for the next day. When they arrived, Rea Jaure was with them. In the séance, the voice of Fletcher, using Ford's vocal chords, again reported a message from Houdini, containing the nine words and explaining how they made up the evidential word *Believe*.

One of the sitters wrote out a declaration that this was, indeed, the proper message from Houdini, and Bess signed it.

Then, on January 10th, the *Graphic* exploded with another front-page headline:

HOUDINI HOAX EXPOSED!

'Seance' Prearranged by 'Medium' and Widow
—Story on Page 3

(At the foot of the page a blurb announced that *"Booze!" Or the Confessions of a Prohibitionist's Daughter* could be found on page 19.)

The story on page 3 carried the head:

HOUDINI MESSAGE BIG HOAX!

Ford Admits He Got Secret Code From Magician's Widow

The story was by-lined "Edward Churchill," apparently one of the *noms de Gauvreau* of Bob Campbell. It began:

The GRAPHIC today is in a position to expose one of the most monumental "psychic" hoaxes ever perpetrated on the American public—the purported communication from the spirit world of Harry Houdini to his widow, Beatrice. Evidence gathered by this newspaper shows that the sensational message was carefully rehearsed prior to its "premiere."

The GRAPHIC further reveals that Mrs. Houdini, who professed only a slight acquaintance with Arthur Ford, the "medium" through which the "message" passed, has been a close friend of his for a year or more.

The truth of the affair is that Rea Jaure, a GRAPHIC reporter, prepared her story twenty-four hours before the seance was held.

Miss Jaure held up her information pending an opportunity to get all of the facts in connection with the hoax, rather than publish a premature and inconclusive story. . . .

Why the *Graphic* ran the story of the message—which had been prepared twenty-four hours before it happened—without comment was never divulged. Perhaps the *Graphic* editors felt that their readers were by this time used to reading things written before they happened. (Some have doubted that the purchasers of the *Graphic* could read at all and suggest that they bought it only to look at the composographs.)

The story went on to reveal that on the previous evening in the apartment of Miss Jaure, two representatives of the *Graphic* —managing editor William E. Plummer and "Edward Churchill"—were hiding in a breakfast nook which was used to store Miss Jaure's steamer trunks. They went into hiding at 11 o'clock and the Rev. Arthur Ford arrived at 11:20 in response to a phone call from Rea. The conversation between the sob-sister and the medium was given in some detail, as scribbled by the two newshawks hiding in the nook. Rea led Ford to admit having been to a party with her and with Bess a year before. When informed that Rea was planning to reveal that the secret of the code and the message was in her possession twenty-four hours before the séance, Ford allegedly offered her a bribe, then tried to appease her in other ways, to no avail. When asked point blank by the "girl" reporter if he had gotten the message from the spirit of Houdini, Ford allegedly replied, "You know, Rea, I could never have done that."

There was more cross-talk in which Ford admitted that he and Bess were planning a "free lance" lecture tour together.

Finally the reverend got his hat and left hurriedly, but was marked by the doorman of the apartment house as the same man who had been addressed as "Mr. Ford" by Rea Jaure earlier in the evening.

Dunninger pitched into the controversy to defend Bess from the charges of conspiracy with Ford. He pointed out that the secret code which transmitted the letters B-E-L-I-E-V-E was an old "mind reading" code the Houdinis had used in their *musée* days and was printed in Kellock's book where Ford or anyone else could have read it. Further, he informed reporters, Nurse Sophie Rosenblatt, who attended Houdini during his last hours, had heard him murmur the two words *Rosabelle—Believe* to Bess. Miss Rosenblatt might innocently have mentioned the supposed secret message and it could have reached the ears of Ford.

Bess wrote a poignant letter to columnist Walter Winchell (on contract to the *Graphic* but a bitter enemy of Gauvreau), disclaiming that she had done anything to betray her husband's trust.

Ford was called on the carpet by the officers of his church and expelled for conduct unbecoming a spiritualist minister. Shortly afterward he was reinstated.

A mysterious man who admitted to being a fish-peddler and who had a girl friend who knew Daisy White came forward to declare that Daisy had learned the secret message from Houdini before he died.

The story in the New York *Telegram* of January 15th ended, "Little Daisy White at Ford's apartment admitted knowing the fish-peddler slightly but denied everything else!"

In an interview with Bess the Los Angeles *Examiner* of July 22, 1935, quoted her as saying:

"I receive many messages that are supposed to come from Houdini through mediums and strange séances but they never mean anything to me. Very often I go to séances, hoping and praying that the signals Houdini gave me will be heard. No message comes to me while I am waiting to hear."

The name "Rosabelle" was not a pet name of Houdini's for Bess, as was believed. She said later, "Houdini would have called me either Bess or Mike." It was the name of a sentimental ditty which Bess had been warbling in the Coney Island music hall where, on the same bill, were two boys with a trick box. For Bess and Harry, it was "their song."

The Rev. Arthur Ford continued as an eloquent expounder of the religion of spiritualism. I once sat for an hour in the living room of his beautifully furnished home in Coral Gables, Florida, hoping that he could spare me a few minutes for an interview, but the gentleman was apparently too busy—or too cagey—to see unidentified callers.

Wise as a serpent, gentle as a dove. In his autobiography he claims that he was "impersonated" that night at Rea Jaure's apartment and it is quite possible that he was. Plummer and Campbell never actually saw the man whose voice they heard. And Rea Jaure was out to "get" Bess. If she cooked up the whole business it would have, indeed, been a most exquisite revenge. Rea Jaure is dead now. So is Bill Plummer and Emile Gauvreau. And, mercifully, the *Graphic* is no more. Even its back files have vanished from the newspaper room of the New York Public Library!

After years of loneliness and confusion, Bess came into calm waters at last. This was due in large part to a gentleman who acted as her manager—Edward Saint. He was a magician and mentalist from California, and a psychic researcher in the best Houdini "ghost-breaker" tradition. Saint was a dapper little man with a shiny bald head, a waxed mustache and a neat gray Vandyke beard; he wore spats and carried a walking stick with a large "cat's eye" stone in the head, held by a golden bird's claw.*

Time eventually took its toll of the people in this history. Dr. Crandon died in 1938 and the "blond witch" Margery followed him three years later. Bess Houdini suffered a fatal heart attack on February 11, 1943, while on the train from California to New York. Hardeen died in 1945; he alone knew many of the answers to riddles in his fantastic brother's life, but in the war years the energies of writers were turned to other projects and what Dash had to tell is unrecorded.

Daisy White, too, of the mocking eyes and snowy bosom has passed on to "join the majority" as the Victorians used to phrase it. And so has ever-faithful Jimmy Collins.

All that remains of Houdini now are the files of letters, the trunks of handcuffs and keys, the stored apparatus with which he "cast the glamourie." But the legend promises to live when all the handcuffs have been devoured by rust.

Into fifty-two years he packed enough stormy living for a dozen lifetimes. That he was a magician everyone knows. At straight magic he was often strangely inept. At his specialty he was magnificent. He was an expert underwater swimmer and high diver, a master lock-picker, a pioneer aviator, magical historian, movie stunt man, psychic investigator, author and editor, genius of publicity, intimate of presidents, entertainer of kings, vaudeville headliner for twenty years. He was charitable and vindictive, generous and penny-pinching; like a little boy he would forget to wash his ears and change his clothes— Bess had to nag him to keep him presentable. He never refused to play a benefit, without pay, for the inmates of asylums and

* One of Ed Saint's most ingenious devices for proving to a group of psychic investigators that they were not qualified to detect fraud was his trick of making the pans of a precision balance move when it was sealed in its glass housing. He did it by dumping in a number of fleas from the hollowed-out end of a pencil. The fleas, while invisible to the investigators, weighed enough to depress the sensitive pans of the balance jumping on and off. At the end of the experiment Saint had the glass case opened and reached his hand into it for some plausible reason. The fleas vanished up his coat sleeve. They were human fleas, secured from a friend who ran a flea circus.

prisons. Too vain to wear glasses in his later years, he carried a magnifying glass for casual reading. A nonsmoker, he kept his fingers busy by rolling a half dollar over and over his knuckles, one of the most difficult flourishes in magic. He was too absent-minded to drive a car. Fascinated by cemeteries, he extended his grave-visiting to the tombs of his friends' parents. Athlete and showman, collector and pamphleteer, Houdini lives on in legend noted for but one thing:

To the generations that have risen since his death he is "the man who walked through walls."

OPINIONATED BIBLIOGRAPHY

ABBOTT, DAVID P.—*Behind the Scenes with the Mediums.* The Open Court Publishing Co. Chicago. 1907. Basic textbook for magicians and mentalists on billet reading methods. If mediums have also learned their stuff from it this is no fault of the author's.

ALEXANDER, C.—*The Life and Mysteries of the Celebrated Dr. "Q."* Nelson Enterprises. Columbus, Ohio. 1946. Reprint of an earlier work, copyrighted in 1921 by C. Alexander. The first textbook on the technique of the vaudeville crystal-gazing act, together with an encyclopedic collection of magical data, including anecdotes of early handcuff kings.

ANONYMOUS—*Revelations of a Spirit Medium.* Facsimile edition published by Kegan Paul, Trench, Trubner & Co. London. 1922. With notes by Harry Price and Eric Dingwall. Much of the material was available prior to 1922 only in Hereward Carrington's *The Physical Phenomena of Spiritualism,* excellently written and illustrated with photographs. Carrington's book is, in all probability, based to a large extent on the material in the *Revelations.*

BOSTON, GEORGE L., and PARRISH, ROBERT—*Inside Magic.* The Beechhurst Press. New York. 1947. Fascinating chapters on magical history in the United States with a section on "Harry Houdini and the Escape Legend," drawn apparently from the recollections of Jim Collins. This must be read with the thought in mind that Collins may have embroidered a bit on his anecdotes of the Boss.

CANNELL, J. C.—*The Secrets of Houdini.* Hutchinson & Co. London. 1932. The author, a British journalist and amateur magician, writes with devotion to Houdini's memory. Some of his explanations, notably of the challenge mail-bag escape, are real contributions to magical lore. Other "explanations" are fantastic, such as his method for the "working" panel of the underwater box, and his explanations of the vanishing elephant, the milk can, and the brick wall. No source is given for the methods explained; it is probably Goldston.

CARR, JOHN DICKSON—*The Life of Sir Arthur Conan Doyle.* Harper & Brothers. New York. 1949. Stirring account of the life of Britain's "last medieval knight." Carr, mystery writer, historical novelist, and swordsman, is the ideal biographer. The book makes no mention of Houdini.

DUNNINGER, JOSEPH—*Inside the Medium's Cabinet.* David Kemp and Company. New York. 1935. Excellent firsthand account, by the successor of Houdini in exposing psychic fraud, of Nino Pecoraro and others of like ilk, with two revealing chapters giving many of the details of the Arthur Ford "Houdini message" intrigue.

ENCYCLOPAEDIA BRITANNICA, 11th Edition, *"Conjuring."* Article signed "H.H." written by Houdini. Half of the article concerns the most significant development of the art in recent years; namely, the challenge escape illusions of Houdini.

ENDORE, GUY—*Methinks the Lady . . .* Duell, Sloan and Pearce. New York. 1945. Suspense novel with psychoanalytical setting, containing a brief reference to Houdini from a Freudian standpoint.

ERNST, BERNARD M. L., and CARRINGTON, HEREWARD—*Houdini and Conan Doyle/ The Story of a Strange Friendship.* Albert and Charles Boni. New York. 1932. Annotated correspondence of the two great figures in the spiritualism controversy. According to collectors of Houdini letters, the correspondence has been extensively edited.

EVANS, HENRY RIDGELY—*History of Conjuring and Magic.* International Brotherhood of Magicians. Kenton, Ohio. 1928. Treasure house of data on magic, magicians, and productions. It contains the original Heller mind-reading code, used in the Houdini message.

FAST, FRANCIS R.—*The Houdini Messages* (pamphlet). Privately printed. 1929. Fast, a sincere spiritualist, was a friend of Arthur Ford's and was present at the séance at which the first Houdini message came through. The pamphlet is a defense of Ford and Beatrice Houdini.

FORD, ARTHUR, and BRO, MARGUERITE HARMON—*Nothing So Strange.* Harper & Brothers. New York. 1958. Enigmatic as al-

ways, Ford's life story is charitable, plausible, and in spots deeply
moving, as in the section dealing with his recovery from alco-
holism by means of a program which almost inevitably leads to
a genuine spiritual awakening. The author of the present volume
can do nothing but wish the Rev. Ford continued health, happi-
ness, and success in every honest endeavor.

GIBSON, WALTER B.—*Houdini's Escapes and Magic.* Blue Ribbon
Books. New York. 1930. The most available source for the
modus operandi of Houdini in handcuff escapes, challenges, and
prepared devices.

GIBSON, WALTER B., and YOUNG, MORRIS N., M.D.—*Houdini on
Magic.* Dover Publications. 1953. The editors have performed a
valuable service in collating many of Houdini's own writings
which appeared in pamphlets and books now rare. The illustrations, including photographs from the McManus and Young
collections, are plentiful; many never had book publication before. The bibliography is excellent.

GOLDSTON, WILL—*Sensational Tales of Mystery Men.* Will Goldston. London. 1929. Salty memoirs dealing with the great escapist, among others; written apparently to offset the saccharine
flavor of the Kellock "Life." Goldston depended on his memory
and is not too accurate in dates and other pertinent facts. As a
convinced spiritualist, Goldston was probably bitter about Houdini's slam-bang denunciations of all spiritualism as bunk.

GREEN, ABEL, and LAURIE, JOE, JR.—*SHOW BIZ from Vaude to
Video.* Henry Holt and Company. 1951. Famous chronicle of
show business as reported in the columns of *Variety.* There are
only two mentions of Houdini, the first, regarding his "jumping
out of airplanes in England," is an error. There is no mention
of Blackstone or Thurston. As a round-up of news from the
variety theaters by years, it is an invaluable source book.

HOLDEN, MAX—*Programmes of Famous Magicians.* Max Holden.
New York. 1937. This pamphlet, a labor of love by its compiler,
is worth its weight in gold to magical historians and provides
fascinating reading for all devotees of the art.

HOUDINI, HARRY—*The Adventurous Life of a Versatile Artist.*
Pamphlet sold at performances. Biographical material contributing to the Houdini legend but also useful for checking dates and
locations.

—*Elliott's Last Legacy*. Edited by Houdini, compiled by Clinton Burgess, illustrated by Oscar Teale. Adams Press Print (278 W. 113th Street). New York. 1923. A collection of odds and ends from the notes of Dr. James William Elliott, one of the cleverest amateur card manipulators and magical inventors. Interesting as a side light on Houdini: in his introduction he states that he regards himself as a card manipulator without peer. He also tells one of the funniest stories of magic, regarding his visit with Dr. Elliott, to an old magician who was a devoted performer on bells, rung with hammers, and the doctor's impish insistence that the old man give them a concert in the early morning hours. The account of this concert reveals Houdini's lively sense of humor. The boyish self-praise of the introduction is another character revelation. One of the most interesting chapters is a list of musical compositions suitable for various magical moods, tricks, and routines.

—*Houdini Exposes the Tricks used by the Boston Medium "Margery"* (pamphlet). Adams Press (278 W. 113th Street). New York. 1924.

—*Life, History and Handcuff Secrets*. Pitch book, sold at the performance. A few simple handcuff "secrets" are given with illustrations.

—*Magical Rope Ties and Escapes*. Will Goldston (no date).

—*A Magician Among the Spirits*. Harper & Brothers. New York. 1924. Popular history of the spiritualism movement from the Fox sisters to Houdini's own activities in exposing frauds. It contains a full account of the famous automatic-writing message given him by Lady Jean Conan Doyle.

—*Miracle Mongers and Their Methods*. E. P. Dutton & Company. 1920.

—*The Right Way to Do Wrong*. Pamphlet. 1906.

—*The Unmasking of Robert-Houdin*. (Privately printed). New York. 1908. Actually a pictorial history of magic, copiously illustrated by reproductions of old engravings and handbills from Houdini's collection.

HOUSE OF REPRESENTATIVES, Hearings before the Subcommittee on Judiciary of the Committee on the District of Columbia, Sixty-ninth Congress, first session, on H.R. 8989 (*Fortune Telling*)

February 26; May 18, 20, 21, 1926. Government Printing Office. Washington. 1926.

JARRETT—*Magic and Stage Craft*. Hand set, printed, and bound by the author. 1936. A 400-copy edition, one of the pithiest, saltiest and most uninhibited books on the art of magic, by one of the great illusion inventors of all time. Guy Jarrett's opinion of Houdini was not flattering. While he gives the weight of Daisy White (118 lb.) he does not list her "measurements," so necessary nowadays in judging a girl's personality. He does mention that she had quite a pair. . . .

KELLOCK, HAROLD—*Houdini/ His Life-Story by Harold Kellock from the recollections and documents of Beatrice Houdini*. Harcourt, Brace and Company. New York. 1928. First serialized in *American Magazine,* this is the authoritative volume for the chronology of Houdini's life. Except for an explanation of the map on the slate which so mystified Theodore Roosevelt, it keeps Houdini's secrets intact.

LAMBERT, R. S.—*Exploring the Supernatural*. McClelland & Stewart. Toronto. 1955. Sprightly written tales from Canadian folklore and history by a Canadian newspaperman, including an historical survey of the Shaking Tent of the Ojibwa medicine men.

McCULLOUGH, EDO—*Good Old Coney Island*. Charles Scribner's Sons. New York. 1957. History of the "magic island" by a descendant of one of its founding families.

MULHOLLAND, JOHN—*Quicker Than the Eye*. The Bobbs-Merrill Company. Indianapolis (no date). Excellent history of magic for the layman, including a chapter on American Indian magic and one on magical greats, including Houdini. Mulholland was a close friend of the Escape King and his tribute is a warmhearted one. It is to be hoped that Mr. Mulholland will someday produce a book devoted entirely to Houdini. He has much to tell.

PRICE, HARRY—*Leaves from a Psychist's Case Book*. Victor Gollancz. London. 1933. The famous British ghost hunter collected a hundred photographs of Margery's phenomena, taken during séances by flash. From them he made lantern slides. When these were projected and studied by Prof. William McDougall, the savant had recourse to his medical training; tiny fragments of Margery's ectoplasmic pseudopods had been pinched off without the medium's knowledge. They proved to be the lung tissue of "some animal." Regarding the spirit hands supposedly formed of teleplasm, McDougall "declared that every hand, pseudopod, or alleged psychic extrusion was cut out of the organs of various animals. In the omentum of a sheep he pointed out the chief characteristics, such as veins, etc. He revealed to us pieces of lung formed into various shapes, and showed us where the knife, in carving out the 'teleplasmic forms,' had cut across the tracheal arteries and membranous ducts. It was like listening to a lecture in anatomy!" The skill with which these hands had been sculptured from lung tissue indicated the work of someone trained in the use of a scalpel; also, Dr. Crandon's brusque refusal to allow his wife to be tested by Harry Price under strict controls casts doubt on the doctor's innocence of complicity in the Margery mediumship.

PRINCE, WALTER FRANKLIN—*A Review of the Margery Case*. The American Journal of Psychology, Vol. xxxvii, pp. 431-41, July 1926.

PROSKAUER, JULIEN J.—*The Dead Do Not Talk*. Harper & Brothers. New York. 1946. This expertly written, compact book by a past national president of the Society of American Magicians, is one of the indispensable reference works on the inside of the "spook racket." Two of its chapters are particularly noteworthy, "Psychic Revelations—and Where They Come From," and "Working a Hostile Town." These contain data never before available in book form. For much of his material the author gives credit to Miss Rose Mackenberg, Houdini's chief investigator of psychic frauds. The chapter on "How to Trap Mediums" gives the experiences of the author in performing Houdini's milk-can escape with the aid of Jim Collins, and the spiritualists' insistence that such escapes are due to dematerialization.

REEVE, ARTHUR B.—*The Master Mystery*. Grosset & Dunlap. New York. 1919. Novelized from the Houdini serial and illustrated with stills from the film.

RINN, JOSEPH F.—*Sixty Years of Psychical Research*. The Truth Seeker Company. New York. 1950. Written a few years before the author's death, this is an old man's book, full of the inaccuracies with which age often tricks the memory. Its most valuable contribution is the reprinting of clippings from Rinn's scrapbooks, many of them dealing with Houdini.

SARDINA, MAURICE—*Where Houdini Was Wrong*. Translated and edited with notes by Victor Farelli. George Armstrong. London. 1950. A reply by a French engineer and amateur magician, to Houdini's *Unmasking of Robert-Houdin*. To this project M. Sardina has brought a wealth of painstaking scholarship. The style is cautious and without passion, as befits the scholarly approach. The author's only real mistake is in assuming that anyone outside of France takes Houdini's blast at the great French conjuror seriously.

WILLIAMS, BERYL, and EPSTEIN, SAMUEL—*The Great Houdini*. Julian Messner. New York. 1950. Lively "story of Houdini" for young readers, following the legend as told by Kellock. The authors, however, did some original research and the book is in some respects an addition to Houdini lore.

Other sources used in the present work are clippings from Houdini's own scrapbooks, the press books of Joseph Dunninger, an article by Rea Jaure in *Science and Invention Magazine* of April 1929, Houdini letters in the Christopher Collection, Houdini receipts and miscellany in the Radner Collection, programs and pamphlets from the Rawson Collection, photostats of material in the Pfisterer Collection, pamphlets from the collection of Jay Marshall, the author's own files on Houdini, augmented by material from the archives of Martin Gardner and Dr. John Henry Grossman, and the invaluable correspondence on the subject of Houdini and escapery in general with The Amazing Randi.

BH836G   cop.2

Gresham.

   Houdini, the man who walked

through walls.

BH836G   cop.2

Gresham.

   Houdini, the man who
walked through walls.